The American
Response to
Professional Crime,
1870–1917

Recent Titles in Contributions in Criminology and Penology

The American Response to Professional Crime, 1870–1917

LARRY K. HARTSFIELD

CONTRIBUTIONS IN CRIMINOLOGY AND
PENOLOGY, NUMBER 8

Greenwood Press
Westport, Connecticut • London, England

141132

Library of Congress Cataloging in Publication Data

Hartsfield, Larry K.
  The American response to professional crime, 1870-
1917.

(Contributions in criminology and penology, ISSN 0732-
4464 ; no. 8)
  Bibliography: p.
  Includes index.
  1. Crime and criminals—United States—History—19th
century. 2. Crime and criminals—United States—
History—20th century. 3. Crime and criminals—United
States—Public opinion—History. 4. Public opinion—
United States—History. I. Title. II. Series.
HV6783.H37 1985   364'.973   84-22549
ISBN 0-313-24503-7 (lib. bdg.)

Library of Congress Catalog Card Number: 84-22549
ISBN: 0-313-24503-7
ISSN: 0-732-4464

First published in 1985

Greenwood Press
A division of Congressional Information Service, Inc.
88 Post Road West
Westport, Connecticut 06881

Printed in the United States of America

10 9 8 7 6 5 4 3 2 1

For their patience, understanding, and love this is
dedicated to
Kyle, Aaron, Emily and, most of all, to
Susie

Contents

Acknowledgments

I have incurred numerous debts in the writing of this work. I would like to thank the staff of the Humanities Research Center at the University of Texas at Austin who graciously helped me locate fugitive sources and pointed out such useful areas as Houdini's library of crime. This study could not have been written without the help of Chris Hanson, who handles Inter-Library Loan Services for the Perry-Casteñeda Library at the University of Texas. She expended untold energy in filling my numerous and often difficult requests.

Shannon Davies read an early draft of chapter five; her knowledge of medical history helped in both pointing toward fruitful areas of inquiry and steering me away from blunders. I would also like to thank Alfred Crosby for helping me keep this work in its true perspective. William Stott and Horace Newcomb read the manuscript and made valuable suggestions. Jeffrey Meikle gave the work a particularly acute reading both for style and substance. I owe William Goetzmann special thanks. He helped in focusing this topic at its conception and made valuable suggestions on several occasions. Additionally, he kept my mind engaged through his excellent teaching and brilliant conversation.

Robert M. Crunden was closely involved throughout the writing of this work and read several drafts closely. I would like to thank him not only for the acuteness of his readings and observations but for continually stimulating me to look in new directions. His aid extends back to my early career, for he was the stimulus behind my interest in this period of American civilization. He also allowed me to peruse the manuscript of his book *Ministers of Reform* before publication; this helped me focus my own ideas and provided much of the underpinning for my argument.

I would also like to express my gratitude to Norman and Maxene Bonds for both the understanding and support that they have given over the last few years. I owe debts too numerous to count to my parents, Hess and Dorothy Hartsfield. They encouraged my interest in ideas from an early age and continue to do so. They have provided support in innumerable ways over many years, and have encouraged me to keep working when obstacles have arisen.

Finally, and most importantly, I want to thank my family for both understanding and enduring. Kyle, Aaron, and Emily have given me love and a joy that has helped me to move toward my goals. There is no adequate way to express what I owe to my wife, Susie. She has contributed insightful readings and helpful suggestions while also serving as proofreader and editor. She has willingly made frequent sacrifices so that I could pursue this work. Above all she has given me constant support and love.

The American Response to Professional Crime, 1870–1917

Introduction: The Metaphysics of Bank Robbery

At eleven o'clock on the hot Friday night of June 27, 1869, George White and Mark Shinburn sat, stripped to their underwear, in a basement office at the corner of Fulton and Greenwich Streets in New York City. On the steps of the same building the janitor, with a crowd of neighbors, was trying to find relief from the heat. White and Shinburn anxiously waited for the janitor to go to bed; one floor above them sat the vault of the Ocean Bank.

White had begun planning the robbery in 1867 when he found one of the bank's clerks, John Taylor, sorely pressed for cash to take care of debts he had run up at John Morrissey's famous gambling den. Although Taylor was congenial to the plan White proposed, he assured White that it was a physical impossibility. White, however, was certain that he could rob any bank, no matter how well protected. In the guise of a Philadelphia banker he visited the vault maker in Rochester; he then established an insurance broker's office in the floor beneath the bank. After two unsuccessful attempts he and his partner felt certain that this time they would succeed.

Finally, the janitor retired and the two men set to work. By two o'clock Saturday morning they had broken through the floor of the bank president's office and, using the light of a cigar, moved their tools, including a 125 pound hydraulic jack, to the upper floor. Having already obtained the combination, they quickly opened the vault and removed a package containing $100,000 that Taylor had hidden within the vault. This they passed to one of their outside men; the package was insurance money they could use to bargain with the bank for their freedom if they were apprehended at work.

The burglars then entered the vault, closed its doors to hide their activity, and attacked the safes. After rifling the safety deposit boxes for cash and negotiable bonds, they turned their attention to the receiving teller's safe. Not until eleven o'clock Saturday morning were they able to complete drilling through the steel over the bolt of the safe's locks, but finally the bolts were sprung and the safe's contents placed in the burglars' satchel. The paying teller's safe was much stronger and the two thieves had worked so long without food that they were too tired for hard drilling. They tried to wedge the door of the safe open with the jack but failed and returned to the drill. After completing half of the drilling, exhaustion forced them to admit defeat. They removed their tools, closed the vault, and departed with one and a half million dollars in their satchel.

After cleaning up and having a meal, White and Shinburn strolled over to Detective Jack McCord's home to report their success. McCord was less than pleased when he discovered that they had not completed the job. The thieves slept for about four hours and at three o'clock Monday morning returned to the vault. They now had too little time to succeed by drilling so once more decided to rely on the forces designed to protect society. After inserting explosives in the seam between the jamb and the door of the safe, they had their confederate outside the bank turn in a fire alarm. As the fire engine clattered past the bank, the burglars blew the safe. White and Shinburn emptied this second safe, but White performed one final act before leaving the vault: he dropped a bundle of $200,000 into the rubble surrounding the safe. He hated both leaving good money and the potential damage of this "careless" act to his reputation, but he had promised Taylor to leave enough money to keep the bank from failing.

The two burglars left the bank about fifteen minutes before it opened; a coach, team, and driver from White's fashionable livery stable waited at the corner. After this coach dropped them at White's home, he sent it to police headquarters to convey the detectives who would investigate the robbery to the bank. Although Detectives McCord and Kelso were angry about the $200,000 left behind, their share of the loot must have helped them to maintain the theory that the bank's looters had been a gang of western burglars. The total take from the robbery was $2,907,300. The burglars dropped $850,000 in non-negotiable securities on the steps of police Captain Jourdan's precinct-house; the securities were useless to the thieves but not to the rightful owners. Subtracting this and such business expenses as assistants, rent for the basement office, and the police left White and Shinburn $1,575,000 to divide.

These genteel burglars who tunneled from an underground basement to successfully attack one of the bastions of American civilization are representative of the thieves who dominated the American vision of crime between the Civil War and World War I. Most Americans of this time were certain that just below the surface of American life, a class of men existed who threatened the very foundations of their civilization; these criminals posed a new threat to a nation just emerged from a war to preserve the union. The threat was particularly dangerous since these men so often mirrored values shared by most Americans, such as professionalism and a belief in material wealth as the primary measure of success.

Following the Civil War professionalization became one of the major themes of American civilization. Increasingly, different groups turned to the concept of professionalism with its emphasis on formal training, special skills, and esoteric knowledge as a way of defining the self and its place in a fluid society. Like other groups, thieves also found this notion attractive; professionalism helped the thief to separate himself from other deviant or criminal groups. For example, these thieves argued that they were fundamentally different from such criminals as murderers and claimed to abhor the use of violence. Since their offences were directed at property, they held that they belonged in the mainstream of American life and often professed a belief in the values of their civilization.

Other groups in America also found the notion of professionalism useful when applied to crime. The symbiotic relationship between White and Shinburn and the detectives sworn to protect society is typical of the position of the professional thief in America. Just as he took what he wanted from the upper world, the upper world used him for its purposes.

The importance of the professional thief grew steadily in the literature written after the Civil War; the variety of literary responses to this figure provides insights into American civilization between 1870 and 1915. From Defoe to Dostoyevsky the literature of criminality has long held an honored place in Western literature, and in America from 1870 to 1915 the professional thief dominated this genre. This figure and his transformations served as ready-made symbols of both the shortcomings and virtues of American life.

While the professional criminal dramatized himself in innumerable autobiographies, he also functioned as a figure of inherent interest for many writers; for others he was a figure to be used in the pursuit of specific goals. The essential relationship between the professional thief and these authors parallels the relationship between the Ocean Bank burglars and the detectives in its symbiotic nature. The professional thief figured centrally in several realms of discourse; these included works based on the techniques of autobiographical, historical, journalistic, fictional, and academic writing. While these approaches used different methodologies and rhetorical strategies, the notion of the professional criminal remained central to the works. He was a figure who engaged the American imagination at all levels.

The literary presentation of the criminal self by the professional thief was one of masks designed to suit an audience's expectations. The deception at the base of the criminal's life carried into his autobiographical writings. These writings were dramatizations which the thief used to "stage" both himself and his role in society. The poses that he adopted changed according to his perceptions of what his audience desired. Did they want a figure of heroic status, a Byronic outsider who saw deeper into reality than they, or did they want an underdog who pointed up the cruelty of injustice, poverty, and hypocrisy? He could fill either of these roles and did, thus reinforcing widespread social beliefs. He reinforced his civilization's move toward professionalization by providing detailed accounts of his tests, his apprenticeship, and his specialization. Additionally, society granted the criminal a special role as critic because of his status as outsider, a role that allowed him to point to the darker side of American life, and he gleefully noted the parallels between his world and the "respectable" world. The criminal took his cue for the presentation of self from what his society wrote about him. He found in the writings of detectives, journalists, novelists, and intellectuals a multiplicity of parts.

Just as the professional thief used his civilization, his civilization used him. The social position of the detective was an unsettled, ambiguous place during the Gilded Age. His work was unsavory and took him into the foulest areas of American life. Like his more favored counterparts, however, the detective wanted to carve a place for himself and his occupation in American society. The professional thief became his passport to respectability. The detective wrote about the thief's skill, his daring, and the threat he posed to individuals unskilled in the ways of evil. His countrymen needed a professional with special skills and knowledge to protect them from this awesome figure. The detective offered to fill this dangerous, demanding role.

The professional criminal played an important part for writers interested in exposing cancerous growths below the surface of American life. These writers shared little but a common desire to unmask fraud and corruption and to expose the hideous reality behind the mask. Both rural and urban Americans partook of this impulse for exposé although each approached it from a different stance. This literature of exposure became a subgenre of nonfiction and attained its most brilliant expression after the turn of the century.

As the nation entered the modern era, many citizens were frightened at the prospect that stretched before them. Rural Americans were especially worried about the urban centers that were assuming an ever-increasing importance in national life. To those who still found a source of value in the agrarian ethos, these cities appeared as a threat to the foundations of America's democratic institutions. More specifically these cities seemed to function as a source of corruption that could infect the small towns of America if citizens were not on their guard. The professional criminal was an urban product who threatened trusting country folk under his guise as the confidence man or sharper.

Many books appeared in this era that were designed both to expose this urban criminal and protect the country folk he preyed upon. These books are valuable for the insights they provide into American values during a transitional period in our nation's history.

The greatest achievements of the literature of exposure, however, were the urban exposés. The muckraker became the representative figure for progressive reform, and he too used the professional criminal. The aspect of professional crime that most intrigued the muckraker was the league between the thief and officialdom. The exposé of this league provided one rationale for the muckraker's call for the social regeneration of the nation.

These years also witnessed the adoption of the professional thief by the American novelist. The professional criminal had long held a prominent place in fiction; he was central to the early picaresque fictions and figured in the writings of such English authors as Daniel Defoe, Henry Fielding, Charles Dickens, and Wilkie Collins. He also appeared in such early American novels as Hugh Henry Brackenridge's *Modern Chivalry* and Charles Brockden Brown's *Arthur Mervyn*. During this era, however, he assumed a new role in the American novel. He found a central place in popular literature soon after the Gilded Age as the increasing popularity of the detective novel reflected the changing position of American detectives. In more serious fiction he moved from a supporting role designed mainly to provide texture to the backdrop of urban life to a position at center stage. Progressive novelists found the professional criminal fascinating. They tried to present the human side of the professional criminal, and he became an important fictional illustration of the crucial nature of developmental processes in shaping human personality.

This use of the professional criminal as a figure to build theories upon was also important to American intellectuals worried about crime. These intellectuals viewed the professional criminal as the most dangerous of the "criminal classes." He became one of the battlefronts between established fields such as medicine and newer disciplines such as sociology as each group attempted to consolidate its influence in American life. These two camps represented strongly contrasting uses of evolutionary thought among American intellectuals. On the one hand, physicians quickly fastened onto the doctrines of the new "science" of criminal anthropology fostered by the Italian psychiatrist Cesare Lombroso. This approach to crime was biological and stressed the role of heredity in shaping personality. Lombroso was most important for his theory of the criminal type which held that criminals were essentially a different species of humanity from modern man. This non-human status resulted either from atavism or degeneration. On the other hand, these biological theories were anathema to thinkers in the social sciences, for they denied the possibility of improvement under the guidance of the intellect. These social scientists developed an alternative set of theories stressing the role of environment in the shaping of human personality while arguing optimistically that environment could be engineered to produce better humans. The debate between these groups penetrated beyond disciplinary bounds as progressive reformers and novelists seized on the hope offered by the social scientists as a means of organizing their plea for a spiritual rebirth in the United States.

These various writings all shared a concern for such questions as the origins and nature of professional crime. What was there in America that lent itself so readily to the genesis of crime? How could this problem best be approached and contained? The thief served as a symbol for these writers of the hidden evils threatening American life. Although the professional criminal used the writings of the upper world to shape a mask that fit its preconceptions, he continued his depredations unscathed. Like most Americans he simply wanted to pursue his profession. In his own eyes the major difference between his calling and other occupations was in the size of its compensations and drawbacks. Potentially, wealth was always within his grasp, but so was complete failure and imprisonment. The fascination of Americans with this figure during these years is closely tied to this quality of risk. He became a symbol of both America's promise and danger.[1]

1   From Rogue to Victim

AUTOBIOGRAPHY AND THE PROFESSIONAL CRIMINAL

The criminal autobiography has been a subgenre of American literature since the Puritans. Traditionally these narratives took the form of confessions and were almost always concerned with murder.[1] The work of Edgar Allan Poe bears witness to the widespread knowledge of this genre and its conventions. Such Poe stories as "The Black Cat" parody the murderer's confession and its use as a moral fable to illustrate the results of an individual's turn from community values. *The Memoirs of the Notorious Stephen Burroughs of New Hampshire* (1811), is one of the earliest autobiographies of a professional rogue in America. This book helped initiate a new style of criminal autobiography in America, a style that concentrated on the exploits of the thief instead of the villainous acts of the murderer. Following the Civil War a trickle of autobiographies by professional thieves became a steady stream which flowed throughout the period and is still flowing today.[2]

Several forces contributed to the emergence of the professional thief's autobiography as popular literature. One was the impulse for exposure that dominated so much American writing in the late nineteenth and early twentieth centuries. Another was the American public's fascination with "great" men and, later, with "typical" men, a fascination that spilled over from the respectable world to the underworld. Also, during this period America began its shift toward becoming an urban rather than a rural nation. The professional thief represented one of the more exotic species of the urban habitat. Perhaps the most important element in the emergence of the thief's autobiography as popular literature, however, was the growing stability of crime as a profession. The war consolidated the profession of theft in America. For the first time huge sums of money could be made by such practices as burglary. The techniques of the professional criminal became more sophisticated as a result of his adjustment to changes in law enforcement and technology.

Also, after the Civil War, the notion of professionalization became central in many areas of American civilization, in crime fully as much as in medicine or law. A key element in the development of this concept of professionalism was the role of status, of one's standing within a profession. Autobiography played an important role in defining status for the professional thief. One of the most important ways for a thief to define his status was to contribute new techniques to the profession. By detailing his innovations, the thief partially realized one of the primary impulses behind most autobiography—the writer's belief that for some reason he is worthy of special interest.[3] The retired professional sees changes occuring in his profession and perhaps fails to recognize a thread of continuity binding past and present. He thus presents himself as an example of a passing life-style. He is, of course, also aware of his peculiar position in the eyes of the world due to his membership in the hidden world of crime. This angle of vision becomes an essential part of his rhetorical strategy. Whether he presents himself as a daring adventurer or adopts the pose of the underdog, the professional thief brings a new viewpoint to the examination of society.

In addition to satisfying the curiosity of more conventional citizens, the thief may also hold himself up as an object lesson in morality. Again, this is part of a conscious rhetorical strategy designed to elicit sympathy from his audience. On the surface, he warns of the consequences of a life such as his. This reinforces social values and thus fulfills one of the demands of any popular art. At this level the thief and his life function as a moral exemplum designed to illustrate the evils attending the life that strays from the conventional path.

These writings also exhibit one of the elementary motives of autobiography. Memoirs usually celebrate the author's deeds.[4] By adopting the persona of a reintegrated member of his civilization, the retired thief can explain his actions—actions that from his perspective are always misunderstood. He thus provides a memorial of his actions for a generation that would otherwise misunderstand them. He also insures that posterity will remember his deeds.

A major part of the rhetorical strategy of these criminal autobiographers is the promise to deliver the inside story and correct false assumptions or distorted accounts of particular crimes. Professional thieves write autobiographies to justify their existence as criminals, to clarify their role as participants in a particularly spectacular crime, to assert their innocence of crimes for which they have been falsely accused, to reveal the innocence of a falsely accused individual, or to receive proper credit as the innovator of a specific criminal technique. This stance of setting the record straight is a rhetorical technique that aids these authors in gaining the trust of their audience.

For all of the above reasons, autobiographies by professional thieves emerged as popular reading material for many Americans after the Civil War. These autobiographies provide insight into both the thief's vision of himself and his profession and also his notion of what his audience believed about crime.

THE MODES OF CRIMINAL AUTOBIOGRAPHY

The autobiographies written by professional criminals between the Civil War and World War I fall into two general modes. The mode chosen by a particular author is usually determined by two things: the author's position in his profession and his purpose in writing. One type is fundamentally a tale of stirring adventure motivated by a strong impulse toward self-justification. The second major class of criminal autobiographies is essentially comprised of social documents. These writers primarily want to present the social context of the professional thief and, perhaps, suggest solutions to the problem of the professional thief. The first class is typical of the autobiographies written by thieves before the turn of the century. The second type was usually a product of the years after 1900.

The adventure-story autobiographies are strongly influenced by the traditions of both the picaresque novel and the rogue's biography, genres stretching back to the Renaissance. The authors of these autobiographies stood near the top of their profession—the expert bank burglar, safe-cracker, forger, or counterfeiter. The autobiography is typically a product of the declining years of the retired professional. It pretends to warn the public to avoid this life-style, and the authors usually include a pious statement of their hope that a close study of these pages will enlighten bankers and other legitimate businessmen about the weaknesses of their establishments and hence enable them to better defend themselves against thieves. These disclaimers are at best perfunctory, and the authors devote most of their vast energies to narrating picaresque adventures. The emphasis is on the author's skills, professional innovations, reputation, and status in both the under and upper worlds.

These autobiographies are built around an episodic narrative structure. Adventure follows adventure chronologically with complete chapters usually devoted to the narrator's more masterful exploits. The style vacillates between flat journalistic prose and sensational, melodramatic prose with the occasional use of such standard devices of nineteenth-century serial literature as the cliff-hanger in ending chapters. The writer who most clearly approaches the archetypal rogue in his ironic narrative is Langdon W. Moore; his autobiography enjoyed wide popularity throughout the 1890s. Perhaps the most skilled of this group of autobiographers is George M. White, whose *From Boniface to Bank Burglar* appeared in 1904. These works are typical examples of this picaresque mode of autobiography.[5]

This picaresque style is representative of the thief's autobiography during the Gilded Age. Both White and Moore write because they are fascinated by their own lives. No one has urged them to provide a picture of their world for the edification of society. As *individuals* they believe their lives have value.

In contrast to the picaresque autobiographers, those writers who produced social documentaries had a very different vision of themselves and their profession. This second type of autobiography is representative of the Progressive Era. These books were usually either a collaborative effort with a journalist or a result of a minister's or reformer's urging. The authors of these books are generally younger than those of the first group and have either "squared it" or are attempting to do so.[6] They are also much lower in the criminal hierarchy. They belong to the group of petty hustlers, house-breakers, and yeggs who furnish the labor that a captain of crime needs to carry out his ambitious schemes. These writers are concerned with documenting the social context of the professional thief and devote more space to analysis of the thief's milieu than to narration of specific adventures.

These books illustrate the growing importance of the social sciences in all areas of American life after the turn of the century. They are more closely allied to both the muckraking exposé of the underworld and the sociological novel than to the picaresque literature of the professional rogue. These writings concentrate on such concerns as the steps which lead to the underworld, the status structure of the underworld, the techniques of different types of criminals, the life-style of criminals, the reform school and prison, and the methods of leaving the underworld. A strong reformist impulse directed toward the slum, the reform school, and the prison underlies these writings. Typical of this class of autobiographies are Hutchins Hapgood's collaboration with Jim Caulfield, *The Autobiography of a Thief*, and "Wellington Scott's" *Seventeen Years in the Underworld*.[7] These works are much more "earnest" than those of the earlier period and are quite often drenched in self-pitying sentiment; usually they lack both the irony and sense of pride in profession that mark the books of the first-class professionals. These autobiographers strive to create a mask of genuineness and "true democracy" that will provide a link between their lives and the broader stream of American civilization.

The development of a persona is one key to these two classes of autobiography. The mask that an autobiographer adopts determines how he will present his story, what he will present, and how his audience will respond. The changing nature of the persona adopted by the criminal autobiographer provides insights into changes in the perception of the profession of theft by its practitioners; it also gives insights into how these thieves viewed the civilization's concept of their work. This change is essentially from the persona of a genial rogue to that of an underdog.

Both styles of autobiography illustrate the shaping power of the dominant fictional aesthetic on the dramatization of the self. The works chronicling crime during the Gilded Age draw on the traditional novel's emphasis on a strong central character as protagonist. They are close to the fictional tradition of the picaresque with its episodic structure and outsider as hero. These works bear a strong resemblance to Daniel Defoe's *Moll Flanders*, William Thackeray's *Barry Lyndon*, and Wilkie Collins' *A Rogue's Life*. The second type of autobiography illustrates both the growing importance of the social sciences in American civilization and a new public belief in environmental determinism. They are more closely allied to such "sociological" novels as Emile Zola's *Rougon-Macquart* series and the work of such American novelists as Frank Norris, Theodore Dreiser, and Stephen Crane. These works emphasize background and the role of developmental processes in shaping human personality.

One of the best ways of viewing the differences in these two modes of autobiographies is by examining the different presentations of similar themes. These different presentations of shared themes also provide insights into shifts in the way that these criminals perceived themselves and their role in American life and in the way that the culture perceived them. The most important of these themes are the birth of a sense of otherness, the self-image of the professional thief, and the exposé of parallels between the underworld and legitimate society.

THE CRIMINAL AS OTHER

From the criminal's point of view the most decisive element in the road to professional crime is the birth of a sense of otherness, of alienation from legitimate society. This sense of otherness may arise from either of two root sources—sources which reveal broader changes in the way Americans viewed both crime and the etiology of the criminal. Those thieves near the top of the profession whose careers began in the 1850s or 1860s present the injustice of legitimate society as the fundamental cause of a sense of otherness. This provides a rationale for the thief's declaration of war on society. Those thieves whose careers began in the 1880s or 1890s present the sense of otherness as the result of a gradual process rooted in environment and education. This developmental process culminates in the criminal's entrance into the underworld.

The expert bank burglar typifies the aristocratic criminal's declaration of war on society during the Gilded Age. This declaration results from a perceived injustice; it can, perhaps, best be visualized as a deconversion experience. Since St. Augustine's *Confessions* the conversion experience has been central to the structure of autobiography. This deconversion experience is the criminal version of the traditional turning point; it restructures the course of the criminal's life and alters his personality in a radical way.

Langdon W. Moore, for instance, came from a respectable family. His childhood held nothing more disreputable than an excess of vital spirits. In early adulthood he opened a grocery store in Boston, but fell victim to the seductions of gambling. For Moore, gambling initiated a journey toward deconversion and a life of crime. After the loss of his store due to gambling debts, Moore moved to New York City and became a professional gambler. Three years later, in 1856, he returned to Boston for a brief visit. In recounting this visit, Moore adopted the mask of the wronged innocent; he claimed that he was falsely arrested for "shoving the queer," or passing counterfeit notes. The charges were eventually dropped, but the experience of injustice had radically altered his attitude toward society; following his release Moore informed his lawyer "that I would make it cost the people of Massachusetts one hundred thousand dollars for each and every month they had allowed the officer to keep me in jail on a wrong identification." He rebuffed his father, who had found a job for him in New York, by saying, "I will never do another day's work until I am compelled to do it for the state." Moore then proceeded to become an expert counterfeiter, a career he would follow until he became a safe-cracker and bank burglar. In his account of this deconversion experience and his turn to crime, Moore adopts the stance of an innocent man who has the right to avenge himself on a hostile world.[8]

George White's deconversion parallels Moore's but is even

more abrupt and carries a tone of sincerity which Moore's lacks. White opens his autobiography in 1864 with a portrait of himself at the significant age of thirty—an honest hotel proprietor in Stoneham, Massachusetts, whose life is "flowing like a placid river." After a false arrest for the robbery of the Walpole Bank, White found himself behind bars for the first time in his life, unmercifully hounded by one of the victims of the robbery. In describing the persecution he suffered as "an innocent man," White dwells on his increasing alienation and the destruction of his former self. This psychological examination assumes a metaphysical dimension as he describes such things as a recurrent daydream: "I was being sifted, as it were, through a sieve of the finest mesh, that part of me left in the sieve being transformed into all that was vile, and my pulverized self passing through, all the good in me, being blown to the four winds of heaven."

The sense of persecution increased after one of the actual burglars plea-bargained his release from jail by agreeing to return his portion of the theft while White was left to languish unjustly. Eventually White's sense of being unjustly wronged leads him to declare that "I would no longer willingly submit to such inhuman treatment; that I would be a law unto myself, and that I would accept the consequences, be what they might." He then broke out of jail and fled to New York City.[9]

In New York, White battled down the inner voices urging him to "plunge into the swift-flowing current of vice" (White, 68) and obtained an honest job as a clerk in A. T. Stewart and Company's retail dry goods house. Unfortunately, due to the earlier injustice, White is no longer master of his fate and soon encounters an old Boston acquaintance. White knows this "friend" will turn him in to the police for the reward, and he leaves the store just in time to escape capture.

In his view White has now become the quintessential victim: backed into a corner with nowhere to turn, he is like a pursued rabbit compelled to seek the first cover that offers. This is the critical period when good and evil fight within him for the last time, but, with no other alternative, he looks up Billy Matthews, a man who had testified as a character witness for Max Shinburn, the actual mastermind behind the Walpole Bank robbery. Matthews introduced White to a gang of safe burglars, and "thus was forged the first link in the chain that was to fasten me to a criminal career for many years" (White, 77).

White typifies the honest man driven into a life of crime because of society's injustice. The metaphors which he uses to describe his life up to the assumption of crime as an occupation generally focus on life as a stream or river and seem particularly apt; White views himself as having little control once he has been taken into the snare of the law. He can exert little power to divert the course his life has flowed into, and his means of escape are outlawed—as in his jail break. Only by actively entering the profession of crime can White once again regain control of his life. The necessity of maintaining individual control overrides any sense of social obligation to a world which seems dedicated to one's destruction. This helps explain White's use of the role of the outsider, the "other." In a hostile world, the man who fights back is the individual who remains free. The value of freedom, whether it be moral, social, or physical, is central to White's persona.

Another notable feature of White's autobiography is that it begins with his first arrest. The reader knows little about his parents, family, friends, or background except that they are respectable. He thus poses the threat that if this could happen to him, it could happen to anyone. More importantly, this technique underscores the changed nature of his life after he becomes an adversary acting against society. This is a new life for which his earlier existence has little meaning.

This first mode of autobiography with its picaresque structure and sharp delineation of the birth of otherness and the importance of this otherness as justification for crime is typical of those criminals at the top of their profession. After the turn of the century a different mode of autobiography appeared, one strongly influenced by the progressive impulse. The urban environment and its effect on the individual provided a major impetus for Progressivism. Most progressives were environmental determinists who believed that personality resulted from a gradual developmental process. The individual adapted to his environment as best he could, and this process of adaptation determined his personality. Tied to this belief in environmental determinism was an optimistic faith that people could alter bad environments; by changing the conditions of the environment one could change the people these environments produced. This belief held special importance for the cities with their cancerous slums, the environment progressives held most responsible for the genesis of criminals.

Under the pressure of Progressivism a new persona emerged that portrayed the thief as an underdog in the struggle for survival. The thieves who made use of this changed persona were generally younger men who had "squared it" for one reason or another. Their retirements were not due to age but to moral regeneration, religious conversion, disgust at their lack of success, or drug or alcohol addiction which vitiated their ability to operate successfully. Like the first group of autobiographers, these present a sense of otherness, of alienation from legitimate society, but no longer is the development of otherness the result of a sudden deconversion experience. Reflecting the progressive concern for environmental determinism, this new style of autobiography as social document emphasizes the developmental process which culminates in alienation. These autobiographies reflect the emphasis of Progressivism on organic growth; they detail in depth the childhoods of their authors and the step-by-step formation of the sense of otherness.

In 1902, Josiah Flint Willard introduced his old roommate, Hutchins Hapgood, to Jim Caulfield, a pickpocket, burglar, and drug addict who had recently been released from prison. This meeting resulted in an "as told to" book, *The Autobiography of a Thief,* in 1903. This work is one of the earliest examples of this new style of criminal autobiography as social document, and ranks as one of the most significant examples of the literary subgenre of the criminal memoir. Over a period of several months Hapgood interviewed Caulfield concerning his career. Hapgood then organized the story and published it with introductory and concluding comments. The book has close ties to the muckraking movement and reflects the era's pervasive interest in factual detail.[10]

Josiah Flint Willard reviewed the book in 1903 and, even though he had a proprietary interest in its success, claimed that for the first time a thief had been truly frank in his revelations.[11] In his

own autobiography, *A Victorian in the Modern World*, Hapgood
argued that this book was important because for the first time
it presented the criminal as human rather than as a sort of curiosity. He believed that the book and its methods resembled
Defoe's *Moll Flanders* and *Robinson Crusoe*.[12]

The work opens with the true note of progressive honesty
and exposé as Caulfield explains, "I have been a professional
thief for more than twenty years." These years have been about
evenly divided between prison and grafting, but he claims that
he was a good pickpocket and knew "many of the best crooks
in the country." He then asserts that he has left the "business"
and will tell his story with entire frankness: "I shall not try to
defend myself. I shall try to tell merely the truth."[13] Hapgood's
own autobiography reveals that Caulfield had not left the business but returned to it soon after the collaboration was ended.
Caulfield used the royalties that were supposed to give him a
new start in life to buy cocaine and good clothes that would
improve his effectiveness as a pickpocket.[14]

The structure of this autobiography reveals a new public understanding of how someone could grow up to be a professional
thief. The autobiography traces the developmental process
through both childhood and prison experiences. This is in clear
contrast to the earlier picaresque autobiographies which present
either a childhood of honesty and industriousness or leave childhood out altogether. No longer is the birth of otherness presented as a sudden experience due to society's injustice; it is
now a developmental process keyed to the criminal's childhood
and adolescence. Several factors such as an over-active imagination, the lack of outlets for boyish mischief in the urban environment, and peer pressure contribute to Caulfield's choice of
crime as an occupation, but the fundamental cause is
environmental.

Jim Caulfield came from a respectable lower–middle-class family which produced a policeman, hod carriers, and grocers as
well as Jim, the only lawbreaker. Caulfield locates the origins of
his deviance in his sixth year. He began to "tap the till" in his
brother's grocery store at the request of older boys who provided
companionship and matinée tickets in return. This first step on
a career of deviance, unchecked effectively when discovered by

indulgent parents, led to future thefts of clothes, money, and household items. During this early career Caulfield lived in a good neighborhood, but the urban environment remained central to his criminal acts. He asserts that the primary reason for these thefts was a desire for excitement and laments that if he had only grown up in the country he would probably have been satisfied with bird's nests and fish (Hapgood, 19).

Environment became even more important when Caulfield's family moved to Cherry Street; here, he argues, the wreck of his life occurred. At the end of his block stood a saloon that served as the headquarters for a band of professional thieves, the Old Border Gang. These "great men" fired his imagination and became his role models. At the age of thirteen, under the tutelage of an older "pick," he began a two-year career as a "moll-buzzer," a pickpocket who specialized in robbing women. At fifteen he was arrested for the first time, spent ten days in the Tombs, and emerged a confirmed thief; here he first met "de mob" and received sophisticated training in criminal techniques, but, even more important, "I began definitely to look upon myself as a criminal." He has now labelled himself as "other," as criminal. This new self-image was reinforced when he was released. Although he was a disgrace in his family, the other boys in the neighborhood treated him with new respect and admired him as a fighter who had "done time." The prison experience established his place as a member of the underworld; he now began to form professional connections and obtain introductions to older grafters who further refined both his technique and sense of professionalism (Hapgood, 45, 60).

This is a striking change in the presentation of the trip toward crime as an occupation and the development of the status of outsider. In addition to the new stress on environment and educational development, the prison experience takes on an added dimension for the progressive thief. Unlike the entrepreneurs of the earlier period, Caulfield makes no claim that he was unjustly imprisoned and thus had a *right* to revenge himself on society. He resents the experience, to be sure, but for him it serves more as confirmation than conversion, establishing his credentials and reputation. Like the older men, however, Caulfield comes eventually to a sense of himself as outsider; shaped by his environment, career, and prison terms he develops into an individual who hates society and seeks revenge on it (Hapgood, 196–97).

"Wellington Scott's" *Seventeen Years in the Underworld* appeared in 1916, near the end of the Progressive Era. This book is drenched in the orthodoxies of progressive thought on human nature. It also, however, looks toward the modern world. While it repeatedly emphasizes the importance of environment in producing the criminal, this is but one of a number of contributing causes. As in the other autobiographies, the notion of otherness, of alienation from the mainstream culture, is a central concept. Scott comes from a strictly middle-class environment and has no economic reasons for turning to crime; indeed, his father moved the family to the suburbs when the old neighborhood began to decline in order to remove his son from potentially bad influences. Scott became a criminal through the search for a sense of community.

Following the family's move to the suburbs, Scott discovered he was nearsighted. Myopia became the ultimate catalyst for his future career. At the age of fifteen, friendless in a new environment, he was forced to wear spectacles, and this altered his psychological environment. At his new school "the jibes of the boys and the half-concealed smiles of the girls" made his life miserable: "The poison of melancholy . . . and the rancor in my heart made me alien from their fellowships." He turned from this miserable life to the warm fellowship of the poolroom, acquired a passion for gambling, and made friendships that "led into the complex shadows of the underworld."[15]

Scott emphasizes the developmental process that begins in the environment of the poolroom. The first step was a weakening of his will, followed by petty theft, and, eventually, a stretch in reform school for forgery. Prison served as the final alienating episode for Scott just as for Caulfield. Scott entered the jail to await trial on a forgery charge as an "amateur in crime" and stayed there for three months—in close contact with professional thieves.

From jail he went to reform school where "the environment, the indiscriminate mixture of the boys, regardless of their ages or evident depravity . . . steered me toward the rocks of a wretched career"(Scott, 30). Here the notion of environment takes the foreground in Scott's analysis for, ironically, this institution designed to rehabilitate youthful offenders through a pure and corruption-free environment is actually one of degeneracy and crime. Scott launches a strong attack on the state for allowing this, placing the blame for most professional crime on the community. His hatred for the reform school extends to the society that allows it to exist; by the time his period of confinement was over, "My mind had formed by association and environment a desire and determination to live entirely in the underworld. I would live by my wits; I would prey against society" (Scott, 48).

The persona of the professional thief as autobiographer has undergone profound changes by the close of this era. The essential elements in his presentation of self and his evolution toward crime as a profession have crystallized into the concepts of environmentalism and alienation from his civilization—an alienation that leads the outsider to search for community wherever it may be found. The earlier entrepreneurs saw themselves as "other," and apart from the mainstream of the culture, yet at the same time viewed their ambitions and goals as essentially the same as those of other Americans. Their methods were different, but they were, if anything, more honest than "respectable" members of society, for they did not try to hide their graft under a hypocritical veil of morality and justification.

Wellington Scott, however, is not simply a genial rogue, aware of his special status and enjoying the privileges it conveys upon him. He is fundamentally the outsider, one of the dominant symbols of twentieth-century thought. Lynn Harold Hough, who wrote the introduction to Scott's autobiography, related that Scott often talked of standing in front of a strange house in a strange city at supper-time: "Within he would see the father and the mother, and the happy little children, and all the bright light of home. He would turn away abruptly and walk into the dark, trying to forget it" (Scott, 5). This image sums up the changed persona of the professional thief at the close of the era. Scott does not present himself as a dashing, heroic figure whose deeds are worthy of remembrance. Rather, he is an alien, cut off from the values of family, home, warmth, light, and community. He has become a voyeur shut off from anything more than a view of the promises of American life. He does not write to provide a stirring narrative but to expose the path that leads to crime and the desolation at the end of the path. The rogue has become the victim.

AUTOBIOGRAPHY AND SELF-IMAGE

The deconversion experience is closely related to the thief's self-image; his vision of himself as alien marks both his vision of self and his presentation of that vision. Again, strong differences in self-image and persona separate those thieves who operated soon after the Civil War from those who came to maturity during the Progressive Era. The earlier thieves took pride in their deeds and achievements. They were also proud of their status within the profession. After the turn of the century the self-image of the professional thief underwent a transformation. No longer was the self an object to be celebrated. These later thieves began to adopt a role that stressed the persona of the helpless victim, without choice or alternatives. The dominant image in the presentation of their lives became a vision of something "wrecked" or destroyed, of a loss of control (Hapgood, 71, 100). This shift in persona involves both a changed notion of society's beliefs about the nature of professional crime and a different caste within the profession.

The vision of crime as a profession is central to the persona of both White and Moore. They are jealous of their status and reputation within the world of professional crime. Each stood at the top of the profession and each reiterates his innovations and contributions to the profession. Professional jealousy also emerges in frequent attacks on rivals for their lack of skill and dependability. Referring to the planning of the Ocean Bank robbery, for example, White stresses how important it was to work with the best men in the profession, for "no loud-mouthed, Jack Hartley crowd of grafters, with their wagon loads of English pattern-made tools, would fill the bill" (White, 242–43).

This contempt for less successful burglars is an important element in self-image and self-justification. Both White and Moore attribute the occasional problems they do have with the law to associating with burglars who are unprofessional and unreliable. As a corollary to this, both are continually dropping the names of well-known thieves with whom they have worked. White, for instance, was extraordinarily proud of his long partnership with Max Shinburn, whom Allan Pinkerton presented as "a very brilliant and exceptional instance of a professional criminal having won considerable fame from a series of masterly bank and bond robberies, marvelous prison escapes and the like, in America, and then crowning all by a final escape sound and safely to Belgium." Pinkerton had good reason to admire Shinburn since he was "about the only criminal that ever escaped me [Pinkerton] in my nearly a third of a century's ... career."[16]

The key to the pride of this class of bank burglars was their dedication to the profession and the skill they subsequently developed. For instance, Moore states that when he decided to drop counterfeiting and take up bank burglary, "for the next few months I devoted my whole time and attention to the Lillie and Yale bank locks." Moore is especially proud of the fact that his Lillie is on exhibition at New York Police Headquarters. Inspector Byrnes gave this lock notoriety in 1884 when he stated in *Harper's Weekly* that Moore "had so studied combination locks as to be able to open them from the sound ejected from the spindle." Moore also visited safe manufacturers where the owners gave him tours and explained how safes were constructed. He then purchased several safes for experiments and "soon solved the problem of lockpicking by putting pressure on the bolt" (Moore, 67–8). With his new mastery, Moore encountered little difficulty opening any safe he attacked.

White was an even more dedicated professional than Moore. After he and his partner had one of their periodic fallings-out, White became convinced that new skills were vital for success in his business. He was sure that lugging around three hundred pounds of cumbersome tools was not the final achievement of his profession. With a nod toward the glamourous treatment professional crime increasingly received in the popular press, White stated: "No doubt, if the newspapers of that period had woven the romance about the burglar that we read of today ... I would have been dubbed the 'Ethical Burglar,' for I began a diligent, systematic study into the theoretical and practical aspects of the subject of bank-looting." Like Moore, White purchased many combination locks and spent months studying their mechanisms. He writes that eventually he "could pick every lock, work out every known train of numbers, and had mastered the finest system in the use of high explosives; and, what was of far greater importance than all, I had evolved a tiny instrument scarcely more formidable than a finely tempered piece of very small steel wire" (White, 204). This wire White dubbed the "little joker." It was a thin wire ratchet that the burglar placed under the plate of a combination lock. When the dial was turned, the mechanism notched the ratchet and enabled White to determine the numbers of the combination. He could then play with the numbers until he determined the correct sequence, a process that took only about thirty minutes. This study also gave White skills in observation: he asserts that following his researches he could usually know the combination of a safe simply by watching someone open it from a distance. White soon renewed his partnership with Shinburn and found that Shinburn too had been developing new techniques and more efficient methods. Together they went into bank safe robbing with new energy: "I tapped on the rock as with a magic wand, and out came a golden stream" (White, 207).

The presentation of self by these aristocrats is a celebration of individuality and success. Their views of themselves and their place in the world closely parallel those of more legitimate entrepreneurs. A key element of the persona adopted by these writers is the mask of an entrepreneur whose values, with a few major exceptions, are in close harmony with the prevailing ethos of American civilization. This is especially true of what might be called public or civic virtues. Moore, for instance, is proud of the large number of men he employed during his career as a counterfeiter. With pride he notes that his help "were men who never indulged in intoxicating liquors, always kept their heads level, and had plenty of nerve" (Moore, 63). He glories in the fact that in his entire career as a counterfeiter, only one of his employees was ever lost to the law; this employee spent only eighteen months in prison before Moore was able to obtain a pardon for him. Moore also emphasizes the "fact" that he never received goods from a robbery in which force had been used

(Moore, 65–66), and both Moore and White are proud of having sworn never to take another man's life even though it might cost them their freedom.

The added spice that the continual danger of their profession gives to their lives also contributes to the celebration of self among the master thieves. They are men on the edge of imprisonment, violence, or death. This becomes an essential element in the excitement of the profession. As White asserts, the greater the risk involved in a particular job, the greater the desire of the bank burglar to "beat it"; White even contends that the man who stays in the ranks of the professional bank burglars does so as much for the excitement as from desire for gain (White, 233–34). The continual presence of danger is a strong element of the persona of adventurous rogue that these aristocrats adopt.

The self-image of the autobiographers who began their careers near the turn of the century is a sharp contrast to that of the master thieves. These later thieves belonged to the working class of professional crime. Several changes in the life-style of professional thieves reflect this altered self-image: the presentation of prison and prison experiences, the use of drugs or alcohol, the role of violence in the profession, the disappearance of innovation and inventiveness, and the changed role of risk in the criminal life.

The professional burglars of the Gilded Age rarely dwell on their prison experiences, presenting them as simply an unpleasant element of the trade. When, as in Moore's case, prison experiences are presented in some detail, the purpose is not to show the debilitating effect of prison but to reinforce the persona of the individual in charge of his life. His experiences in prison do not destroy him; instead, he uses them to destroy corrupt wardens through his influence in the outside world and thus exerts control over his fate even when he is supposedly powerless.

In contrast to these master thieves, men such as Jim Caulfield and Wellington Scott dwell repeatedly and at length on the quality of their prison experiences. The prison, in effect, becomes the school for the progressive thief. Here he learns the skills of his profession and forms ties to older professionals who will aid him in practicing these skills when released from prison. Caulfield's refrain after each of his many releases from prison becomes "What can I do?"; he blames his inability to stay straight on his lack of a legitimate trade and the distrust of society for ex-convicts. Typical of his attitude on his release from a prison sentence is this statement: "The only thing I could do well was to graft; and the only society that would welcome me was that of the underworld" (Hapgood, 208–9). Rather than celebrating his status as other and as a warrior against society, he rationalizes his career as the only choice open to him. Due to his environment, experiences, and status as an ex-convict, he has no choice but crime; theft is all that he knows.

Another change in the persona of the professional thief as memoirist is his attitude toward drugs and liquor. The master thieves of the earlier era prided themselves on their control—on abstinence from drugs, and use of liquor only when it would not interfere with their work. These later thieves, however, blame many of their problems on drug dependency and alcoholism. These thieves of crime's laboring class view drugs and liquor as central to a thief's life.

This is at least partially a result of a changed attitude toward risk and danger. Unlike earlier thieves who enjoyed the brinksmanship of living on the edge throughout their careers, these later thieves resent it more and more as they grow older; they search for release from anxiety in whatever means are available. When Scott discusses the peculiar calling of the "yegg," he states: "His greatest passion is drink; he will 'slop up' (get drunk) whenever the opportunity is offered" (Scott, 79). Caulfield began to use opium in a search for added stimulation to a jaded consciousness, but after he had become an addict he thought the opium had ruined him: "I became dead to almost everything that was good." He realized the dangers of drugs when, under the influence of opium, he almost murdered a partner who tried to cheat him in dividing the take from a robbery (Hapgood, 238). The opium also caused him to lose his ambition as a thief; he eventually spent his time smoking and stole only to get enough money to buy the opium. The essential note struck in these later autobiographies is the boredom of crime; no longer is the "high" of the risk present; it simply becomes a job with the same drawbacks as any other job. After Caulfield's second term in prison, he spent seven months before taking his third fall. He acknowledges that the graft was good in these seven months, but he had lost his ambition for a hustling life due to opium, bad health, and the study of philosophy. The excitement was gone and theft had become merely a job; hence, he turned to swindling, the easiest form of graft, even though it did not stir his imagination (Hapgood, 286–87). These authors would willingly leave the profession if they could; indeed both these later autobiographers at least claim to have retired from crime in middle age.

The whole notion of the professional nature of the calling has also undergone profound changes. No longer are these thieves proud of their innovative contributions to the craft; now reputation becomes a matter of one's associates and one's standing in the rogues' galleries scattered around the country. Caulfield drops the names of big-time burglars into his autobiography with regularity even though he never worked with these people and knew them only in prison. His tone becomes almost nostalgic as he looks back toward an earlier golden age of crime.

The changed role of violence typifies the changes in the profession. Although the threat of violence was always present in these callings, men such as White and Moore prided themselves on never harming another person. They even refused jobs where a night watchman would have had to be silenced. By the close of the Progressive Era these compunctions had disappeared. Violence emerged as an increasingly important tool in the thief's repertoire until it became central to the profession. A crime such as safe burglary, once considered scientific, degenerated into a matter of crude force.

The increased importance of violence is evident in the replacement of the old style bank burglar by the yegg, a tramp thief who used the role of hobo as a cover for his crimes. Scott describes the life of a yegg as one "of stirring adventure," but one in which study and mastery of skills is hardly necessary. For Scott, violence is simply a part of the trade. Even here there is a certain pride in violence as a professional skill used only under certain conditions. Scott claims that the yegg never uses violence for pleasure, against women, or simply to obtain money: "On the other hand, if a life should stand between him and liberty, he would unhesitatingly take that life." Even in the use of murder as a tool, Scott maintains a sense of professional caste, for he claims that the yegg "never degenerates to the cruelty of the stick-up man" (Scott, 80).

The callousness in the use of violence, even when qualified in the ways Scott indicates, is a new element in the world of the professional criminal. This points to a widening gulf between the values of the professional criminal and the rest of his culture, a new and frightening lack of empathy for his victim or the innocent witness. While this ready use of violence has always been associated with such criminals as the footpad or mugger, the higher levels of the profession had viewed it with repugnance. Perhaps one reason for the increasing violence associated with all kinds of professional theft following the turn of the century is the growing distance between the criminal and the ethos of his civilization. He no longer shares the culture's values, and his alienation makes it harder to view his victim as an object of empathy. He becomes simply an obstacle standing in the criminal's way, an obstacle to be removed as expeditiously as possible.

THE PROFESSIONAL THIEF AS SOCIAL CRITIC

Another important element in these autobiographies is drawing parallels between the underworld and the upper world and exposing the corruption riddling American society and institutions. These thieves considered this corruption endemic; indeed, they could not have operated successfully without the collaboration of the police and the willingness of victims to settle for a partial return of stolen booty in return for a promise to forego legal prosecution. A key element of the rogue's persona since the early picaros has been his vantage point. This enables him to see the baser side of respectable society with remarkable clarity. One justification for a life of crime is a social system that perpetuates poverty and injustice. As Lincoln Steffens told the nation in *The Shame of the Cities*, the police, politicians, and businessmen are the true criminals.[17]

White and Moore, in spite of their status as "other," subscribe to most of the values of American culture. For example, following his first successful bank burglary, White succinctly sums up the rags to riches success mythology. A week earlier, he had possessed only five dollars; now he owns over forty thousand: "I felt myself growing so satisfied with having this money, gained through crime, that I tried to crush the feeling." He is unable to "crush" his feeling of satisfaction and presents himself almost as if he were a character from one of Horatio Alger's novels who, because of his "pluck and luck," has risen from the bottom of the social heap to the top (White, 128). White does not see or present himself as having a value system that differs radically from that held by the rest of the country. He is simply more straightforward in going after what the rest of the nation desires—wealth.

These first-rank burglars found themselves living double lives marked by conflicting value systems. This helps explain the ease with which they adopt the personas of "respectable" captains of industry. White funneled most of his money into a legitimate business, a fashionable livery stable in New York City which he kept in his wife's name. He used his correct name in his dealings with the legitimate world but adopted the telling alias of George Bliss for use in his true vocation. White's position in the upper world was so secure that he worked as a professional bank burglar for about eight years before his wife discovered his profession. He maintains that her discovery of the truth was one of his most painful experiences (White, 402).

The ability to move easily in the world of legitimate enterprise is central to both the work of the first-class burglar and his persona. Both White and Moore are from solid middle-class backgrounds. The camouflage of respectability thus fits them comfortably. Neither of them is quite convinced that there is really anything wrong about their profession. They are pursuing the goals of practically everyone else in their civilization—they are simply less hypocritical and more direct in their course from rags to riches.

Although this vision of the interchangeability of the two worlds is central to their persona, the imagery of their writings reveals a chasm separating the two worlds. White's language reveals the gulf between these worlds when he discusses his professional achievements. During his first robbery he was associated with a brutal gang of lower-class bank robbers. This gang tried to gain entry to the bank by using a one-armed gashouse watchman to "work the sympathetic dodge" on the bank's guard. All of White's references to this terrified man describe him as a "tool," a dehumanized object to be used in the same manner as the other tools in their burglar kit. These descriptive images also reduce him to something mechanical, without life or feeling. For example, White says that he presented a ludicrous picture with "his teeth chattering like a fast-working sewing-machine needle," and that "as a tool, he responded to our bidding with the same directness that a needle responds to a magnet." Throughout the account of this robbery, one of White's few experiences with actual human brutality, he seems compelled to create a sense of distance, a sense of unreality which negates the true force of the cruelty.

Just as his images distance him from the gang's terrorized victim, his presentation of the gang relies on the conventions of melodrama and creates a sense of aesthetic distance. He presents the gang's leader, "Tall Jim," as a stage villain who hisses his words when angry, thus turning the whole episode into a piece of theater rather than reality. This distancing of the self from violence not only confirms White's own distaste for it, but also points to the necessity of the victim's dehumanization before violence can be usefully employed. The victim must become "other," less than human, and thus a suitable object for violence (White, 86, 89, 90).

Both White and Moore use the parallels between the two worlds as a justification for their careers. Moore repeatedly makes half-serious, half-humorous references to the American work and profit ethic. For instance, he explains that he passed counterfeit as a "little outside speculation" while simultaneously scouting a targeted bank since "[Moore and his gang] did not want to allow an opportunity to make a dollar to go by unimproved" (Moore, 79). The exposure of corruption is, however, a more serious enterprise, almost a righteous undertaking. These burglars are incensed by the betrayal of trust even though this same betrayal of trust allows them to pursue their careers. White recounts his discovery of police corruption in ten pages that detail his initial shock at this corruption. His first, instinctive response was dismay, for, though he had been "driven" to crime through persecution, he found it abhorrent to split his loot with a traitorous officer "in the employment of the people" (White, 172). This presentation of police corruption as treason runs throughout his autobiography. He continually names names and gives the amounts of pay-offs. White also points to several jobs that the police set up for him and asserts that he could never have operated successfully without the "patent safety switch" provided by the New York Police Department's Bank Ring (White, 403, 463, 313). One reason these burglars see the betrayal of trust as such a heinous thing is the cornerstone of underworld ethics: loyalty. The unpardonable sin for these thieves is the betrayal of trust by "squealing." Without this trust, overrated though it may be among criminals, the outlaw is in a much more vulnerable position.

Moore makes the same accusations against policemen; he too considers them guilty of betraying a public trust. Moore concludes his autobiography by asserting: "I reported to the licensed thieves, for more than six years, every robbery I committed, and the amount of money and valuables stolen; and I gave them their 'square bit' out of all the stealings, for police protection" (Moore, 645). He argues that the public needs to learn it does not take a thief to catch a thief and that it can obtain better results from honest men than from rogues.

Money is the great panacea for the professional thief. Moore states that money figures in the "prosecution" of all crimes except murder and that he never feared prison while he had money. The greed of policemen is also one of the forces that keeps a professional thief busy: "I was called fast, but I could not steal fast enough to feed a lot of licensed thieves and my family" (Moore, 645). This betrayal of trust is thus much worse than a straightforward attack on property, for betrayal of trust undermines the foundations of society itself. In spite of their status as other, these men accept the values of their civilization. They see parallels between their form of theft and that of the great entrepreneurs of the Gilded Age, and they share an admiration for their achievements even though this admiration is tinted by jealousy at their legitimate status. In a way, the burglars highlight these cultural values by carrying them to their logical extremes. If the amassing of a great fortune is the ultimate goal, what does it matter whether it be theft from a bank or theft from the powerless? This theme was soon to surface as one of the major thrusts of much progressive social reform.

Just as he differs in other major themes from the earlier autobiographers, the criminal of the Progressive Era differs in his view of the upper world. He too draws parallels between the two worlds, but the persona of the progressive criminal is much more alienated from the values of the culture. He delights in exposing the hypocrisies of the "moral" upper class and views corruption as much more endemic to the American system. Caulfield, for instance, joyfully recounts an occasion when he "nicked" a small knife from an "aristocratic woman"; the rivets of the knife turned out to be magnifying glasses for pictures that would have "made Comstock howl" (Hapgood, 210). This minor vice represents the veil of hypocrisy in which the "legitimate" world drapes itself. It also reinforces a changed self-image. Earlier thieves preferred to concentrate on such notable robbers as Cornelius Vanderbilt. The hustler is content to point out the harmless indiscretions of the middle class.

Caulfield also recounts numerous examples of the police corruption which allows the thief to operate with immunity, but this is less important in his eyes than the generalized social corruption that extends from cold preachers in large churches to prison guards. His attitude is that at least one thief can trust another thief's word and that there are few honest men anywhere, in or out of the world of graft. Far worse than the professional thief is the man who has made his wealth by destroying the lives of those without power, for these men do the greatest harm to society even though they may never have broken the law: "I am not trying to excuse myself or my companions in crime, but I think the world is a little twisted in its ideas as to right and wrong, and who are the greatest sinners" (Hapgood, 195). Thus, even the pickpocket-burglar who suffers from "astigmatism of the conscience" (Hapgood, 309) is infected with the temper of reform and redirects the focus on deviance from his subculture to the society as a whole.

Scott follows the same tack in presenting the injustice of the upper world. In his view, the fact of crime is less important than its size. Society is foolish to expect professional criminals to reform when the petty thief sees the embezzler who has wrecked a bank and destroyed hundreds of lives come to prison "with a paltry sentence of a few years." In the prison, the petty thief quickly discovers that crime does pay if one only commits a large enough crime. He sees the big thief working in a soft clerical position while he labors under a harsh contract. The result is, of course, that "the little crook tries to become a big crook" (Scott, 52–53). The unfairness of the criminal justice system thus contributes to the increase of crime as well as the destruction of the criminal.

Scott also draws parallels between the criminal and the honest citizen; once again the focus of these parallels has shifted, and the shift reveals the influence of progressive thought. Scott is less concerned with justifying the criminal by pointing to corruption in society than in reuniting him with the human family. He points out that criminals are not very different from anyone else; they possess the same emotions. They work, love, and have ideals. The criminal does not belong to a distinct class. For Scott "the great fact in the formation of criminal tendencies ... is environment," and society must accept its responsibility for crime. If social conditions were better, America would have less crime (Scott, 112–16).

These autobiographies are typical of the criminal autobiography from 1870 to 1917. They reveal striking changes in the ways Americans viewed professional crime and the ways the criminals viewed themselves. One of the most telling of these changes is the shift in the nature of the form from a picaresque tale of adventure to a social document. The purpose of the first is entertainment while that of the second is reform. The autobiographies point up a growing concern for the environment and its shaping influence, an important part of progressive thought, as well as placing a new emphasis on developmental processes. Where the reader of the Gilded Age discovered how professional thieves operated successfully, the progressive reader found out what made the professional thief. The public persona of the professional thief and his self-image also changed dramatically during this era. Other notable differences involved the changing nature of professional theft and the growing acceptability of violence. Throughout the period the professional thief as autobiographer maintained a relish for pointing to parallels between the worlds of crime and respectability and exposing both police corruption and the moral hypocrisy of the upper world.

These criminal autobiographies provide a glimpse of the "golden age" of professional crime. After World War I this type of crime went into a decline. The crime corporations that resulted from Prohibition diminished the role of the individual entrepreneur and "small businessman" in the profession of crime.

In the Hands of the Detectives; or Unravelling a Tangled Web

THE BIRTH OF THE DETECTIVE

One July afternoon in 1847 a small boy interrupted Allan Pinkerton's work with the information that H. E. Hunt, owner of the general store in Dundee, Illinois and one of the more important men in the village, wanted to see him. Pinkerton strolled into town barefoot and bareheaded, wearing a checkered shirt and bleached-out overalls. Hunt and another village merchant, I. C. Bosworth, explained that they wanted Pinkerton to do "a little job in the detective line." Pinkerton protested that he knew nothing about detective work: "My line is the cooper business," he told them. Hunt finally persuaded Pinkerton that he could do the job and explained that they were suspicious of a stranger in the village. Someone had recently passed two counterfeit ten-dollar bills in the community; this stranger had asked directions to the house of a man suspected of passing the counterfeit. Pinkerton again began to protest: "How would I know they were counterfeit? I never saw a ten-dollar bill in my whole life." Hunt produced samples of both the genuine and the false bills for Pinkerton to study; he left the store and walked down the street to the local harness shop where the stranger's saddle was being repaired while the stranger waited at the local tavern.

Eventually a well-dressed elderly man entered the shop. This respectable person was the stranger Pinkerton was waiting for. After mounting his horse, he studied the unsophisticated villager admiring his sleek roan, then asked for directions to "Old

Man Crane's house." Crane was the suspect individual. His suspicions confirmed, Pinkerton walked beside the mounted stranger until they were outside the village. Pinkerton then confided that hard money was difficult to obtain and he was looking for a scheme to bring in cash.

The stranger introduced himself as John Craig, a farmer from Vermont. The two men reached a ravine in the wilderness of this still sparsely settled region of northeastern Illinois. Here they paused and Craig asked several suspicious questions while Pinkerton acted the part of a slow-witted lout not averse to making a crooked dollar. Finally, Craig agreed to sell Pinkerton $500 worth of counterfeit ten-dollar bills for $125. The meeting would take place in an unfinished building on the outskirts of Elgin, Illinois.

Pinkerton hurried back to Dundee, where Hunt and Bosworth rounded up the cash. He met Craig in the basement of the rough structure. After a brief conversation, Craig took Pinkerton's cash then asked him to step outside for a moment. When Pinkerton returned, Craig had vanished, but the counterfeit was waiting under a rock. Pinkerton returned to Dundee, dog-tired and sure that he was not born to be a detective: "The little cooper-shop, my good wife, and our plain homely ways, were, after all, the best things on earth."

Pinkerton was not the sort of Scotchman who would leave a task half done, however. He knew that for a successful arrest and prosecution, Craig must have the counterfeit on him when arrested. Pinkerton arranged to make a larger buy in Chicago. He then arrested Craig, but the counterfeiter mysteriously escaped from jail, leaving a richer sheriff behind.

This episode eventually led to the founding of Pinkerton's private detective agency in Chicago in 1851. His reputation for catching Craig spread until he had so much detective work to do that he was "soon actually *forced* to relinquish the honorable, though not over-profitable, occupation of a cooper for that of a professional detective."[1]

Pinkerton presents his first adventure as a detective in symbolic terms that emphasize the temptations facing the detective as well as highlighting several themes of mid-nineteenth century American culture. Appropriately, the corruption comes from the older East into the unspoiled purity of the West where it poses a threat to virtuous communities of small merchants, laborers, and farmers. Pinkerton paints himself as the yeoman laborer, barefooted, bareheaded, and unsophisticated, asked to trap the "keen man of the world." Pinkerton emphasizes his strong feelings of inadequacy, a strategy that underscores one of the themes of this adventure: that untutored virtue will always triumph over the most sophisticated villainy.

Pinkerton dramatizes the meeting between the barefooted yeoman and the sharply dressed easterner with a rhetoric filled with religious echoes. Pinkerton's temptation occurs in the wilderness, the archetypal setting of the struggle between good and evil. Although Pinkerton emerges from the struggle with his virtue intact, he asserts that even though he has never been shaken in his determination to bring a criminal to justice, the memory of his own temptation tempers his response to lawbreakers: "I can never think of one undergoing the first great temptation to crime whether he has resisted or fallen, without a touch of genuine human sympathy." He has been fundamentally changed by his encounter with crime and, in spite of his triumph, has gained added insight into those he will hunt for the rest of his life. He leaves the encounter with these ideas "playing back and forth like a swift shuttle through my mind." This image of weaving presents the essential fabric of a detective's life as the threads of all strata of human activity are inextricably mingled in his experience.[2]

This account also centers around one of the central issues detectives faced in pursuing their careers—deception. Deception surfaces repeatedly in this narrative. The crime Pinkerton faces is counterfeiting. This crime is a form of fraud; it relies on a deceptive appearance hiding an empty reality. John Craig's appearance is deceptively respectable. He is dressed soberly, has gray hair, and seems to be about sixty-five years old. Pinkerton himself must play a deceptive role to pierce Craig's false surface and bring the real criminal to justice. Pinkerton acts the role of a slow-witted, dishonest laborer to trap the sophisticated actor aping virtue. Even justice is deceptive; when Pinkerton finally lodges Craig in jail, Craig escapes by buying off the symbol of society's quest for order—the sheriff.

Pinkerton is but one example of a class of authors who assumed an increasingly important role in the presentation and
definition of professional crime for Americans after the Civil
War—professional observers. These professionals were either
private detectives or policemen who used professional thieves
to enhance their own standing in American life. In the last thirty
years of the nineteenth century, the status of the American detective underwent profound changes. Detectives emerged in the
late 1840s and early 1850s in America as new preventive police
forces replaced the old constabulary. These earlier constables
had developed extensive practical knowledge of crime in their
work as thief-takers. Although the power to arrest criminals had
been transferred from the constables to the new patrolmen, constables made a place for themselves in the new departments
through their knowledge of the underworld, which gave them
an edge in recovering stolen goods. The result was the detective
system.

These new detectives encountered strong opposition at first.
The police forces that had replaced the constables were built
around the concept of crime prevention. One reason for their
development in American cities was that reformers hoped this
would eliminate the abuses in the old constable system. Both
constables and detectives went to work only after a crime was
committed. Reformers feared that detectives, like the earlier constable, would have an interest in the generation of crime. They
also hoped that the new police forces would be so effective in
reducing crime that detectives would be unnecessary. These
hopes died quickly and, despite public hostility to the constable-
detective, the success of professional criminals required his presence. In June 1845 one of New York City's ex-constables, Gil
Hays, established his "Independent Police" as a response to the
reorganization of the police system in New York. This was the
first private detective agency in America. Other agencies appeared in St. Louis (1846), Baltimore (1847), and Philadelphia
(1848). Allan Pinkerton established his agency in Chicago in
1851.[3]

The detective's function was essentially the recovery of stolen
property, although he also secured evidence for divorce cases
and located missing persons. Generally the detective worked for

a reward or a portion of the recovered goods as well as salary. To be successful he needed a wide acquaintance in the professional underworld. This opened the way for obvious abuses, and practically every criminal autobiographer gave accounts of detectives who specialized in gaining access to legitimate institutions to plan robberies for underworld associates to execute.[4] If the pursuit by the official police became too intense, the detective would step in and either return the stolen goods, splitting the reward with his confederates, or serve as the middleman in working out a deal to return part of the stolen property for a promise of immunity from prosecution for the thieves.

This problem of the criminal detective also surfaced in practically every examination of the underworld not written by police officers or private detectives. This theme attacks the league between professional thieves and private detectives as well as the detective's propensity for blackmail and extortion. Edward Crapsey, in *The Nether Side of New York*, argued in 1871 that the mysteriousness surrounding private detectives was not romantic but shielded "beasts of prey"; "shadows" darker in reality than the metaphoric slang implied. Crapsey called for the suppression of the institution of private detectives through a boycott, since their methods were so corrupt and interwoven with crime. He believed that the system itself was "naturally at war with the fundamental principles of justice." Detectives made their living primarily from the distrust of employers for their employees and the distrust of a spouse for his mate. Even more dangerous than this fostering of distrust was the detectives' willingness to "turn a dishonest penny by recovering stolen property, which they can only do by compounding the crime by which it had been acquired." This undermined the very foundations of law; detectives "are a peril to society."[5]

Other writers attacked private detectives for different reasons. The most notorious criminal lawyers in America during the nineteenth century were William F. Howe and A. H. Hummel, who operated out of New York's Bowery and were known as the "fixers" for the underworld. Their book, *In Danger; or Life in New York* (1888), contains a long attack on detectives; unlike Crapsey they are not interested in exposing detective criminality. They simply want to puncture the inflated egos of American detectives. A detective's success depends on his acquaintance with a particular class of criminals. Howe and Hummel assert that ninety percent of all cases are worked through the "squeal" of a thief or ex-thief and that most private detectives depend for their livelihood on breaches of the "moral" rather than the social law—such as marital infidelity.[6]

Still another approach to the darker side of detective work comes in Morris Friedman's *The Pinkerton Labor Spy*. The premise for this attack is ideological. Friedman argues that the methods of the Pinkerton Agency are opposed to American institutions. Although the Agency has a reputation for honesty, it is built on "skilful and systematic misrepresentation of facts." The Pinkertons have "perfected a system of espionage, calumny and persecution of labor ... more intolerable and pernicious than the universally detested and infamous Secret Police of Russia."[7]

Although the detective continued to carry a somewhat unsavory reputation, he also began to assume celebrity status in post-Civil War America. Several factors were behind this rise in status. One was the success of such "incorruptible" detectives as Allan Pinkerton. Also, after 1880, Thomas Byrnes achieved notable results from his reorganization of the Detective Bureau of the New York Police. Additionally, the detective came to the fore in popular literature as a romantic figure of skill and daring after the Civil War. He obtained a firm foothold in the American imagination through such fictional avatars as Old Sleuth, Cap Collier, and Nick Carter.

The most important cause behind the detective's rise in the minds of the public, however, was skilful self-dramatization. A torrent of books purporting to reveal the secret life of the real detective flooded the American market between 1870 and 1900. Although hacks trying to capitalize on a favorable market produced many of these, actual detectives wrote others. The motives behind these writings ranged from vanity, as in Pinkerton's long series of adventures, to simple advertising as in Thomas Furlong's *Fifty Years a Detective*. Among these writings were, however, honest attempts at presenting the detective's life. The motivation behind such books was often an attempt to clean up the unsavory odor that hovered over the job. These writers were participants in the move toward professionalization that dominated so many areas of American civilization after the Civil War. In order to claim the status of professionals, these detectives needed to prove that they could provide a specialized service to the community—a service that called for esoteric training, skills, and knowledge. They also needed to demonstrate the necessity of their calling. For this they needed a worthy adversary.

They found their opponent in the professional thief, a figure they used to elevate their own position in American life. They presented the professional thief as a highly skilled warrior constantly alert for opportunities to prey on an unprotected public. Only a skilled detective could bring this worthy to bay. These detectives developed a specialized vocabulary and often adopted the mask of a critic in their presentation of crime; on occasion they became aestheticians of crime. The central use of the thief by these professional observers was to improve the detective's image—an image that dominated their conception of self and their role in American civilization.

THE LITERARY ROGUES' GALLERY

The Rogues' Gallery must be one of the oddest forms of literature ever written. It developed in the years following the Civil War and was a curious hybrid of the old Newgate Calendar style of collective criminal biography and a newer, more scientific analysis of criminals. The genesis of the literary Rogues' Gallery was the use of photography in law enforcement. In the 1850s detectives realized how useful this new process could be in their jobs. Until then the only way detectives could gain knowledge of a criminal's appearance was through the process called "showing up." If a detective spotted a criminal he already knew, he would pick him up on suspicion and take him to headquarters. All the available detectives would then be summoned to study the criminal so that they too would recognize him in the future. This cumbersome process had obvious flaws in the amount of time it involved, the possibility of a faulty memory, and the violation of a suspect's civil rights. Major cities and large private detective agencies such as the Pinkertons soon began to take advantage of the new technology of photography. When suspicious persons were picked up, their photographs would be taken. These would be placed with photographs of other local criminals. These compilations of criminal photographs were called rogues' galleries. A detective could study the photographs in his spare time or show them to the victim of a crime in hopes that he could identify his assailant.

The literary Rogue's Gallery was an attempt to disseminate the detective's information to the public. Two works provide the best examples of this subgenre produced by professional observers: *Criminals of America; or, Tales of the Lives of Thieves Enabling Everyone to Be His Own Detective*, by Detective Phil. Farley (1876) and *Professional Criminals of America*, by Thomas Byrnes, Chief of Detectives in New York City (1886). Both books were collections of photographs or illustrations of professional criminals.

The works occupy a peculiar middle ground between narrative and analysis, a middle ground which reflects the detective's own peculiar status in American society. Although only ten years separate the publication of these books, the shift in their styles and themes reveals much about the changing imaginative response to American crime. This shift involved the movement of crime as a mental concept from the realm of an extraordinary "imaginative fact" to the notion of crime as an accepted fact in the country. Farley's book represents an era when the police occupied an ambiguous position in their culture. The police were still uncertain of the role they would play in a developing society. Byrnes looks forward to the modern era. His approach is more "scientific." Byrnes presents crime as a social fact; Farley presents it as a social curiosity.

Even the statement of purpose with which each author prefaces his work reveals this change. Farley, for instance, claims he is writing "to prevent crime; aid in the detection of criminals; show the young and inexperienced some of the pitfalls that await them.... In tearing the veil of romance from vice, and laying bare the skeleton head of the monster in all its hideousness, I consider I am still doing my duty." His major goal, however, is actually to entertain his readers with a view of lower-class life in the city—a realm that would not come into its own in American writing until the 1890s. Farley's book serves mainly as a series of case studies in the horrors of a thief's life of "lonliness [sic], constant fear, doubt, remorse, despair, imprisonment, degradation, and incessant labor."[8] The use of illustrations to prevent criminals from escaping detection is clearly secondary.

Byrnes, however, does not see his primary goal as exposing the horrors of a life of crime; he writes to prevent the successful operation of skilled criminals and thus to protect society from those who would prey on it. His goal sounds a bit naive to the modern reader as he contends "that there is nothing that professional criminals fear as much as identification and exposure." He holds that if criminals were widely known their depredations would suffer a severe setback: "With their likenesses within reach of all, their vocation would soon become risky and unprofitable."[9] Byrnes offers his book as a public service in the aid of preventing crime arising from established professionals. This also points up the changing persona of the detective. Byrnes never doubts that detective work is a profession. By presenting his specialized knowledge, he is serving his community. Farley, however, has no illusions about the special skills of the detective, as his subtitle ironically indicates.

Another striking difference between the two works lies in their areas of emphasis. Byrnes does indeed present a portrait gallery of America's major thieves. His book has two major divisions. The first section is a detailed examination of the methods of professional thieves in the traditional mode of the criminal anatomy; the second presents the photographs and biographies of slightly over two hundred of America's most dangerous criminals, including major forgers, confidence men, and bank burglars.

Farley's book, however, says nothing about the most important thieves in America. His book is organized haphazardly and presents short examinations of the methods of thieves, biographies of petty shoplifters, pickpockets, and fences, and anecdotes from the lives of petty criminals. The only thief approaching major-league status in Farley's book is Spence Pettis, "the meanest and most cowardly thief in America." This Pettis was a renegade and snitch, an outcast among the aristocrats of crime and hence suitable for inclusion in this book.

When Farley's book appeared, the *New York Times* gave it high praise as a valuable tool for the city's protection, asserting that "it contains nearly 150 portraits of some of the most notorious, clever, and therefore dangerous of the thieves of the metropolis." Books of crime were generally taboo for genteel readers in this era, and the reviewer was careful to stress the moral impetus behind the work: "We are no advocates for sensational literature, but the narratives here are true, while at the same time they fix the reader's attention; and the morals to be drawn from them are neither few nor destitute of force."[10]

In spite of these assertions from both Farley and the *New York Times* about the importance of this book, Farley avoids his true subject, never dealing with successful thieves. Ironically, this detective, who seemed dedicated to exposing thieves for the good of the public, was one of the more corrupt detectives in American history. When Max Shinburn was arrested in 1868, George White states, "Detective Phil. Farley was among the first to hear of the arrest of Shinburn . . . and he hurried to me with the facts."[11] White further claims that Farley was a member of the "Bank Ring" of the New York Detective Bureau and that he, along with Chief of Detectives John Irving, and Detectives McCord, Radford, and Kelso, received $17,000 each as their share of the spoils following the Ocean Bank robbery in 1869.

Farley's activities among the criminal elite were not confined to bank burglars. Following the Bank of England forgeries, perhaps the most famous theft of the nineteenth century, George MacDonald, the engraver for the gang of youthful American forgers, attempted to return to America on the steamer *Thuringia*. The directors of the Bank of England, knowing of the rampant corruption in the New York City Detective Bureau, retained the Pinkerton Agency to capture MacDonald on his arrival in New York. After a bizarre boat race, the police launch outdistanced the Pinkertons. Detective Farley and Chief of Detectives Irving barricaded themselves in MacDonald's cabin, refusing to allow the Pinkertons entry until MacDonald had split over $160,000 between the two. Much of the money from the forgeries was in gold sovereigns, and Austin Bidwell later relished his thoughts of what the scene in the cabin must have been like. The Pinkertons and federal marshals were pounding on the door of MacDonald's cabin "morally sure that Irving and Co. had plucked their bird." The two detectives knew that "any appearance of pockets bulging out might lead to disgrace, so, while they hated to leave any, for their fingers itched for all, yet they were forced to that cruel self-denial."[12]

Bidwell, one of the masterminds behind the Bank of England forgeries, asserts that Farley and Irving introduced him to crime. These detectives approached him while he was a struggling broker on Wall Street in desperate need of money. They wanted him to sell a batch of stolen bonds in Europe, and, although at first he demurred, Bidwell eventually agreed to serve them. The money was so easy that, at the detectives' further urging, he left Wall Street for a life of crime.

This, perhaps, is the explanation for Farley's failure to deal with major crime and criminals. Unquestionably, he was deeply involved with them; yet, one wonders why he would write a book for the public's "benefit" that professed to expose the methods of criminals. Farley is not hypocritical in what he does present. He often adopts a persona sympathetic to criminals, presenting the sentimental side of the burglar or the burglar as family man, yet he rarely names one in active practice. Farley's relations with the underworld were ambiguous, and this ambiguity is continually expressed in his writing. Farley's primary purpose was actually not to prevent crime but to relate amusing stories and to entertain an audience.

Farley treats the methods of several classes of criminals in some detail: burglars, house-breakers, silk and lace thieves, confidence men, pickpockets, sneak thieves, hotel thieves, pocketbook droppers, and till-tappers. He also presents such criminal operations as the pawn-ticket game, banco, and check-raising. His presentation is laced with judgments aimed at his perceived audience's expectations, such as in the assertion that the housebreaker is the most daring and desperate of thieves. This threat to the sanctity of the hearth is presented in a way that reinforces the importance of the detective to his society.

Farley's anecdotes provide several insights into what a practicing detective believed the American public would find interesting about crime. Farley had soaked up many of the popular literary currents of his time. When he assumes the persona of entertainer he naturally falls back on these stock story types. One problem here is precisely how much of this is due to Farley and how much, if any, to an unknown collaborator. In its review, the *New York Times* reports that he originally planned to work with the aid of a commercial writer, but this writer failed to keep his commitment so that Farley was forced to write the book himself. Whatever the source, Farley's stories are essentially criminal variations on popular magazine short story patterns. Farley adopts these structures with few changes; the alterations he makes are designed to tailor the patterns to criminal life. Among the forms he uses are sentimental love stories, humorous love stories, and mistaken identity stories. He also presents variations of the consolation literature so popular in the mid-nineteenth century as well as horror stories patterned after such fictional exposés as Eugene Sue's *Mysteries of Paris*. Farley even manages to include sentimental poetry.

These stories highlight the distance between the lower classes and the ideals of American elites. The anecdotes themselves are memorable for occasional vulgarity mixed with realistic details of lower-class life; they usually suffer from sentimentality or heavy-handed attempts at humor. Practically all of the "love" stories are based on adultery and its near discovery; these turn on misunderstanding, deception, confusion, and the threat of discovery. These stories aim to narrate a humorous presentation of the love life of the lower and/or criminal classes. They are notable as early presentations of these classes in popular American writing, but the presentation is steeped in literary conventions governing the use of the lower classes for comic purposes stretching back to the Renaissance and contain nothing truly innovative. Farley uses his comic anecdotes primarily as a technique to vary the flow of his narrative; these stories generally provide relief for the reader after analytical passages. Farley does not consciously model these passages on such predecessors as Elizabethan drama; he is simply participating in a literary convention governing the use of low life that has a long history.[13]

Several major themes concerning professional theft emerge from Farley's *Tales of the Lives of Thieves*. Farley plays up the misery that generally accompanies the end of a thief's life. He also examines the pattern of a professional career in crime, placing stress on the importance of choice in the profession of theft and outlining the process of tutelage and apprenticeship that turns a thief into a professional. Several anecdotes are built around the professional thief's vanity concerning reputation. In spite of his own romanticization of crime and criminals, Farley recurrently emphasizes that the reality of crime is worse than generally portrayed by the uninitiated imagination.

Unlike most earlier writers of criminal biography, however, Farley does not concentrate on the most barbaric and savage crimes he can discover to present in a sensational fashion. With Farley professional crime is becoming a social fact, a social institution. He presents crime as a normal and eternal element of urban life even while he invests it with a heavy imaginative coloring. The urban environment is a threatening place, especially for the provincial villager untutored in the ways of vice. Farley usually presents this threat as one to property. Crime, for Farley, means theft. His concentration on property crime reveals the nature of his vision of "normal" crime as well as his perception of what is most important and hence most interesting to his audience.

Farley views violent crime as somehow aberrant, foreign to the American criminal; in confirmation of this he draws a brief sketch of Jesse Pomeroy, the famous child-murderer of the nineteenth century. Pomeroy, himself a child, brutally slew four other children. Farley agrees with the finding of the jury that Pomeroy was insane; Pomeroy finds a place in the book "because there has probably never before been known a juvenile possessed of such murderous and fiendish proclivities."[14]

Inspector Thomas Byrnes shares Farley's emphasis on property crime in his *Professional Criminals*. Byrnes adds a strong aesthetic element to the presentation of crime, often adopting the role of the critic in his analysis. Byrnes is much surer of his place in American life than Farley. He assumes the persona of a professional on the first page of his work and never drops it; this persona strongly colors both his method and his imaginative vision of crime.

Thomas Byrnes was the most famous American police detective of the nineteenth century. He was born in Ireland in 1842, came to New York as a child, and joined the New York City Police Department in 1863. By 1870 he was a captain and from 1880 to 1892 he served as head of the Detective Bureau. In 1892 he was appointed superintendent of the police department, a post he held until forced to resign in 1895 by a newly elected reform administration.[15]

Lincoln Steffens, in his *Autobiography*, recalls that "Tom Byrnes was a famous police chief; few people ever saw him; he was only a name, but there were stories told about him, of his cunning, as a detective, as a master of men, as a manhandler of criminals, and as a retriever of stolen properties—stories that filled the upper world with respect and the lower with terror."[16] As an example of Byrnes' prowess, Steffens relates a story of having his pocket picked after being paid one Saturday afternoon. Byrnes asked Steffens how much money was in the envelope, how it was addressed, and what lines of cars Steffens had ridden, then promised he would have Steffens' money on Monday morning, "and on Monday morning Byrnes handed me the envelope with the money just as I had received it from my paper."[17]

Byrnes achieved his success and reputation by training his detectives to become connoisseurs of crime and criminal technique. In Julian Hawthorne's *The Great Bank Robbery* (1887), a fictionalized account of the robbery of the Manhattan Savings Institution on October 27, 1877, based on the "Diary of Inspector Byrnes," Hawthorne uses the analogy of a literary critic to describe Byrnes' technique. He argues that just as a critic familiar with contemporary authors can usually guess who wrote an unfamiliar passage, "so can an efficient detective divine, from the manner in which a safe has been attacked, and the character of the marks left upon it, something pointing to the identity of the operators." Since the number of first-rank bank burglars is small, most skillful detectives are familiar with their methods.[18] Hawthorne worked with Byrnes on this detective novel; the presentation of the detective as a professional possessing esoteric knowledge and skill reinforces Byrnes' rhetorical mask in *Professional Criminals*.

Byrnes also established a network of "agreements" with the underworld in which criminals agreed to operate outside of New York City or at least outside of its wealthy areas. For example, he established his famous Dead Line in March 1880 to stop the depredations of pickpockets, sneak thieves, and forgers in the

Wall Street district. If a known thief were found south of Fulton Street, he was "dead." Detectives would pick him up on sight and, if he could not explain his presence, he spent time on Blackwell's Island. If he had legitimate business in the district, he obtained a pass from a detective before heading downtown.[19] Byrnes clearly viewed his job chiefly as the protection of the city's business and respectable classes.

Though only ten years separate the appearance of Farley's book from the first edition of Byrnes' *Professional Criminals of America*, several major changes are evident in both Byrnes' book itself and the public response to it. *The New York Daily Tribune* opened its review by noting the "morbid" interest every class of society has in "the strange phases of criminal life" and praising Byrnes for not exploiting this interest in a sensational way but rather making legitimate use of it "to interest his readers while he puts them on their guard against the methods of the criminal classes that flourish on every hand." The *Tribune* went on to assert that Byrnes' book "will be to the police what a literary dictionary is to the public" and that he had admirably succeeded in his chief aim of protecting the public. The *Tribune* also noted the consternation that had been produced among the crooks in the city since the publication appeared with its excellent photographic portraits taken from the New York Rogues' Gallery.[20] Indeed inclusion in Byrnes' book became a mark of standing among thieves, for Caulfield relates at one point that before he took his second fall, he was grafting with "Jack T.——, who is now in Byrnes's book and is one of the swellest 'Peter' men (safe-blowers) in the profession"; on another occasion, Caulfield refers to the book as the Hall of Fame.[21]

The New York Times began its review by immediately separating the book from sensational narratives about crime; it was "not a cheap book with red paper covers and remarkable woodcuts purporting to reveal the lights and shadows of all the mysterious places in the great city of New York." The *Times* went on to quote from an interview with Byrnes, who felt the book would be "of great value to chiefs of police, detectives . . . banks, hotel and boarding housekeepers, commercial houses, and, in short, to all persons liable to contact with criminals."[22]

The first section of Byrnes' book provides a fascinating view of the professional urban underworld of the late nineteenth century. Byrnes' accounts of the techniques of criminals are so explicit that they almost become a primer for the would-be thief. His accounts are detailed and exact, and he gives the names of the major practitioners of each branch of crime. The changes dictated by the altered persona of the writing policeman reflect the increased drive for professional recognition. Among the topics Byrnes covers are bank burglars, bank sneak thieves, forgers, hotel and boardinghouse thieves, sneak and house thieves, store and safe burglars, shoplifters and pickpockets, confidence and banco men, fences, sawdust men, and mock auctioneers.

Throughout his analysis, Byrnes adopts a rhetorical strategy that underscores his admiration for the skill and daring of the best men in each specialty; they are worthy opponents of the first class, and he will not sully this image with presentations of the "low" classes of crooks such as river thieves, butcher-cart thieves, or garroters (muggers), though some of these do find a place among the biographies in the second half of the book.

Not only does Byrnes allow his appreciation for the skills of these men to show, but he continually makes what can only be called aesthetic judgments of their technique and style. This adoption of an aesthetic pose reflects Byrnes' self-image as a man of special abilities engaged in a battle with skilled opponents. The aesthetic judgment of crime also points to a changed vision of the nature of crime among Americans. Since Poe's introduction of the locked-room mystery in "The Murders in the Rue Morgue," the fictional presentation of crime increasingly dealt with the processes behind the commission of a crime. This approach downplayed an older vision of crime as sinful, as an offense against a moral order. In fiction the portrayal of crime moved toward an emphasis on the intellectual interest in the way a crime was executed: how ingeniously was it planned and carried out? This fictional move also stressed the role of the detective; he became the specialist that society needed to protect itself from sophisticated criminals. The influence of this new fictional attitude carried over to the nonfictional presentation of crime. Detectives were quick to seize on this trend for it glorified their role; they realized its inherent possibilities for improving their position in American society. Byrnes makes repeated use of this technique in his analysis of crime.

Of all thieves, first-class bank burglars and forgers hold the top rank for Byrnes. Writing of the bank burglars who "head the list of mechanical thieves," Byrnes states "there seems to be a strange fascination about crime that draws men of brains, and with their eyes wide open into its meshes." He argues that a criminal needs rare qualities to become an expert bank burglar, a specialization of the highest order. He then states: "The professional bank burglar must have patience, intelligence, mechanical knowledge, industry, determination, fertility of resources, and courage—all in high degree." This description could apply equally well to any successful middle-class professional engaged in legitimate enterprise. Byrnes creates a worthy antagonist who calls forth the highest skills of the detective's profession. He presents the constant study the bank burglar must maintain to achieve proficiency and then begins a discussion of the aesthetics of bank burglary. Byrnes describes various techniques for breaking into banks and safes such as picking locks, using wedges, using various explosives, and deciphering combination locks. He reserves his greatest praise for the "little joker" used by Shinburn and White.[23]

Following his anatomy of the divisions of the professional underworld, its hierarchies, and its techniques, Byrnes appends a short discussion of the use of photography in police work as a preface to the photographs and biographical sketches. Byrnes uses this section to examine some popular misconceptions the respectable classes hold about thieves. The burglar is not "low-browed, sullen, with stealthy glance and hunted air . . . as fancy and romance have pictured him." Photography is an invaluable aid to the police because many criminals "carry no suggestion of their calling about with them." This is where the public makes its mistakes: "Their idea of burglars . . . have been gathered from books, and they look for Bill Sykeses and Flash Toby Crackitts, whereas the most modest and most gentlemanly people they meet may be the representatives of their very characters." He asserts that almost all the "great criminals" lead double lives and "some of the most unscrupulous rascals who ever cracked a safe or turned out a counterfeit were at home model husbands and fathers" (54).

Byrnes thus raises the theme of appearance and reality, a theme he rams home throughout the biographies. He uses this essay on photography as a transition from the romantic portrayal of the criminal underworld to the romantic portrayal of the criminals themselves. At the same time, he shows the constant threat these hidden members of society present to the unwary, and emphasizes the necessity of skilled detectives for the protection of the populace. He states his opposition to criminal anthropology, just beginning to assert its influence in America, by claiming that physiognomy is no guide to the criminal classes; even though some of the lower grades of thieves such as low burglars are "hard-looking brutes," it is never safe to judge by appearances (55). Byrnes must discredit the notion that anyone can discern a criminal simply by observation. This poses a threat to the importance of the detective as the specialist best able to guard society against crime.

An undercurrent of melodrama flows through the biographies themselves as Byrnes relates exciting incidents in a thief's life. Unlike Farley, Byrnes does not lose sight of his major goal: the presentation of America's major professional thieves. His rogues are drawn from all geographic regions, although the emphasis is on New York and the Northeast. Each biography follows the same pattern. First Byrnes gives the thief's true name, his aliases, and various specialties in crime; next comes the "description," simply a short collection of vital statistics such as age, place of birth, and physical description, including scars and tattoos; finally Byrnes narrates the thief's "record."

The "record" of each thief is actually a short biography which describes a thief's background, arrest record, major criminal exploits, and standing in the world of crime. The "record" usually ends with Byrnes' personal judgment on the accuracy of the photograph and a connoisseur's judgment on the thief's level of skill. For instance William Beatty, alias Billy Burke, a burglar and sneak, is "a mean thief, and is called by other thieves a 'squealer' " (157–58), while John Jourdan, a safe blower and sneak thief, "is considered one of the cleverest men in America in his line" (155–56).

Although the "record" of each thief is at first appearance simply a description of the rogue's history in the underworld written in direct, straightforward prose, closer inspection reveals Byrnes' varied use of these records to provide both moral instruction and moral titillation. These biographies function as either moral allegories or cautionary tales that reinforce the values of the dominant group in American culture in the latter nineteenth century. Repeatedly a thief's record opens with the assertion that he is from a respectable background and family, as in the case of Langdon W. Moore, whose parents were "very respectable people" (84). Byrnes usually says little more than this. He adopts a rhetorical strategy based on the repetition of a pattern for its effectiveness. The road to crime these once respectable men traveled warns that a respectable background is no defense against a life of crime. These tales help the reader gain insight into the unstated moral premises of the late nineteenth century.

Solomon Stern is typical of one pattern: he began to run with a fast woman, stole from his family's business to satisfy her greed, and was finally cast out of his family. Stern degenerated quickly after departing from the asylum of the family. He was soon a confirmed drinker and professional thief. Ex-Governor Moses of South Carolina and William Gray, the son of a United States senator, provide another pattern. This is one based on the abuse of position and business relationships; these men fell because they were unwilling to work gradually to amass a fortune but tried to make it too rapidly. After abusing the "sacred" relationships of business, these men were forced to turn to crime as a career.

Saddest of all, however, is the case of William Gilman. Gilman was not a professional thief, but Byrnes inserted his story since "Gilman's false step will stand forever as a warning to others" (294). Gilman symbolizes the most common of crimes for the businessman; he embezzled company funds for his own speculations and, when he could not cover his thefts, was discovered. He made a full confession in "one of the most affecting scenes ever witnessed in a courtroom." Although "every eye in the courtroom was moistened" by Gilman's confession, the judge, realizing his duty to society, sentenced him to five years hard labor. Byrnes provides the even sadder denouement in Yantic

Cemetery at the open grave of Gilman's wife: "While in prison his daughter had died, and he was released in time to attend the funeral of his wife, whose heart had been broken with sorrow over her husband's sin" (294). Gilman thus destroyed the sanctity of the family as a result of his failure to adhere to the strict morality of business, losing both a wife and daughter who were unable to bear his shame.

Byrnes inserts entertaining anecdotes of criminal life throughout these "records." Unlike Farley, Byrnes has little use for sentimentality; his anecdotes are drawn from the thief at work rather than in his leisure time or love affairs. Generally these anecdotes serve as an understated warning of the inevitability of capture for the criminal, no matter how skilled or careful he may be. An example of this is found in Byrnes' "record" of the celebrated Max Shinburn's arrest in Viveres, Belgium, in 1883. American prisons had been unable to hold Shinburn, and he had returned to his native Germany following the successful robbery of the Ocean Bank. Strapped for funds, he and Charley Bullard decided to hit the provincial bank in Viveres. In spite of their care, which Byrnes describes in detail, they had forgotten to relock the gate to the yard of the bank, and a night watchman discovered the open gate. The thieves had done nothing in the bank but survey it for the next night's robbery; when the police examined the bank they could discover nothing out of place. They were about to release the two when a locksmith noticed a small plug of wax in the keyplate of the bank's lock. A matching plug was in Shinburn's pocket. Two minor details thus brought Shinburn's downfall and a sentence of seventeen years, six months in prison (255–56). The "records" provide not only accounts of the thieves but also an implicit didacticism that reinforces contemporary social values.

These rogues' galleries are curious blends of the old and the new in their approach to crime and criminals. Both make use of illustration, anecdote, and biography, and both are, in some ways, closely linked to older styles of crime writing such as the Newgate Calendars. The contrasts between the works are more revealing than their similarities. Farley's work looks back to an age when crime was still something alien to the accepted American experience, something Americans found interesting because it was outlandish and different. Farley's book typifies an earlier age when both police and professional criminals were still working out their roles in society. Neither group had yet established a self-definition or group identity. This uncertainty finds expression through Farley's inability to stick to his purpose; he takes a shotgun approach to the presentation of criminal life and hopes that something will hit the mark. In contrast, Byrnes exhibits a strong sense of self and a discriminating vision of professional criminals. His persona of a dogged, determined professional who never leaves the trail until he has caught his criminal mirrors the structure of his writing: he keeps the main goal always before his eyes. His book, with its attendant photographs and biographies, freezes a moment of the past and a section of a vanished urban America; he gives modern Americans a glimpse of a forgotten part of our past.

THROUGH THE EYES OF THE DETECTIVES

Professional observers also produced anatomies of the professional underworld. These anatomies are strongly analytical "dissections" of professional crime. The writers of these anatomies are not overtly concerned with the problem of reducing crime; professional theft is simply a fact, and the best protection against it is knowledge of how criminals work. One can then at least hope to guard against them. These writings have a strong kinship with the rogues' galleries but differ markedly in their emphasis and techniques. The rogues' galleries presented the criminal as an individual, but these writers prefer a study of the criminal as a representative figure or type. Also, the rogues' galleries describe an underworld in stasis, frozen for an instant and lifted from the flow of history. These writers present the dynamic of historical change in their analyses. Both the *New York Times* and the *New York Daily Tribune* singled out this historical consciousness in reviews of *Recollections of a New York Chief of Police*, by George W. Walling (1887).[24] The added dimension of historical analysis provides an interest for the modern reader that the more static descriptions lack. One obtains a notion of the dynamic interplay between criminals and such opponents as police, bankers, or safe manufacturers and thus sees how each contributed to the evolution of the other. These writers are aware of such themes as the ways in which technology changes both crime and the social response to crime.

The tone of these works also contributes to their interest. Unlike reformers who view this world from the outside, these writers have been intimately associated with professional criminals on an almost daily basis. This close contact has removed the aura of strangeness from the underworld and, paradoxically, given these writers the possibility of achieving a measure of aesthetic detachment. Thus, instead of a tone of naive wonder or moral outrage, these works are often suffused with humor and irony. Allan Pinkerton, for instance, recounts a case of professional jealousy between two rival gangs of bank burglars in New York City. In 1875 the Scott-Dunlap gang had plans to burglarize an uptown bank while a gang led by George White had targeted a downtown bank for a burglary at about the same time. To prevent the increased security that would follow a bank robbery and thus frustrate his own plans, George White dressed the members of his gang as policemen. They drove the Scott-Dunlap gang away, leaving the field open for White. White's rivals, however, learned of his ruse and tipped the police to White's operation. White's gang managed to escape the police raid, in spite of considerable shooting, but thus, Pinkerton chortles, two large bank burglaries "were prevented through nothing more or less than what was hoped to be a very excellent trick by one notorious set of rogues upon another."[25]

Along with the added dimension of irony, these writers provide aesthetic criticism of various professional criminals. Repeatedly these authors make judgments on style among the gangs of professionals, ranking these gangs according to technique, daring, courage, and planning. Walling for instance, after first asserting that "there can be no doubt that burglary is a fine art," points to the successful bank burglar as "a king among thieves, and so far as the skill and cunning which he exercises are concerned, he undoubtedly earns his reputation."[26] Not only do the most intelligent among criminals follow this branch, but they also have "more than ordinary mechanical skill, an amount of energy and patience that is phenomenal." They spend thousands of dollars on tools, experimenting with new technologies, and devotedly learning "every detail of their occupation." Walling argues: "Thus it is that every succeeding year adds to the knowledge of the criminal, and makes absolute protection against detection seem possible" (236).

Walling presents George Leslie, Jimmy Hope, and Max Shinburn as examples of burglars whose skill he holds in awe and then narrates some of their accomplishments as supporting evidence. In contrast to the art of these burglars he also presents the operations of the several "mobs" who had contemplated robbing the Manhattan Savings Bank before a group of first-class burglars did so in 1877. These earlier schemes were "brutal, coarse and vulgar," involving "the forcible overcoming of those who guarded the bank at night" (263).

Pinkerton makes use of the same sort of aesthetic discrimination and states: "Expert and professional bank robbers are a distinct and exclusive fraternity, and under no circumstances are to be classed with dishonest practitioners in the lower grades of crime." These professionals have no rivals and rarely rob anything less than a bank. Pinkerton believes that the demonstration of their skill is as strong a motivation for these thieves as profit: "Their ruling ambition is to perform their work in the most skillful and perplexing manner possible." They take a special joy in "leaving behind them indisputable evidences of their dexterity and skill in the calling which they have adopted."[27]

In no other type of writing concerned with crime does this aesthetic element assume such prominence. One cause for the adoption of the critic's stance is the author's need to create adversaries worthy of his own skill. A second reason is the theme of the contrast between appearance and reality that continually surfaces in these books. All of these authors insist that both the public and the academics are mistaken in their concept of who a criminal is and what he looks like. Pinkerton, for instance, states that "among the criminal classes to-day are to be found men of powerful minds, of strong will, and of educational advantages which, if correctly applied would have enabled them to make their mark in the professional and business circles of the community." Unfortunately, these men have turned their great talents to "base purposes."[28] Walling asserts that it is a preconceived and ill-founded notion held by the vast majority "that men who war upon society must of necessity bear the brand of their evil doings on their brows." He takes on the biological doctrines of criminal anthropology, arguing that "with few exceptions, the men who have been accredited with the most daring violations of the law have been persons who could not have been marked by the most learned physiognomist as of accomodating morals" (Walling, 321).

Walling also raises the theme of the double life that the most skilled criminals lead. The anonymity of an urban center like New York makes the assumption of two roles easy. The tendency of Americans to form close relationships in spite of knowing little or nothing of an individual's past aids this anonymity.[29] De Tocqueville had noticed this fluidity of personal relationships in America fifty years earlier; he attributed it to the frontier and lack of established communities in America. Americans, who stressed the future rather than the past, often considered this fluidity a virtue. On the frontier quickly established relationships were perhaps necessary to provide any sort of social cohesion, but this could cause major problems in an urban environment infested by such threats as the confidence man. Pinkerton, for example, points to a bank burglar (probably George White) who hinted that he worked for the United States Secret Service. Not only did his social acquaintances accept this but also "the young and beautiful lady to whom he was married, and . . . all of her high-toned relatives."[30] Benjamin Eldridge and William Watts point to White's great social influence in New York, his fashionable livery stable, and the attempts made by prominent New Yorkers to keep him out of prison. They also comment on Max Shinburn's refined manners, cultivation, and mastery of several languages.[31]

Eldridge and Watts, however, are unlike other professional observers. Writing near the turn of the century, they are less confident that one cannot tell a criminal simply by appearance. Criminal anthropology became a fad of sorts among American intellectuals in the 1890s; these writers must grapple with its doctrines to prove that as professionals they are knowledgeable about all areas of crime. These authors have read the criminology of their time and discuss it at length, thus adding an intellectual dimension to the persona of the detective. They point out that they have treated "rascals" in their book; these "rascals" bear no relation to the infrequent monsters who absorb the energies of the criminal anthropologists. One can guard against the professional criminal since his acts are governed by the rational motive of profit. The monster or born criminal is a different sort; his actions are completely irrational and no specialist can help in protecting against him.

Although they contend that they are unqualified to discuss Lombroso, Eldridge and Watts argue that his influence is due to the apparent novelty of his ideas even though criminal anthropology "is hardly more in principle than the stretching of the theory of evolution beyond any conclusions reached by Darwin." The authors summarize Lombroso's theories of heredity and atavism but assert that it is impossible to determine the importance of heredity. Instead they argue that such causes as a degrading environment, the impulse of vicious temptations, and the lack of honest employment are more important than heredity as causes of crime. As a final attempt to discredit Lombroso, Eldridge and Watts quote the French criminologist Louis Proal to prove that physical distinctions between the criminal and the honest man do not exist.[32] Eldridge and Watts express the notion of development in environmental terms; although "the professional criminal is a product of evolution," this evolution is one of skill and conscience instead of biology. The rogue's progress from rung to rung on the ladder of crime is from the wayward boy, to the petty thief, to the weary and bored clerk seeking escape in gambling, to the professional thief and forger.[33]

Still, the power of the anthropological theories of crime was so widespread by the mid–90s that Eldridge and Watts could not simply toss out the notion of judging by appearances. They assert that a detective develops an extra sense which occasionally allows him to judge by appearances. This, however, is an occupational skill sharpened only by long practice. They then present the work of Galton and one of the odder experiments in the history of photography: composite portraiture. This technique involved the superimposition of several photographs on one another to produce a composite photo. For instance, if one wanted a portrait of the pickpocket as a generic type, he would fuse the photographs of fifty pickpockets. This would produce a portrait in which certain features were blurred while others were sharp. Those which remained sharp in the composite would be generic for the pickpocket as a type—for instance, a narrow forehead or high cheekbones. Thus, the individual could quickly be placed in the proper category. Eldridge and Watts express the qualified hope that this technique could be a future tool to help detectives place unknown individuals and incidentally illustrate how conversant they are with even the most avant-garde of criminological experiments.[34]

Among the other themes raised by the professional observers, two are particularly revealing about the detective, his status in American culture, and the insights into American society that his vantage point provided. These themes are the detective's vision of the American economic system and the detective's response to the glorification of his role in American life. The detective was, in a sense, a mediating figure between the underworld and the legitimate world. This position provided him with a unique view of American civilization. Practically all professional observers in this period shared Farley's sympathy with workers. Like him they found the start of many criminal careers in employers who failed to pay a living wage, thus forcing employees into petty pilfering. Even the union-busting Allan Pinkerton, a radical Chartist during his youth in Scotland, occasionally criticized the American economic system. Most of these writers adopted a persona sympathetic to the poor and the conditions that forced them into a life of crime.

Walling, for example, argues that not only is there "no such thing as hereditary viciousness" but that there is "something radically wrong in our social system." He further asserts that want drives most people into crime and contends that education in crime by professional thieves accounts for far fewer criminals than "the fact that young men of much more than average ability are fairly driven to thievery by want, and also the fact that they can see no way of making an honest living in the immediate future."[35] Pinkerton not only echoes this sentiment but adds the lament of the great loss to society implicit in the loss of brilliant talents to a career of crime.[36]

This identification with labor points to the working-class roots of the detective. Before ambitious detectives and policemen became involved in the drive for professional status, they considered themselves part of the laboring class and identified principally with this group. Later, as they began to view their duties as essentially the protection of the interests of the propertied classes, this class identification, though still present, weakened considerably. As one would expect from this pattern, the strongest attack on the American economic system came from the earliest work by a professional detective following the Civil War, *Knots Untied*, by George S. McWatters (1871).

McWatters was known in New York City as the "literary policeman" on account of his frequent anonymous contributions to journals and newspapers as well as his friendship with literary men. He was an habitué of Pfaff's, the beer cellar frequented by Walt Whitman, William Dean Howells, Artemus Ward, and Bayard Taylor. McWatters was born in Scotland, raised in northern Ireland, and, after a stay in London, emigrated to Philadelphia where he studied law from 1848 to 1849. From Philadelphia he went to California to prospect for gold. He then lectured for a traveling panorama, acted as agent for the actress Laura Keene, became a private detective, and finally joined the Metropolitan Police in 1858. In 1870 he resigned his position because of police corruption and official lack of sympathy for the poor; his literary friends obtained a post for him in the New York Customs House.

McWatters' book is a compilation of true detective stories; the presentation of criminals and their methods is incidental and occurs within the narrative framework. Although the work does contain some analysis, this is generally confined to introductions or to short "philosophical" digressions. McWatters says that one of his strongest interests has always been various sociological problems, especially the questions of human suffering and crime. His implicit sympathies with the underdog are clear throughout these narratives, for he argues that society creates the crime it punishes and that all men are thus responsible in some measure for the crime a society experiences.[37] The strongest attack on American society comes from the biographical section which precedes the narrative. McWatters declined to contribute an autobiography, for he refused to 'vaunt himself.' The publishers then secured the services of one of McWatters' friends in journalism to provide a biographical sketch as well as insight into McWatters' central ideas.

Certainly one cannot simply attribute the notions found in the biography to McWatters. However, this journalist claims to be an old personal friend of McWatters, and his assertion that McWatters has long been interested in reform and the problems of the working class finds support in McWatters' published writings in newspapers. The biographer uses extensive quotation from these writings to establish McWatters' credentials as a reformer interested in socialism.[38]

The biographer's attack on the American system is twofold. First he excoriates American greed; he argues that unbounded materialism is undercutting American values. Second he focuses on the perversion of American republicanism as a result of the development of a "master-class" erected on a corrupting sense of privilege; this denunciation is built around the imagery of class conflict.

The attack on American greed begins by detailing the corruption of the New York Police Department and municipal government under Fernando Wood. These conditions not only caused McWatters to resign from the police force; they also accounted for a dramatic increase of crime. This growth in crime has made it appear more respectable; it is undermining the foundations of American life: "Crime is no great stain to any man in New York if he but have money, or is in the 'line of making it fast' " (52).

The theme of class struggle provides the text for the remainder of the biographical section. The author takes on the class of industrialists spawned by the Civil War, presenting them as a tyrant class. He details the sufferings of the outraged republican masses "trampled into the dust by the powerful robbers of society in their mad greed for wealth, or cheated by pious and talented hypocrites out of their moral as well as physical rights" (74–75). Here, he argues, McWatters makes his true contribution for the future historian of the new order: "What a *resumé* of crime and outrages of all kinds will that of the nineteenth century be for the historian of the fortieth century to make" (69).

The biographer concludes with a call for changes in the American social structure that would insure that the right to life, a right of all people, would be attained; this will not happen until the people organize and each individual receives all he deserves. The only class of real worth is that composed of the laborers, not the "chief villains and the worthless tyrants" who now "enjoy all the honors, and are shielded by the laws in robbing from and exploiting upon the poor, the laboring classes" (70–71). This biographer makes strong connections among crime, greed, and the destruction of republican values in his analysis of the causes of crime.

McWatters' book also begins the glorification of the detective's role that evolved during this period. In a review of *Knots Untied*, the *New York Times* states one reason for the interest Americans felt in detective life. The reviewer asserts that the lives of detectives are "necessarily fraught with exciting events and incidents, and their stories when well told have a charm for nearly everyone."[39] Much of the detective's appeal for Americans in the late nineteenth century came from the sense of romance that seemed part of the detective's daring deeds. Another source of appeal was the detective's penetration of a hidden and exciting stratum of American civilization.

Walling, for instance, recalls that in 1836, when he was thirteen, the famous Helen Jewett murder case first attracted him to police work. He joined the force in 1847. Walling introduces his book by stating that "no fiction could be so rich in sensational incident as the true record of the lives of great criminals" and argues that the tales of the great lawbreakers are moral warnings. Their careers almost invariably follow the archetypal tragic structure of a rise to glory and respect with a final, dreadful downfall. These tales thus serve also as examples for a money-grubbing culture not too particular about where the money comes from.[40]

Early memoirists such as McWatters celebrated the melodramatic nature of the detective's life. Later writers toned down the melodrama and stressed, instead, the cold intelligence a detective needed in a threatening world. In spite of his belief that "police detection has become almost an exact science," McWatters places his primary emphasis on the *art* of detection: case after case in his account revolves around the motif of disguise.[41] The theme of disguise reinforces the theme of the problem an individual faces in distinguishing the reality behind appearances. This problem was a central theme of much of the early subliterature about the detective. Though early writers like McWatters emphasize the use of disguise, the authors such as Pinkerton and Walling who followed him take pains to discount its importance.

While McWatters argues that the life of a real detective is much more "romantic" than the wildest novels of the "sensation school,"[42] Walling contends that the work is prosaic. One of the goals Walling wants to achieve is to correct popular misapprehensions about detective life and the threat these misconceptions pose to the status of the detective as professional. He argues that while the detective of romance "is a superlative being, endowed with such prescience, fitted out with such a wonderful brain and gifted with so many more senses than the average man," the character of the actual detective is likely to be misunderstood. Walling contends that in the ordinary world the slow, hesitating man is much more fitted for detective work than the quick-witted man. A detective needs the ability of pausing before taking a conclusive step because detection is essentially rational and closely resembles a game of chess. Walling also stresses the element of chance in the detective's occupation. In Walling's view luck is more important than clues in successfully solving most cases. Walling argues that in spite of the advances in detective skill, advances by criminals have outdistanced them. Each year it becomes more difficult to catch the professional criminals who truly test the detective's mettle. Unlike those of the fictional world, actual murders are not often the work of clever criminals and are usually solved quickly. Outside the domestic circle, a blunderer or novice who does not know how to hide his tracks most frequently commits murder from the urge for profit. Theft is the crime that most fully draws out the detective's skill. Still, Walling is not averse to playing up the exciting aspects of detective work; like McWatters, Walling believes that the detective must have the same skills at disguise and impersonation as an actor.[43]

Writing in 1878, Allan Pinkerton also examines the role of the detective, and the changes the profession has experienced since he adopted the calling in 1851. During these years, Pinkerton says, he has observed the rise of a group of people who view the detective as an almost supernatural being who leads a mysterious, exciting life. Most of these people have developed a strong desire to become detectives. Pinkerton protests that these would-be detectives pester him unmercifully with letters inquiring about jobs as detectives. He has come to believe that a vast audience clearly wishes to go on stage, become authors, or turn detective. Pinkerton puts their letters in his "lunatic file," advising these would-be detectives to "let well enough alone." Such dreamers should remain at their mundane jobs and attend to them "faithfully and honestly." Certainly they might become successful detectives, but for each one who succeeds in the task, "a thousand fail utterly and completely—or, worse, become blackmailers and vagabonds, if not actual thieves and criminals." This is the crux of detective work for Pinkerton: it is a righteous calling; the most important attribute for a successful detective is "the clean, healthy, honest mind, using clean, healthy, honest methods, and those persistently and unceasingly."[44]

PARADIGMS OF THEFT

The best of these criminal anatomies by professional observers was written by Benjamin Eldridge and William Watts, of the Boston Police Department. *Our Rival the Rascal* appeared in 1896; the title indicates the tone these authors follow throughout. The contest between the forces of law and those of professional crime is presented as a good-natured rivalry from which the most skilled participant will emerge the victor. The book is a broad survey of the world of professional crime and such related topics as police methods of arrest and identification, academic criminology, criminal women, treatment of criminals, and technological advances in locks, burglar alarms, and safes. The authors are concerned solely with the professional criminal who aims at property. The goal of protection underlying this book dictates the focus on professional crime since such crimes as murder usually occur under the spur of uncontrollable passion. Murder, while dreadful, is not a regular pursuit society can guard against; theft is.[45] The authors reveal their attitude toward the professional criminal by referring to him as a "rascal" throughout the book as well as in the title. This emphasis on rascality lends an almost playful air to the work; the authors downplay the threat these criminals pose to the person and emphasize their threat to property. They become less of a danger than an annoyance, and Eldridge and Watts use images normally associated with pests or vermin, such as "swarm" or "infest," when describing professional thieves. These rogues seem far removed from villainy.

Eldridge and Watts adopt a paradigmatic method in presenting the grades, methods, and habits of professional criminals. Occasionally chapters open with a satiric portrait of the honest citizen trembling with dread before the advance of a noxious rascal, but usually they begin with a literary or historical allusion to the type of crime about to be presented. A brief historical analysis follows which forms an undercurrent through the remainder of the chapter. Next, the authors describe the methods and technology typical of this style of criminal specialization; finally Eldridge and Watts reach the heart of each chapter: an Emersonian presentation of representative criminals and crimes from the nineteenth century that stand as typical of each specialty. The authors include short biographies of these representative men as well as photographs and accounts of their criminal exploits. In this portion the writers amplify the technology, methods, and historical evolution of this field of criminal endeavor.

"Knights of the Road" is typical of their method. Here Eldridge and Watts present the famous figure of the highwayman. The chapter opens with a brief portrayal of the romantic figure of the highwayman in history and "yellow-covered romances"; the authors then assert that while he still exists in some isolated sections of the country, he has practically disappeared—at least in this familiar guise. However, the machine sneaks into even the garden of crime; the very technology responsible for the death of the old gentleman highwayman, the railroad, has given birth to another incarnation of the same criminal, the train-robber, who has "gone far beyond any bravado or daring of the old school of highwaymen" (250).

After briefly examining the train-robber as a type, Eldridge and Watts trace his historical evolution from the Reno Gang, who in 1866 invented this style of crime in southern Indiana, to

similar bands such as the James Gang. Train robbery soon became more sophisticated, and later gangs were composed of
specialists; each usually included one expert safe blower or burglar skilled in the use of dynamite and one member who was
able to handle a locomotive. Eldridge and Watts treat such specific methodological questions as how and why the opening of
a safe on a train differs from opening one in a store. On a train
time becomes the crucial determinant, while in a store the central
problem is noise.

After this discussion of organization and method, Eldridge
and Watts narrow their focus to the two most notorious gangs
of the last ten years, the Hedspeth Gang, which operated in the
Midwest until 1892, and the Morgan Gang, which preyed on
the South Atlantic states until 1895. The members of these gangs
and the methods they employ are presented as typical of the
character and devices of all train-robbers: thus, the paradigmatic
method in which the part stands for the whole. The authors also
discriminate between the work of the amateur and the professional, noting that the amateur always reveals his status by a
stupid blunder, but the professional is adept at avoiding detection.

Eldridge and Watts carry the paradigmatic method to the length
of isolating and examining anomalies, such as Oliver Curtis Perry,
a "young fellow with pensive brown eyes, effeminate voice,
almost invisible mustache and general air of weakness," who at
the age of twenty-six singlehandedly robbed an express car on
the New York Central Railroad in 1891. A year later, having
squandered his booty, Perry attempted a second robbery on the
same train in the same state. This act of hubris was responsible
for his downfall and imprisonment (265–75).

Eldridge and Watts make several points about the nature of
professional crime. Some specializations such as picking pockets
have remained static. This branch of crime depends on human
skills closely linked to such arts as magic, skills passed down
from generation to generation. Other crimes such as burglary
have undergone major changes during the century. Many of
these changes were innovative responses to new technologies.
As the profession of burglary changed, the internal caste system
of the specialty also experienced alteration. Eldridge and Watts
note that the lines of caste division between various types of

burglars are not as sharp in 1896 as they were thirty years earlier when the craft of burglary was rigidly ranked according to the skills of the individual burglar (65). A good example is the later career of Max Shinburn. After his arrest at Viveres, Shinburn had friends circulate his obituary in American newspapers. Eldridge and Watts report however, that in 1892 there was "a singular revival of country bank burglaries here after the marked cessation of such offenses since the days of the great Manhattan Bank robbery" (50). These robberies showed a master's hand, especially in the skilful use of nitroglycerine, and one of the men eventually arrested was an elderly man with a German accent, Baron Max Shinburn. One of the reasons the Pinkertons captured him was that all of the expert detectives in America became convinced that stories of Shinburn's death were false since "the phenomenal brain and hand that had reconstructed the burglar tools of America and successfully perpetrated some of the greatest robberies ever known, were alone adequate to the expert adaptation of dynamite to burglary" (50–51).

Although his skill caused his capture and a sentence to Dannemora, a hospital for the criminally insane, Shinburn's final innovations formed a legacy that contributed to the development of the yegg. The transfer of targets from rich urban banks to smaller country banks is one indication of the pragmatic adaptation which professional thieves practiced so well. As urban banks developed extensive protective devices, these thieves shifted to the more vulnerable rural banks. They also moved away from a reliance on mechanical ingenuity to the cruder but more effective device of dynamite.

Eldridge and Watts present the safe robber in a transitional phase as he moved from the aristocratic bank burglar to the yet unnamed yegg. This transitional figure is youthful, between twenty-five and thirty-five years old; he commonly uses the disguise of a tramp or traveling salesman; he shows little discrimination in his choice of targets; and he practices almost exclusively on rural banks, stores, and post offices where he rarely obtains more than a few hundred dollars in cash or postage stamps. Although he carries a few light tools to help obtain entry into the targeted building, he relies almost exclusively on explosives to open the safe. These explosives do not require the complicated apparatus the earlier safe blower needed for the use of black powder. These transitional burglars also pride themselves less on their skill in opening safes than the older burglars did and no longer have a sense of pride in leaving their signatures behind. Eldridge and Watts point out that not only are these new-style burglars less accomplished than the "better class of bank burglars," but they are "less inclined to shun a deadly fight or brutal assault on the way to their booty" (73). This is perhaps the crucial element in the evolution of this more modern criminal, and Eldridge and Watts express a sense of strong repugnance at this new willingness to use violence: "They almost uniformly carry loaded revolvers and, at times, other weapons and will shoot to disable or kill with ugly recklessness" (73). The reliance on violence along with the blurring of rank and the use of explosives rather than ingenuity and imagination all point to one of the major themes in the evolution of burglary: as the older burglars died or retired, their vision of professionalism was replaced with one that placed greater emphasis on practicality and less on such old-fashioned ideas as honor or individual skill. The pragmatic response of these newer professionals was a reaction to improved technologies for law enforcement and advances in the protection of property.

The professional thief proved invaluable to detectives eager to improve their standing in American society. Detectives used thieves in a variety of ways as they attempted to define their occupation, self-image, and role in American life. In the professional thief these detectives either found or created an opponent they considered worthy of their skills. The thief also served the detectives as they pondered such problems as the deceptiveness of reality and the role of deception as a part of their occupation. These detectives-turned-authors worked to define a representative persona they could adopt when addressing the American public, and again the thief played an important role. The interplay between the thief and the detective helped both groups to establish a sense of identity and purpose.

The View from Above: Upperworld Explorations of Professional Crime

THE HOUDINI SYNDROME

Just as the professional thief was driven to expose the hypocrisies of the upper world in his autobiographical writings, the upper world felt the need to examine this subculture an urbanizing America had spawned. The result was a literature of exposure ranging from the sensational revelations of a cheap story paper to sober academic analysis of the nature of theft. The growth of analytical literature is reflected in works like Frank Wadleigh Chandler's *The Literature of Roguery* (1907). Chandler's study is a two-volume literary history of rogues that ranges from antiquity to his own day and touches all the literatures of Europe. Chandler lumps all nonfiction about crime into the "anatomy of roguery"; he examines both the historical development of this form and its connection with imaginative literature. Chandler defines the anatomy of roguery as "an essay descriptive of the grades, cheats, or manners of professional criminals," and argues that it includes beggar-books, conny-catching pamphlets, prison tracts, revelations of criminal mysteries by the repentant, canting lexicons, scoundrel verse, and modern sociological studies of crime.[1] The term "anatomy" has been used in a figurative sense for logical dissection or analysis since Aristotle; this term originally meant "dissection" in medical parlance but came into common use in English literature in the late sixteenth century.[2] Chandler simply expands the term to stand for any nonfiction writing that examines crime.

American writing about crime includes much more than simple dissection, however. Few authors can resist the temptation to prescribe cures after they have studied symptoms and made a diagnosis. American writers between 1870 and 1917 who examined the world of professional crime wrote about an alien subculture, describing both its folkways and its methods of gaining a livelihood. These "anatomies" are early examples of a form modern readers know as popular sociology or anthropology. The authors often presented themselves as explorers returning from a sojourn in an alien land; their writings are a report from that land.

In the years between the Civil War and World War I a multitude of works testified to American interest in professional crime. These ranged from journalistic exposés such as Edward Crapsey's early *The Nether Side of New York* to the muckraking studies of Josiah Flynt at the turn of the century, and included works as disparate in nature as Charles Sutton's *New York Tombs, Its Secrets and Mysteries* and Harry Schindler's *How the Bank Sneak Works*. These writers represented a broad cross-section of American society including both journalists and criminals as well as the magician Harry Houdini, who contributed *The Right Way to Do Wrong; an Exposé of Successful Criminals* (1906) and the reformer Anthony Comstock, who wrote *Frauds Exposed* (1880) and *Traps for the Young* (1883).

Thomas W. Knox, a New York journalist, published a book in 1874 that stands as representative of the oddities which surfaced in the genre. This work carried the imposing title of *Underground or Life Below the Surface; Incidents and Accidents Beyond the Light of Day; Startling Adventures in all Parts of the World; Mines and the Mode of Working Them; Under-Currents of Society; Gambling and its Horrors; Caverns and their Mysteries; the Dark Ways of Wickedness; Prisons and their Secrets; Down in the Depths of the Sea; Strange Stories in the Detection of Crime.* As the title indicates, Knox's work is organized around all conceivable literal and metaphorical meanings of one concept. He is driven by a need to expose, to bring hidden things to the light. Among the book's topics not covered by the title are the Underground Railroad, the early history of mankind, the Parisian sewers, prizefighting, and borrowing and borrowers. Knox uses an organic metaphor of society as a plant to justify this hodgepodge. He will present the root system; these roots are not only necessary to society but contain a great deal of life. The roots cannot be cut from the plant without the death of the plant's flower; both the moral and immoral life of a great city are "cut and seamed with subterranean excavations."[3] This book appeared early in the era; Knox's ambiguity is typical of the American response to its emerging underworld in the years immediately following the Civil War. Although Knox deserves credit for the broadest interpretation of his subject, his expansive approach is typical of most writers who tried to give a "factual" portrayal of crime. These artists of exposé attempted to present crime in all its multitudinous faces as well as portraits of slum life and descriptions of official corruption.

Two threads are common to the anatomies of crime and criminal life from this era: description and exposure. The persona these writers adopt forces them to describe the activities they are presenting. Most of these authors present themselves as the possessors of secret or special information that has been hidden till now. This description may have a narrow focus as in Schindler's examination of the bank sneak's job or the anonymous *How 'Tis Done*, a description of the various methods used to swindle farmers and villagers. On the other hand, the description may be a broad attempt to cover the entire spectrum of urban vice as in *Darkness and Daylight*, a collection of three anatomies by the reformer Helen Campbell, the journalist Thomas Knox, and Inspector Byrnes. Description is a necessary evil, however. Most of these writers describe their subjects in detail simply because they are presenting unfamiliar material.

The true motivation behind these nonfiction writings is exposure. These authors delight in the belief that they are stripping the mask from fraudulent actions, and many of them include the word "exposé" in the titles of their works. The very term "underworld" with its connotations of things in darkness, things below the surface, took on its central contemporary meaning during this period and became firmly linked to the worlds of crime and vice.

Harry Houdini, "Handcuff King and Jail Breaker," was one of the thousands of Americans interested in crime as well as exposé; in 1906 he published *The Right Way to Do Wrong; An*

Exposé of Successful Criminals. For a man like Houdini, the impulse to exposure is deeply entwined in his psychological makeup as well as in his intellectual interests. His skills could easily have made him a premier thief, for his professional life was dedicated to a career which revolved around hidden techniques akin to the methods of such thieves as pickpockets. He was also famous for his ability to escape from jails. This trick involved more than a display of his skills; it dramatized the frailty of the social institutions designed to protect society from its enemies. Although Houdini made his jailbreaks as part of a ritual of "play," the threat was real. His curiosity about hidden things drove him to investigate such areas as spiritualism as well as crime; indeed a portion of this book is devoted to exposing the devices fraudulent mediums use to trick a gullible audience. Houdini's book is a good representative of this form of nonfiction writing designed to unmask frauds, swindles, and criminal methods. This class of writings employs certain themes and techniques; it represents a literary subgenre that is both representative of a well-defined approach to writing and also symbolic of life: The Houdini Syndrome.

The Houdini Syndrome was a central pattern in the tapestry of American culture during this era of Progressivism and muckraking. Under the guise of muckraking, this literature of exposure dominated the imagination of Americans after the turn of the century. Although muckraking originated with young journalists dedicated to exposing the social problems of modern America, the term soon came to stand for the literary subgenre of exposure.

These young journalists had typically grown up in small towns in the Midwest dominated by a pervasive Protestantism. The value system they had absorbed in their youths faced a shock when confronted with the realities of early modern America: the horrors of urban poverty, the corruption of public men and corporations, and the apparent destruction of traditional American values. These writers became, in effect, preachers exposing the evils of a changing America. With their Protestant backgrounds these muckrakers valued the exposure of evil as an end in itself: once a problem was recognized, good citizens would correct it.

The muckrakers devoted their energies largely to the exposure of social corruption rather than the dishonesty of individuals. This focus on large issues with its corollary of the need for a general social regeneration is the major difference between muckraking and the vast body of exposés produced in America between 1870 and 1900. The earlier writings of exposure called for a personal renewal. This altered emphasis helps explain why even though early pieces of muckraking such as Josiah Flynt's *The World of Graft* and Lincoln Steffens' *The Shame of the Cities* presented the role of the professional criminal, he quickly disappeared from the work of the muckrakers. The professional criminal was a symbol of individual evil, and the problems of modern America were too large for these writers to allow themselves to become sidetracked by the problems of the individual. The professional criminal did, however, move to center stage in the progressive novel. Fiction was a medium that allowed these writers to examine the impact of large social forces on a representative individual.[4]

Although the exposé attained its greatest influence during the progressive years, it was a dominant theme throughout the postwar era and was certainly not confined to the world of crime. Fiction such as *The Gilded Age* (1873) by Mark Twain and Charles Dudley Warner, *John Andross* (1874) by Rebecca Harding Davis, and *Honest John Vane* (1875) and *Playing the Mischief* (1876) by John William De Forest were driven by the impulse of exposure. Nonfiction such as *Progress and Poverty* (1879) by Henry George and *Wealth Against Commonwealth* (1894) by Henry Demarest Lloyd also participated in this thrust.

This theme was not confined to the arenas of literature and journalism. The naturalistic paintings of Thomas Eakins such as *The Gross Clinic* (1876) and *The Agnew Clinic* (1898) reveal the wide appeal exposure had for Americans. Exposure here becomes the aesthetic of Eakins, with his idea of beauty as something based on function and an understanding of function. This corresponded with his obsession for anatomy; the artist must study the muscles hidden beneath the surface before his portrayal of surfaces could be true. In art this impulse for exposure also realized its greatest flowering near the end of the period, with the Ash Can School. John Sloan, William Glackens, and

George Luks brought new subjects into the range of American art with their depictions of the Lower East Side and the Bowery.

The work of such photographers as Jacob Riis also reveals the interest in exposure. His photographs of slum life and the accompanying text in *How the Other Half Lives* helped stir the civic conscience of New York to attempt the alleviation of the worst features of slum life. This motive of exposé touched most areas and philosophies in America; while its chief exponents were reformers, it also found an outlet in works whose impulse varied from art to adventure to recollection.

Although all criminal anatomies shared the basic motive of exposé, they did not share the same purpose, in spite of an almost universal prefacing note stating that the writer's goal was protecting the respectable classes. These writings fall into two groups based on the persona the author adopts to present his exposé: amateurs and reformers. Those written by "amateurs" usually take the protection of the individual citizen as a theme. These amateur writers adopt the persona of an ordinary individual who simply has an interest in crime and wants to warn the public so that it can defend itself against criminals. These writings include the productions of such authors as Houdini. They adopt a literary strategy built on the premise that the ordinary adult, because of his essential honesty, is in the position of a child in a deceptive world. Because he approaches the world straightforwardly, he is no match for the skilful machinations of the professional criminal. Once he has been educated to the deceptive nature of the world, he will become immune to the practices of sharpers. These amateur anatomies are almost always solely concerned with unmasking various techniques of fraud, confidence games, and swindling. The anatomies produced by reform journalists are also centrally concerned with protection; here the emphasis is on protecting society, rather than its individual parts. This includes not only the respectable classes but the slum dwellers as well. The reform impulse usually dominates the theme of protection; the thrust of the reform drive may be directed toward slum areas, prisons, corrupt police and public officials, or basic social institutions. The amateurs want to educate the trusting individual to the ways of a corrupt and deceptive world. The reformers want to make this education unnecessary by changing the world.

EXPOSÉ AND THE AMATEUR

Those authors centrally concerned with the protection of the individual included some of the oddest of the anatomists, yet their writings remain among the clearest in highlighting emerging themes in American civilization such as urbanization and the growing tensions between city and country dwellers. These amateur anatomists assume the personas of avengers unmasking frauds who threaten trusting individuals. This style of writing has a long history in America stretching back to Cotton Mather's *Magnalia Christi Americana* (1702) with its warning about false ministers who assume the cloth and bamboozle trusting churches into supporting them. One hundred years later Stephen Burroughs recounted that when pressed for money he posed as a minister and thus drew support from rural churches. After the Civil War these exposés turned to the city as the source of corruption; these urban centers became sources of infection, oozing putrid waste that threatened the virtuous countryside.

The writers saw themselves performing a civic duty in exposing both the sources of corruption and the fair masks it often hid behind. All these writers claimed that they were writing to protect the trusting individual from the slippery manipulations of fraud. They exhibited little concern for broad social reform, wishing simply to inoculate the virtuous against vice. These authors were, of course, also writing to provide entertainment and to satisfy the audience's curiosity about an unknown area of American life.

Although many of these works, such as those by Anthony Comstock, appeared before the turn of the century, an equal number appeared afterwards and ran parallel to the broader stream of muckraking. A better image is perhaps that they ran below the current of muckraking. Muckraking exposés were tied closely to mass market periodicals and belonged to the mainstream of American culture between 1900 and 1917. These works, however, were oddly divorced from the concerns of modern

America; they recalled an earlier age that stressed the role of the individual alone rather than as part of a social whole.[5]

These amateur anatomies were, for the most part, concerned with various types of swindles or frauds and were especially aimed at a rural audience. A. J. Greiner asserted that "to bunco a man, there is but one thing needful—you must obtain his absolute confidence,"[6] and although the swindles he exposes, which include the "Stock Tank Swindle," the "Electric Lights for Farmers" swindle, and "The Slick Historian" swindle, are mainly aimed at country dwellers, he hastens to reassure his audience that sharp city folks are also suckered by such tricks as the "Swindler with Vicious Dog" and the "Canary Bird Swindle." Writer after writer stresses that the countryman is the usual victim of the confidence man because of his hospitality and trust in his fellows. These writers agree that such qualities are virtues, but, in their role of protector, the writers caution that these virtues must be practiced carefully if one is not to be duped by that sharp product of the urban environment—the bunco man.

The anonymous *How 'Tis Done* opens with the declaration that if the reader will "read these pages carefully, he will have his eyes opened to a condition of things he was never aware of before, and be made acquainted with the fact of the general prevalence of dishonesty, of which he has for a long time been made the unsuspecting victim; for it is a fact that in the farming communities the harvest is reaped."[7] Houdini also views the threat of the swindle as one primarily directed at country dwellers: "When the corn husking is over and the county fairs begin their annual three and four-day sessions in a thousand agricultural centers, a silent army of confidence men and swindlers make ready for their richest harvest of the year."[8]

The farmer is the representative of America's best qualities: faith, trust, optimism. Unfortunately, the city, a symbol of the underside of American civilization for these agrarians, produces germs that cannot only infect but also destroy the trusting individual. Countrymen are accustomed to judge according to appearances. For them appearance is reality since they live a pastoral life in harmony with nature. With the rise of urban centers these honest folk must realize that appearances may be deceptive. This truly signals the end of the agrarian ethos in America, an ethos that necessarily accepted men as what they represented themselves to be.

This theme of the innocent and trusting countryman had become so firmly entrenched in the American popular mind that O. Henry (William S. Porter) wrote a series of humorous stories called *The Gentle Grafter* centered around the exploits of two confidence men fleecing farmers, although in occasional stories, such as "The Ethics of Pig," the bunco-artists are fleeced by the rubes. These stories revolve around such proven swindles as the green-goods game, a con in which the sucker is offered $5000 for $1000. The con-man assures the dupe that the $5000 is indistinguishable from genuine bills because the counterfeit is printed from plates stolen by an employee of the U. S. Treasury. The mark is offered a few genuine bills for inspection, makes his buy, and is then warned not to open his package until he is in a safe place. When he examines his purchase, he discovers that he has bought a batch of brown paper. The confidence man uses a magician's sleight of hand in changing packages.

In "Modern Rural Sports" Jeff Peters and his partner Andy find themselves in southern Indiana with only sixty-eight cents, determined to fleece a farmer. Jeff chooses as bait "some of the new income tax receipts; and a recipe for making clover honey out of clabber and apple peelings; and the order blanks for the McGuffy's readers, which afterwards turn out to be McCormick reapers; and the pearl necklace found on the train; and a pocket-size goldbrick."[9] Instead of the usual sucker, Jeff finds: " 'this one's shook off the shackles of the sheepfold. He's entrenched behind the advantages of electricity, education, literature and intelligence.' " Andy refuses to accept this, for he believes in the design of Providence: " 'Farmers was made for a purpose; and that was to furnish a livelihood to men like me and you. Else why was we given brains' " (41–42). Andy then proceeds to outfit himself as a circus thimblerig man, uses the oldest of all cons, the shell game, and returns with $860—all the sharp farmer had in the house. Andy tells Jeff that when he left, the farmer followed him, and with tears in his eyes thanked him " 'for the only real pleasure I've had in years. It brings up happy old days when I was only a farmer and not an agriculturalist' " (43). This story plays on the nostalgia of a rapidly changing

America for a simpler past and its values. O. Henry serves as an example of the sympathetic urban dweller viewing the simplicity of the rube. Still, he finds truth in the notion of the farmer as an easy mark in spite of his humorous and ironic treatments of the theme. The grafters are usually successful.

Not all of the anatomists viewed the trusting natures of their rural audience as the central cause of its victimization by confidence men, however. To be successful a confidence operation must not only gain the victim's trust, but also appeal to his self-interest. This self-interest could be aroused with the promise of obtaining something for nothing as in the green-goods game or the goldbrick swindle; it could also be aroused by an appeal based on the mark's vanity. Among those schemes directed toward vanity were the map and atlas business and the production of county histories. Both of these games promised that a forthcoming publication would include extended biographies of the "leading" citizens of a county, that is, the marks.

As the author of *How 'Tis Done* noted: "Success is made dependent upon patient study of the foibles of human nature.... It thus becomes a science. Every possible weakness of human nature, every loophole of ignorance,... is studied with utmost care."[10] This appeal to a small town's vanity was based on the premise of the isolation of rural life. This isolation contributed to the development of a provincial sense of self-importance among the inhabitants. The narrowness of the countryman's outlook also became a tool used by the swindler. This emphasis on the barrenness of rural life stands in direct contrast to the agrarian myth. It does bear a strong resemblance, however, to the writings of such regionalists as Hamlin Garland whose *Main-Travelled Roads* (1891) used the aesthetic of literary realism to portray the lives of Midwestern farmers.

Another theme in the swindling anatomies is distrust of the emerging corporations. These corporations were usually seen as an urban phenomenon and many of the country dwellers had a strong fear of them. The best statement of this distrust comes from J. B. Costello, the editor of *Swindling Exposed from the Diary of William B. Moreau King of Fakirs*. This book is an autobiographical exposé detailing such swindles as "Barb Wire Frauds," "The Writing School Fake," and the "Garden of Eden Hoax"; Costello appends an almost paranoid conclusion built on the assertion that the crimes of the "Moreau combine," even when added to the takings of thousands of other professional swindlers, "did not squeeze as much out of the people of the United States as the unscrupulous octopus known as the Standard Oil Company, dominated by John D. Rockefeller."[11]

This book appeared in 1907, not long after Ida M. Tarbell's muckraking *History of the Standard Oil Company* (1906); the cue for the final chapter clearly comes from such journals as *McClure's*. The emphasis on the crimes of the powerful and wealthy became one of the elements distinguishing the Progressive Era's response to crime from that of the Gilded Age. The stance Costello adopts in his denunciation of wealth is built around more than simple suspicion of criminal actions as the source of this wealth. Costello's response to Rockefeller's endowment of thirty-two million dollars to found the University of Chicago gives evidence of complete distrust for the possessor of great wealth. Costello views Rockefeller's action as an attempt to "build up a machine . . . to sing his praise." In addition to extolling Rockefeller's virtue, this university will give him control over a source of public information; he will use this control in an "endeavor to mold over public opinion to the idea that possessors of wealth, no matter how it was acquired, should be looked up to and worshipped as possessing divine rights on earth, (President Baer of the Reading Railroad so declared.)" (214).

Costello's stance is an attempt to awaken the common American to the threat great wealth poses to the democratic traditions of America. As the bank burglars were fond of noting, Americans did tend to be astigmatic about the sources of a man's wealth once he had attained it. Costello argues that Americans must correct this faulty vision. If allowed to continue unchecked, these industrialists will turn the true American, the farmer or laborer, into a slave. Americans will lose their most precious inheritance—freedom.

Closely paralleling the purpose of protection in these amateur anatomies is the usually unstated goal of providing entertainment and satisfying the audience's curiosity about a hidden stratum of American life. These amateur exposés are often oddly naive in their approach to crime. This naiveté presents itself in the crudely drawn illustrations, reminiscent of those found in cheap joke books or comic papers, as well as in such endorsements as those H. K. James (James Henry Keate) uses to preface *The Destruction of Mephisto's Greatest Web or, All Grafts Laid Bare.* . . . These endorsements include the Salt Lake City chief of police, ministers, and a high school principal; one wonders how knowledgeable these preachers were about James' subject: "the crooked methods, the mechanical devices and code systems employed by the professional gambler in order to surely obtain the money of the non-professional player."[12] Perhaps this naiveté is linked to the rural audience these works were directed toward. They illustrate a curious culture lag in their presentation, harking back to the antebellum era.

These amateur works are part of an old American tradition of writings authored by enthusiasts on hobbyhorses. Once astride they will not dismount until fully sated. These anatomies are often microscopically focused; however, they strive for encyclopedic exhaustiveness within narrow limits. For instance, A. J. Greiner presents over two hundred swindles in his book *Swindles and Bunco Games in City and Country*; he also devotes chapters to the experience of a bunco-man and how to avoid him. Greiner presents these in no apparent order; one swindle simply follows another as it enters the author's mind. They range from "World's Fair Employment Agents" to the "Appendicitis Swindle."

Most of these books contain more structure than the analytically episodic form used by Greiner, but these structures remain unsophisticated. James' book on the cheating techniques of professional gamblers alternates structurally between chapters containing detailed exposés of these techniques and anecdotal object lessons illustrating the fate of those foolish enough to be ensnared by the professionals. Both Schindler's book on the methods of the bank sneak and Costello's edition of Moreau's diary follow an anecdotal episodic structure that reveals criminal techniques within the framework of narrative incident. Houdini's *The Right Way to Do Wrong* and the anonymous *How 'Tis Done* are analytic in structure, but the analysis remains unsophisticated. Houdini, for example, generally concludes his chapters by using a joke drawn from criminal life but unrelated to his topics.

Although these writings are unsophisticated, they are permeated with the moral presuppositions of their time. They illustrate a profound distrust of the city as inimical to American traditions. To these writers and their presumably rural and small town audiences, the city represented a perversion of both nature and the promise America offered. These Americans found something unnatural in the urban landscape; they feared that urban corruption would spill over the boundaries of the city into the countryside. These writers also abhorred the accumulation of great fortunes by a few men; this, too, was a subversion of American traditions.

As they surveyed their country these authors had a pessimistic vision of the destruction of a society without fixed classes, a society that offered the hope of economic and social mobility to all of its citizens. In its place they saw the stirrings of a society ordered around a rigid class structure based on wealth; that wealth and its sources were monopolized by a few greedy hypocrites. These industrialists were not content to sap the economic strength of the nation, they would also selfishly usurp the sources of knowledge and pervert even truth to serve their ignoble goals.

PROFESSIONAL JOURNALISTS AND THE
NETHERWORLD OF PROFESSIONAL CRIME

A strong sense of moral outrage motivates the anatomies of the professional underworld written for the purpose of reform. These works partake deeply of the muckraking impulse and expose not only the corruption of the underworld, but also of the upper world. The shared theme is that without the covert sanction of the police and politicians the underworld of professional crime could quickly be eliminated, or at least brought under control. Thus, a major theme in these anatomies is police and political corruption.

Professional journalists wrote the majority of these anatomies. The writings are more closely allied to sociological studies of criminal life than to the earlier spirit of linguistic or literary curiosity found in the amateur anatomies. Henry Mayhew's *London Labour and the London Poor* (3 vols., 1851; 4th vol., 1861) strongly influenced these writings.[13] The fourth volume of Mayhew's work was devoted to crime and included detailed examinations of beggars, thieves, and whores, as well as their autobiographies. Mayhew also included exhaustive classifications of the London underworld. In his presentation Mayhew tried to achieve a photographic realism and included a wealth of sociological detail about roguery.

Mayhew's work influenced American reformers in many areas; he began the attempt to present criminals "scientifically" from a sociological approach. His influence is perhaps most evident in the ambitious *Darkness and Daylight or, Lights and Shadows of New York Life* (1895, by Helen Campbell, Thomas W. Knox, and Thomas Byrnes). This work was extensively illustrated with 251 engravings made from photographs and is notable not only for its attempt at scrupulous and detailed sociological realism but also for its interdisciplinary nature. It includes the viewpoints of policeman Byrnes, journalist Knox, and reformer Campbell. The publishers consciously strove for this multiplicity of vision, arguing that New York was too varied to view from a single stance and that each of the writers provided different insights.

The major emphasis, however, is on the scrupulous realism of this presentation of the dangerous classes, and the publishers repeatedly stress the inclusion of the illustrations. Among the contributing photographers are O. G. Mason, E. Warrin, Jr., Frederick Vilman, and Jacob Riis. The publishers note that "recent developments in photography have rendered it possible to catch instantaneously all the details of a scene with the utmost fidelity."[14]

The photographers spent months exploring the city, seeking "living material on the streets, up narrow alleys and in tenement houses, in missions and charitable institutions, in low lodging houses and cellars, in underground resorts and stale-beer dives, in haunts of criminals and training-schools of crimes and in nooks and corners known only to the police." The subjects of these photographs "would rather have been anywhere else than before the lens' eye" (ix). This joyous exuberance in the realism made possible by the use of photography extends throughout this seven-hundred-page anatomy, as in the caption of a portrait of a "Sly Opium Smoker": "This photograph was made by flashlight in a Chinese opium den on Pell Street when the smoker was supposed to be fast asleep. Subsequently the photograph disclosed the fact that he had at least one eye open when the picture was made" (571). Repeatedly there is a sort of exultant surprise at the wonders made possible by this new technology.

Darkness and Daylight was perhaps the most self-conscious of the reform anatomies, for its writers and publisher were well aware of the tradition within which they were working. In his introduction, Lyman Abbott noted the importance of Mayhew's work in focusing attention on the problems of the modern city— an attention reawakened in England by General Booth's *In Darkest England and the Way Out* (1890) and Charles Booth's *Labour and Life of the People*, which began appearing in the late 1880s. Jacob Riis' *How the Other Half Lives* (1890) contributed to this renewal in America. Abbott praised the realism of *Darkness and Daylight*, stating that it was the most comprehensive picture yet produced of New York City and a "noble" successor in its literary class (37).

Darkness and Daylight was by no means alone in its reformist presentation of the underworld. Twenty years earlier Edward Crapsey's *The Nether Side of New York* (1872) had exposed the world of the professional criminal. Portions of Josiah Flynt's *Tramping with Tramps* (1899) and the whole of *Notes of an Itinerant Policeman* (1900) and *The World of Graft* (1901) also presented the league between the underworld and the legitimate world. The professional criminal played an important role in Lincoln Steffens' *The Shame of the Cities* (1904), one of the premier works of muckraking. These reform anatomies serve as a transitional link between sensational exposé literature and academic sociological studies of crime. They show the strong influence of the aesthetic of literary realism and occasionally grope toward empirical and scientific methods in the analysis of deviance.

Edward Crapsey's *The Nether Side of New York; or the Vice, Crime and Poverty of the Great Metropolis* appeared only ten years after the fourth volume of Mayhew's study of London life—a strong influence on Crapsey's work. Although only the first quarter of Crapsey's book is devoted to professional crime, he presents a vividly detailed picture of New York's underworld immediately after the Civil War. Crapsey's book not only dissects the crime of the metropolis but also examines its causes and its cures.

Unlike other urban anatomists of "mystery and misery," Crapsey maintains a factual tone, avoiding the sensational. He makes an attempt to use statistics (drawn from 1868 to 1871) to bolster his arguments, thus showing the influence of a growing positivism in the social sciences.

When Crapsey's book appeared, the *New York Times* called it an "astonishing revelation" and recommended it for all thoughtful men as an important examination of the Empire City. The reviewer noted that Crapsey was "biased by no pet scheme, nor awed by that respect for constituted authority which influences the reports of regular statisticians." The paper felt it was important that Crapsey pointed out elements below the respectable classes of society "as destructive to its existence as are the earthquake and volcano to the fair face of the earth."[15] John H. Warren, in his *Thirty Years' Battle with Crime* (1875), refers to Crapsey's work as "an intensely interesting account of crime and its haunts in this city" but takes Crapsey to task for underestimating such things as the number of whores in New York.[16] The response of the reviewer for the *New York Times* with his cataclysmic metaphors is especially revealing of a vision of crime as a threat to the entire social fabric in the years immediately following the Civil War. The nation had survived one threat but how would it fare in its battle with this more insidious one?

Crapsey is primarily interested in detailing the history of New York City from 1867 to 1871, a history which "ought to suffuse the cheek of every American citizen with shame".[17] His major themes are the incompetence of municipal government and the subversion of the republican inheritance of America. The study opens with an examination of the causes for the prevalence of crime in New York; this analysis is notable for both its breadth and variety, for Crapsey refuses to place the blame on any single factor or on any single social class. The reasons New York is "a reproach to all the nations" include the city's location on an island, the city's lack of mass transit, the flight of the middle class to the suburbs, and the constant influx of immigrants. Even worse than these are political corruption and the tenement system, which Crapsey calls New York's crowning shame (5–13).

Crapsey places most of the blame for New York's crime on official corruption. He points out that during these wretched years while the public conscience slept, violent crime such as highway robbery and murder did not increase in the city. This is not due to civic virtue or the good administration of the law, but simply to the fact that the thugs have been given places in the city government and found political employment congenial to their temperaments and financially rewarding. However, during this same period crimes associated with professional criminals increased dramatically as pickpockets, confidence men, sneaks, and burglars became both more numerous and more enterprising. Austin Bidwell might attribute this to the increase in currency created by the Civil War, but Crapsey places the blame on the detective system and a corrupt administration of the police courts (11–12). He presents a paradigm of justice applied to the professional thief in New York as "obtaining conclusive evidence of guilt against a thief; arresting him; wresting from him the last possible dollar, and then turning him loose to repeat his crime and again experience its condonement" (45).

This civic corruption infects the entire populace and helps push those hovering on the edge of the law toward a career in crime. At the same time this corruption subverts the republican ideology at the foundation of the city and nation. Immigrants and members of the lower classes look to the city's leaders for models of behavior only to "imbibe from a vicious political system a dangerous disregard for the rights both of person and property" (24). Linked to this problem of civic corruption is the ease with which "respectable" citizens sacrifice public to private good. Much of the blame for the success of thieves belongs to those who "sell their own honor and the safety of the community by shamelessly promising immunity for crime in exchange for all but a small per cent of their stolen treasures" (51–52).

This subversion of republican ideals is especially dangerous for the group of "casual" criminals, a group that includes the marginal professional criminal as well as the legitimate citizen who occasionally "falls" into illegal behavior. This is the group responsible for the city's reputation for lawlessness. These criminals are still amateurs who occasionally drop into crime but have not yet turned to it as a means of livelihood. Crapsey attributes the large size of this group to a life on the borderline of poverty and the effects of drink. These marginal criminals keep the machinery of the law in constant operation. Crapsey argues that these offenders deserve pity rather than censure, for they are usually victims of circumstance. They exist because of the failure of America in responding to poverty. The typical American response has not been to help the poor get a start; Americans react irrationally by passing laws that punish begging with imprisonment. This simply puts the unfortunate in contact with professional criminals.

Crapsey begins his exposé of the professional underworld with the harbor thieves, an early instance of organized crime. Crapsey uses the careers of Saul and Howlett to present the harbor thieves. These infamous pirates were hanged for murder in 1853. Crapsey views the harbor thieves and their methods as an anomaly in American crime. These two youths headed a well-organized band of thieves who murdered their victims to destroy witnesses. With the river conveniently present to receive the bodies, the gang followed this technique for several months before they were apprehended. Crapsey underscores the difference between this easy use of violence and the techniques of the ordinary footpad or burglar. He assures his readers that murder as a cover for robbery has been unknown in the harbor since the execution of these monsters. He stresses the notion that these violent criminals are anomalies in the world of crime. The major themes of his work dictate this strategy of downplaying the threat of personal violence. Crapsey wants to emphasize the role of official corruption in professional crime; his attack is ideological and he needs to drive home the belief that the threat posed by professional thieves is actually of less consequence than the threat posed by corrupt officials. Thieves threaten individuals but corruption threatens the institutions of America.

The analysis of the professional underworld proper has two directions: Crapsey studies in detail the subculture of professional theft and attempts to explain why these thieves succeed. An essential part of his strategy for downplaying the threat of the professional criminal is to humanize him. Crapsey opens his account of professional criminals by attempting to provide a statistical base for discussion. This proves impossible since none of the police officials "knows" anything, and a study of arrest records from official reports is valueless. Still, he is able to make a few assertions. Most of these downplay the sensationalized role usually assigned to professional criminals. He points out that in 1868, of 78,451 arrests, 66,880 were for minor offenses such as drunkenness. Of the remaining 11,000 arrests, most were for such offenses as shoplifting; during the entire year only 303 arrests for picking pockets, 630 arrests for burglary, and 132 arrests for robbery took place. Crapsey then asked the police captains for estimates of the number of professional criminals in their precincts; their replies suggested that not more than 2500 professional criminals of every grade lived in the city (14–15). Having established his factual basis, Crapsey proceeds to the task of analysis. He presents a detailed classification of the modes of professional crime as well as describing the methods and attendant technology of professional criminals.

Crapsey's descriptions of these grades of criminals are notable for his aesthetic judgments as well as his implicit moral criticism. Crapsey applies no moral opprobrium to the forger, simply describing his techniques in a neutral manner. The bank sneak, however, represents "the highest possible criminal development." Crapsey approvingly writes that this sneak has "so much of patient research, so profound a knowledge of character, such readiness of resource, such perfect mental equipoise, that he seems worthy of being that favorite of fortune which his qualities have made him" (15). Other sneaks do not fare this well. Crapsey has little use for the chance sneaks who "stand at the very bottom of the scale of villainy, the scorn of all speculative thieves, the butt of all rascally ridicule, and the aim of all police endeavor. They . . . are all equally without adroitness and originative capacity . . . [but] are poor, aimless creatures drifting helpless about" (18). Crapsey's strategy in making these judgments is to apply the moral values of the upper world to the inhabitants of the under. Thieves are not essentially different from anyone else. What matter if a man be a burglar so long as he is dedicated, skillful, and industrious in his calling? The thieves who deserve and receive ridicule are those who lack originality, planning, discipline, and the ability to make large strikes.

Crapsey closes the descriptive presentation of the professional criminal by returning to the true problem: official corruption.

He raises another of the many "official mysteries" surrounding police headquarters, pointing out that it is ridiculous for the New York Police to claim little knowledge of the extent of the underworld and its inhabitants. He has just accomplished what they have decreed impossible. Crapsey is not simply pointing to police inefficiency but once more toward the pervasive corruption within the department. He emphasizes the suggestive fact that while a regulation exists requiring professional criminals to be photographed for the Rogues' Gallery, the gallery contains fewer than five hundred portraits, mostly of small-time thieves: "No bond-robber, or safe-burster, or thief of high degree, whose name is known in police circles the nation over, has ever been seized by the camera for the official collection" (23).

The second element of Crapsey's treatment of professional crime is an attempt to discover why thieves are successful. Crapsey finds the answer in the New York City Detective Bureau. In spite of the fact that no class is so ruthlessly stripped by both lawyers and detectives as the professional thief, those who belong to the first rank of crime have long since learned how to "square it" and are thus allowed to operate with impunity in the city. Crapsey's ire is directed primarily at detectives. He admires most patrolmen as honest, even effective. This admiration is in keeping with his republican stress on the values of the virtuous laborer. Although he admires the patrolman, he calls for the "utter eradication" of the detective system. It is universally corrupt: "something must be done if thievery is not very soon to become the most profitable and best-protected of industrial pursuits" (52–53). Crapsey's attack on detectives fits into a long controversy over the role of this occupation in the police department.

The use of detectives had been a source of controversy in America's urban centers since 1840, when a six-month inquiry, the first police probe in America, revealed the extent of corruption among New York's constables. This debate became a major issue in the fight by reformers to institute a police force based on the model of prevention, which advocated intervention before a crime rather than afterwards as in the older constable/detective mode of policing.[18]

Crapsey does not simply diagnose; he also offers suggestions for a cure such as making it a felony for a police officer to receive any remuneration beyond his salary. He believes that one of the central threats to American institutions is the lack of control citizens have over their police forces, and the attendant corruption of both the police and the courts. Crapsey argues forcibly against the discriminatory power granted policemen in enforcing such petty offenses as disorderly conduct; this offense is an annoyance but scarcely a crime. He argues that no citizen is safe from arrest on this charge, for "the misdemeanor is a vague if not glittering generality, and depends exclusively upon the fancy of the policeman making the arrest" (27). This offense is simply to be expected in a crowded city, especially in the tenements; it should be eliminated from the criminal code (27). His resistance to the discriminatory power of policemen is a conservative argument which goes back to the debates of the 1840s about the establishment of a preventive force. One of the main arguments against this reform was that the new police would too much resemble a standing army with excessive power over the rights of the individual. For Crapsey, the police abuse of the disorderly conduct charge is an excellent example of the results of this excessive power.

Crapsey attacks not only the discretionary power granted to policemen which allows them to invade the rights of the private citizen; he also attacks the corrupt police court system as the producer of unequalled travesties upon justice. He presents these lower courts as a form of institutionalized extortion. If an individual picked up on a charge of drunkenness appears to have little money, he is summarily sentenced to ten days; if, however, he appears prosperous, the courts will not release him until he has been bled. Not only do the judges want their share, but also the jailers, guards, patrolmen, and detectives.

Crapsey uses the professional criminal as a part of his literary strategy in this exposé designed as an attack on New York's system of justice. He humanizes the criminal so that his threat will appear minimal. This is in direct contrast to police writers who celebrated the professional criminal's skill and courage. While these police authors were trying to solidify their position in American life, Crapsey wants to eliminate it. Using his own experience as a standard, he argues that the ordinary citizen can fulfill the role assumed by detectives at least as well if not better than these "professionals": the true threat to America comes from those sworn to protect her.

JOSIAH FLYNT

Josiah Flint Willard was the most famous criminal anatomist of his era. His first book was an anatomy of the underworld of tramps, and until his death in 1907 he produced a steady stream of fiction, "pop" sociology, and muckraking that dealt with tramp life or the professional underworld: *Notes of an Itinerant Policeman* (1900), *The Powers that Prey* (1900), *The World of Graft* (1901), *The Little Brother* (1902), and *The Rise of Ruderick Clowd* (1903). He is the central figure of the Progressive Era who dealt with the world of professional crime and, in addition to his prolific production of journalism, fiction, and sociology, was an active figure in the literary milieu of the period. Flynt was responsible for Hapgood's introduction to Jim Caulfield and the resulting *Autobiography of a Thief*. He also interviewed such diverse figures as Ibsen and Tolstoy. In London he became an intimate of the British historian and student of decadence Arthur Symons, who contributed the introduction to Flynt's unfinished autobiography; through Symons he became a friend of such decadent *littérateurs* as Ernest Dowson and Oscar Wilde. Flynt also moved easily in the underworlds of Europe and America where he went by the moniker of "Cigarette."

This curious figure with one foot in the world of respectability and one in the underworld was born in 1869 in a suburb of Chicago, where his father was editor-in-chief of a Chicago daily newspaper. Flynt's antecedents were impeccable: his ancestors helped found Concord, Massachusetts; Frances Willard, a temperance leader and feminist, was his aunt. In spite of this respectable middle-class background, he claimed that his earliest memory was of a runaway trip which ended in the village lockup; his life was a series of alternations between respectability and the underworld until his death from alcohol abuse. He spent time in juvenile reformatories and county jails as well as on Tolstoy's farm. He did graduate work in sociology at the University of Berlin and shared the life of tramps riding the rails.

This dual life gave him a unique preparation for the "realistic" sociology he used to present the subcultures of vagabonds and professional criminals.

The core of Flynt's writing was autobiography; his life determined both his subject and his themes. His major concerns were the necessity of experiencing a subject in its actual milieu, attacking the falsity of academic criminology, and exposing the league between criminals and police. Flynt's first book, *Tramping with Tramps*, was a study of hobos, a subject in which he was perenially interested and about which he also produced a novel, *The Little Brother*.[19] *Tramping with Tramps* is strongly flavored by academic sociology; the first chapter, "The Criminal in the Open," lays out the fundamental tenets of Flynt's realistic sociology and contains a biting attack on criminal anthropology. Professional crime plays an important role in the last chapters of Flynt's posthumously published autobiography and provides the *raison d'être* for his muckraking book, *The World of Graft*, an exposé of corruption from the criminal's point of view that originally appeared in *McClure's*.

Flynt uses a pragmatic test of truth in his nonfiction writings. The student of crime must throw away theory and study the criminal as he is. Flynt's title for the first chapter of *Tramping with Tramps* illustrates this practical slant. He emphasizes that the only way to gain a true and "scientific" knowledge of the criminal is to study him in his natural habitat outside of the prison. Flynt contends that this is the major failing of criminology and that the focus on the imprisoned criminal has produced a distorted and illogical view of crime. His approach to the criminal anthropology of the era becomes another exercise in the unmasking of fraud.

Flynt uses a stance that parallels William James' concept of "radical empiricism," James' way of demanding that the individual rely on his own immediate experience to determine the meaning of truth.[20] Flynt argues for the value of his personal experience as scientifically valid evidence "in so far as it deals with the subject on its ground and in its own peculiar conditions and environment."[21] Flynt also adopts the pragmatic method. This method is essentially that of experimental science: the meaning of a theory evolves as it is experimentally tested. This method demands that all claims to truth be publicly verified and withstand the competition of prevailing ideas.[22] The pragmatic approach to truth also emphasizes respect for the complexity of existence by arguing that one must flexibly adopt a plurality of concepts to deal with human problems.[23] Again, Flynt's complaint is that this complexity is precisely what criminal anthropology, with its focus on biology and its search for the biological "criminal type," has failed to recognize.

Flynt also shares the muckraker's notion that if the public were only aware of a problem, it would attempt to solve it. In his autobiography, Flynt writes of his early days in New York when he tried to land a job as a police reporter. He uses this topic to include a brief discussion of journalism and crime. Flynt recommends that newspapers present a daily record of crime in the country as a sort of "criminal thermometer" indicating the nation's "criminal feverishness." This reporting should include "statistics, quiet accounts of crimes committed, anecdotes, illustrative incidents proving no theories, but merely making graphic the volume of crime in our midst." The goal should be an "inexorable display of our criminality" since Americans are without doubt "the most criminally minded nation on earth." Flynt argues that the real function of the crime reporter "should be to keep this forlorn state of affairs ever present in our minds until we wake up and say that this can no longer be."[24] This exposé is built upon an ideal of knowledge leading to action. This ideal is a continually present element in Flynt's work, and is, perhaps, the central theme of progressive muckraking. Implicitly this assumes a beneficent and dynamic view of democracy and human nature. If people are aware of a problem, they will solve it.

The World of Graft, a study of the professional underworld, was Flynt's largest commercial success. Commissioned by S. S. McClure, the book ran as a series of articles in his magazine beginning in 1901, and thus was one of the first documents of progressive muckraking.[25] Flynt approached professional crime and its ties to official corruption as a national problem; its solution demanded the moral regeneration of the nation.[26] Like Crapsey's book of thirty years earlier, Flynt's exposé includes a classification of professional criminals. Unlike Crapsey, however, Flynt simply lists these branches of theft briefly, providing practically no account of their modes of operation. This sort of literary curiosity about the process of professional crime is no longer evident in the work of the professional journalist/reformer, its place having been essentially filled by the amateur. Flynt assumes that most readers are acquainted with the techniques of these professional criminals; his primary interest is in why they follow this path, how they are able to succeed in it, and what they cost the American public.

Flynt adopts a muckraking persona that reverses expectations; he dons the rogue's guise and allows this rogue to have his say about municipal and police corruption as well as the pleasures and pains of the professional thief's life. Flynt's stance is highly moralistic and, in spite of his own experiences as a tramp, he has little sympathy for the " 'boes" and criminals he describes; he is essentially a respectable middle-class WASP. Flynt does share the "mugged" or known thief's contempt for the "unmugged grafter": the crooked cop, the corrupt politician, the embezzling clerk, and the greedy corporate president. These figures are just as accomplished as thieves, and just as deserving of punishment as the yegg.

The World of Graft is organized into four major sections plus a short introduction and concluding glossary. Flynt's purpose is to present the underworld's view of the "upper world's system of municipal defense against crime," since criticism of municipal government has come almost wholly from reformers and upperworld critics rather than those who make their living from the corrupt administration of the cities; these critics have usually recounted in a different vocabulary the argument of the social scientists who have failed to consider the thief "outside of the realm of theory."[27] Thus, Flynt promises the inside story. He presents himself as an anthropologist returning from an unknown country whose book will present an account of his journey and discoveries:

The World of Graft is wherever known and unknown thieves, bribe-givers and bribe-takers congregate. In the United States it is found mainly in the large cities, but its boundaries take in small county seats and even villages. A correct map of it is impossible, because in a great many places it is represented by an unknown rather than by a known inhabitant, by a dishonest official or an unscrupulous and wary politician rather than by a confessed thief, and the geographer is helpless until he can collect the facts, which may never come to light. The most that one can do is to make voyages of discovery, find out what he can, and report upon his experience to the general public.(5)

Flynt adopts the persona of a cultural anthropologist returning from an exploratory journey to reveal the findings of his study of an alien culture. This persona relies on the pragmatic approach of participant sociology. This will be a firsthand account delivered by one who has actual knowledge of this "new" world. Implicit in his adoption of the role of cultural anthropologist is an attack on the physical anthropologists who dominated thinking about crime in 1901. Additionally, this image of exploration underscores Flynt's identification of America as the most criminal-minded nation in the world; only seven years after Frederick Jackson Turner announced the closing of the physical frontier of America, Flynt is pointing to another unexplored country, one that exists in the moral and spiritual heart of the nation.

The first portion of Flynt's analysis examines corruption in Chicago, New York, and Boston. After detailing the extent of corruption in these urban centers, Flynt has a thief who has "squared it" describe why professional thieves leave the underworld. This reformed thief then details briefly the changing styles of police corruption in New York City from the 1870s to 1900. This thief "squared it" by becoming a detective; he provides a historical comparison of the older styles of professional crime with the present styles. The revelations of a former bank burglar, "Big Leary," who has also become a detective, counterpoint the first source's confessions. Unlike the first detective, this second "fly-cop" is on the take and his story relates how an honest cop is corrupted.

One theme which Flynt raises here and returns to throughout the book is the entanglement of professional crime with the "legitimate" American economy; Leary justifies his corruption by arguing that if he did his job properly not only would he make "the Line" (or Tenderloin) hostile, but "see the money that the cab people 'us lose, the laundry people, the places that sells flowers, the theay-tres—yes, an' the landlords, too" (117). Leary maintains that the city benefits from his corruption. Later a professional thief uses the same argument that he is a central part of the national economy: "Take the mechanics what builds safes an' the guys that invents burglar-alarms an' all the things what's used to protect locked-up money and jewels. Where the devil 'us those people be if we guns hadn't given 'em a job?" (155). This problem of the interconnection of the underworld and upper world is the primary theme of the remainder of Flynt's anatomy. The two final sections are concerned with detailing how detectives work and with presenting the thief's "expense account." He also tries to determine how much crime costs the taxpayers and gives recommendations from ex-thieves who have "squared it" on how to correct these abuses.

Flynt's complaint with the current police system is the old complaint of corrupt detectives. Like Crapsey, Flynt places most of the blame for corruption on ignorance and laziness which result in the detective's reliance on underworld informants to solve crime. Flynt's solution is both moralistic and pragmatic. Get rid of all the corrupt patrolmen and detectives and make sure the remainder are both "wise and honest." A good chief should have his detectives learn how to pick pockets, break open safes, do second-story work, handle counterfeit money, and in general learn to be good thieves. He should occasionally send his men out with a mob to see how they work. This practical experience would do away with the need for informants and thus do away with the major source of corruption (144–47).

In addition to this practical approach to detective work, Flynt contends that most of the retired thieves he spoke to suggested that the best way to control crime is to take the policing function out of the hands of the municipalities and give it to the federal government by replacing the old Secret Service (the precursor of the FBI) with a national police force (203). Again, this is almost paradigmatic of the progressive reform impulse which turned from the local to the state and then to the federal government for its reform.

These pragmatic reforms alone, however, are not enough to stop America's "most expensive luxury." A more important and fundamental change is necessary not only in American attitudes toward crime, but also in the corrupting materialism of American life. These two notions are inextricably linked. One "gun" Flynt interviewed stated that he used to read in the papers about how clever he was and that this cheered him up. Like a novelist jealous of his reputation, this retired thief continues to read newspaper clippings of his former deeds and states that "there was a time when I used to think that the public didn't care very much whether I was a criminal or not, so long as I got there and did it cleverly" (209–10).

This ex-thief argues that even though professional thieves steal to obtain the plunder, the public applause of admiring newspaper accounts encourages them. These accounts allow thieves to believe that the public does not really consider them bad but admires their cleverness. This both consoles and heartens the thief. Until this public attitude changes "and a theft is recognized as a theft, no matter by whom committed, it will be exceedingly difficult to reform professional guns." These newspaper accounts turn crime into a form of play; this is why "the gun" stays in his profession for many years (210–11).

Even more necessary than the change in the public's attitude toward crime, however is the need for a change in the materialistic emphasis of American life. As Flynt points out, the unknown plunderer of the upper world costs the public much more than the class of professional criminals, and, while "it seems rather harsh to the Upper World to call a man a criminal who is merely unscrupulous in business or reckless in the management of public funds, . . . the Under World makes no distinction between him and the pick pocket so long as he profits and the public loses by his illegal transactions" (177). This is the same justification for crime that such autobiographers as Langdon W. Moore and George Miles White use; indeed, they take the argument a step further and consider themselves more ethical than corrupt businessmen who carry an additional load of hypocrisy.

One of Flynt's confidants argued that he knew there were good people in the world, "but grafting is somehow or other in the air on this side of the water, and you find it in business as well as in politics." Like the gun, the businessman wants to "make a pile," and he is more than happy to cheat his neighbor to get it: "That's the spirit of things over here . . . and some of the most successful men commercially are noted for having done some very tricky things." This code of morals has a profound effect on the beginning criminal as he casts about for an exciting way to succeed quickly. If this beginner makes some "notoriously big strikes," hundreds of thousands of Americans will speak of him as a "mighty smart fellow" and not as a thief: "He is succeeding in making money quickly, and, as I say, a large part of the public overlooks his methods, and judges merely his performance" (208–09).

This presentation of American attitudes contains an implicit call for a moral regeneration in America. The widespread attitude that it is not important how a man makes his money as long as he makes it not only sustains the criminal in his profession but also undermines the "promise of American life." It perverts the American dream and comes to stand as simply an alternative path from the slum to a better life. In other books Flynt asserts that the majority of professional criminals come from the slums; unfortunately these are the brightest and most adaptable among the poor. Flynt expands this idea with the observations of a thief who points out: "The average gun in this country begins life with about as much chance of getting on honestly as that dirty little boot black over there on the corner" (168). This gun realizes graft does not pay, but it does allow him to have an occasional good time; life in the penitentiary is no worse than life in the tenements. More importantly, *"it's the one profession that as a ragamuffin I've got a fighting chance to win out in, and it amuses me to try my luck"* (170, emphasis Flynt's).

Flynt's implicit argument for a radical shift in American values carries over to his discussion of the nature of professional crime as an occupation. Stealing, Flynt argues, is simply a business for the professional thief "in which the accumulation of money, or rather the acquisition of it, has the same importance that it has in legitimate commerce" (213). As one "dead one" tells him, "We're all in this world to make money ... and I used to get mine my way, and my neighbors got theirs in a different way." This thief sees no difference between his old profession and any other business—the goal of all is to make money. Like other businessmen the thief "studies the market, makes investments, takes chances, and wins or loses, as he has planned well or poorly, and your merchant princes do the same" (213). This is the key to the moral regeneration that will eliminate both official corruption and professional theft in America. As a nation, Flynt argues, we must learn that the ends do not necessarily justify the means.

The year separating the writings of Crapsey and Flynt witnessed the birth of modern America. In these years the Houdini Syndrome became more than simply the literary subgenre of the exposé; it became an approach to life based on the unmasking of fraud, deceit, and corruption. Writers from the legitimate side of society made use of the professional criminal to highlight the sins of both individuals and the nation. Early, "amateur," reformers often used the exposé to present the threat of corruption that an alien, urban landscape posed for the virtuous countryside. These writers saw their primary goal as the protection of the individual. When professional journalists and reformers began to produce exposés at the turn of the century, the focus of the writing shifted in the same direction that the calls for social reform took during this era. As the muckrakers assumed this approach and used it to examine the sins of America, a new sense of the need for social rebirth emerged. No longer was it enough to convert the individual; the new call was for a regeneration of the nation.

4   The Novelist as Shadow

CRIME AND AMERICAN FICTION

Literature has always dealt with crime and criminals, and the subject holds particular importance in the history of the novel. The genre originated as a story of rogues in such picaresque novels as *Lazarillo de Tormes* (1554) where the rascal is the central figure and functions as a mouthpiece for the author's satiric observations on society. In England the history of the novel is intimately bound with professional crime. Defoe's *Moll Flanders* introduced the female professional thief to fiction.[1] Fielding solidified the use of professional crime in the English novel with *The Life of Mr. Jonathan Wild the Great,* a novel based in large part on Fielding's experiences among the London underworld as a magistrate and head of the English police.

American literature is no exception; crime has been a pervasive constant in the nation's imaginative writing since the early days of the republic.[2] Indeed, one good index to changing American concerns about crime is the style of deviance which an era finds most compelling to examine in imaginative writing. Murder has always found a central place in the imaginative literature of America, but American presentations of other modes of deviance have closely reflected shifts in the larger consciousness of Americans. This is especially true of popular literature, but also holds for more serious and thoughtful fictions.

The professional criminal surfaced in the work of America's first professional author, Charles Brockden Brown. *Arthur Mer-*

vyn (1799–1800), perhaps Brown's best novel, deals at length with the character of Welbeck and his criminal career as forger, confidence man, thief, and murderer. *Ormond* (1799) also contains an exploration of the early manifestation of the professional criminal. Both of these novels present crime as something essentially alien to the new republic, for both criminals are originally Europeans who came to America to escape prosecution and thus brought the seeds of corruption with them.

Occasional novels which included professional theft appeared throughout antebellum America.[3] The most famous of these is Melville's *The Confidence Man* (1857), a novel which takes a professional criminal as the central figure in a metaphorical exploration of the American character and such metaphysical problems as the nature of reality, of evil, and of sin.[4] Melville's career as a professional writer began with *Typee*, a narrative of his first serious crime, desertion from his ship, and his flight to avoid prosecution.[5] The use of crime and criminals remained central to all of Melville's writings through his exploration of the nature of justice and sin in *Billy Budd*, the novel he was writing and rewriting at the end of his life.

Not until the years following the Civil War, however, did the professional thief achieve prominence in American literature. Several forces contributed to the thief's changing role. One was the increasing importance of urban centers with the concomitant growth in urban poverty in postwar America. Another was the growth of realism in American literature, with its concern for environment as well as a multilayered presentation of American society. Finally, as industrial capitalism developed, thoughtful Americans questioned the overwhelming materialism that was creeping into all areas of American life along with the apparent beginnings of a class system based only on wealth.

These concerns found growing importance in American literature. The professional thief originally found a place in the popular fiction of the postwar era. In the mainstream novel he first functioned primarily as part of the backdrop of urban life, but with the growth of Progressivism and a new social involvement on the part of American novelists such as Brand Whitlock, Josiah Flynt, and Alfred Henry Lewis, the professional thief assumed a central place in the serious literature of the first decade of the twentieth century.

Popular literature was the spawning ground of the professional criminal in American fiction. In the immediate postwar years the vice and crime of the new urban centers, especially New York City, aroused great interest in the American public. This concern permeated not only sensational magazines such as the *National Police Gazette* but also more sedate ones such as *The Christian Herald*, *The Galaxy*, and *Appleton's*. Urban vice seemed to go hand in hand with postwar expansion. The great attractions of the city for country boys as well as urban opportunities for corruption made the sins of the cities important for all parts of the nation.[6]

This attention quickly moved from magazines to the dime novel and its competitors. Although the dime novel became the bane of judges, teachers, and clergymen, it was beloved of youth like Booth Tarkington's Penrod. By an odd quirk of literary history, these detective stories followed the same path to a place in American culture as that taken by symbolist poetry. Both originated with Poe, then moved to France before returning to America, the symbolist poetry through Baudelaire, the detective/crime novel through Gaboriau. These dime novels formed the subliterary breeding ground that produced the modern crime novel.

Dime novels originated as stories aimed at adolescent boys and quickly became scapegoats when respectable people tried to explain how youths became criminals. The assault on the dime novel often sounds oddly modern, for many of the issues that concerned those in opposition to these stories are still present today for people who worry about the relationship between mass media and the generation of crime. Nineteenth-century attackers included the sociologist William Graham Sumner, Detective Chief Thomas Byrnes, and the ineffable Anthony Comstock, who devoted several chapters of his *Traps for the Young* to "these sure-ruin traps": "the silly, insipid tale, the coarse, slangy story in the dialect of the barroom, the blood-and-thunder romance of border life, and the exaggerated details of crimes, real and imaginary."[7] Comstock presented a brief analysis of the contents of one story paper which included, "six assaults upon an officer while resisting arrest.... A burglary.... A woman murdered by masked burglars.... One confidence operator at work to swindle a stranger. An assault on the highway. A hired assassin...."[8]

The clear threat these writers saw was imitation. The life of the criminal, especially the professional, offered possibilities of wealth and excitement otherwise unobtainable for most American youths. Although it would be several decades before Gabriel Tarde's theory of imitative crime was felt in America, these critics found a sure threat for the naive youth in these stories. Sumner argued that they gave boys a theoretical knowledge of the methods of professional crime. He believed "it is impossible ... that so much corruption should be afloat and not exert some influence."[9] Lombroso's criminal anthropology had not yet emerged as a potent force in American thought, and the notion of personality as plastic and subject to distortion by bad example continued to dominate the typical American's ideas about deviance.

Dime novel detective stories originated as fictional recreations of actual crimes but quickly moved into the realm of pure imagination, although some stories continued to use a small percentage of fact to exploit the interest aroused by sensational crimes. The famous early detectives included Old Cap Collier, Old Sleuth, Broadway Billy, and Nick Carter. These pre-Sherlock Holmes detectives did not stress the minute observation and logical process so beloved by the decadent Holmes and his literary forbears such as Poe's Auguste Dupin. Instead they relied on disguise, physical strength, and brawling ability. Old Sleuth, who first appeared in 1872, gambled, drank, and used underworld slang. The genesis of Old Sleuth provides an interesting sidelight on the fictional transformation of reality. Allan Pinkerton, a model of moral rectitude, served as the source for the racy Old Sleuth.[10]

In these melodramatic novels the professional thief and the professional underworld found a foothold in American literature. These novels, which included such books as *Larry Murtagh Among the Harlem Thugs, A Syndicate of Crime, The $3,000,000 Bond Forgery, The Thugs of Chicago,* and *Karbo, The King of Safe Blowers,* attempted to provide verisimilitude through the use of underworld slang and detailed descriptions of the lower-class urban environment and its fixtures such as beer dives and dance halls.[11] Although the prose of these novels was lurid and their structure based on the crudest cliff-hanger technique, they did present a somewhat realistic portrait of a world hidden from most Americans.

THE YOUNG DETECTIVE STORY IN AMERICA

During the second half of the nineteenth century, the fiction of "roguery" was supplemented and largely replaced by the new genre of "crime detection." The rogue novel was rooted in the picaresque tradition and, after Fielding, was exploited by such English novelists as Dickens in *Oliver Twist*, Thackeray in *Barry Lyndon*, and Wilkie Collins in *A Rogue's Life*. William Gilmore Simms' early novel, *Martin Faber*, typifies the American use of this form. This type of novel was closely allied to the earlier form of the rogue-biography and generally used biography or autobiography as the major structuring device to follow the career of a criminal hero. This form was particularly suited to satire because of the rogue's status as outsider.

The replacement of the rogue novel by the detective novel signals a fundamental shift in the imaginative treatment of crime, for the criminal yields his place as fictional protagonist to the criminal hunter; the exploitation of roguery ceases to be a primary goal. The humorous or ironical presentation of crime diminished as deviance became a greater threat to society, and thus the importance of the detective and the villainy of his criminal opponent was reinforced. The new detective heroes provided a substitute for the rogue in fiction while continuing to allow a graphic portrayal of low life. The appearance of the detective in urban society thus supplied an opportunity for the reversal of point of view in fictional depictions of crime, with the added benefits of appealing to the moralist as the agent of a violated society, to the analyst as an untangler of puzzles, and to the artist as a substitute for Fate.[12]

The detective story could not develop as a form of popular literature until the detective himself developed as a social institution. The occupation of detective also had to become a socially accepted occupation. The two men who contributed most to the rehabilitation of the reputation of detective work in the nineteenth century were probably Thomas Byrnes and Allan Pinkerton. Each "wrote" or collaborated on a series of books based on actual cases he had solved. One of the more important impulses behind their writings was self-advertisement and self-glorification. This was not, however, simple vanity but was motivated by a desire to enhance the reputation of their occupation within society.

Neither man actually wrote "his" stories. Pinkerton discovered the commercial possibilities for the "detective" story in his fifties and turned out a series of eighteen volumes (about three million words) that became best-sellers in the 1870s and 1880s. In a letter of 1876 Pinkerton reveals that he had "seven writers working on my stories." His basic method was simply to sketch the outline of an investigation and then leave it to the scribblers to expand the sketch with dialogue, setting, and physical details. The stories themselves, early examples of the nonfiction novel, are highly melodramatic but fairly accurate, especially when dealing with the detective techniques of Pinkerton himself.[13]

Julian Hawthorne, Nathaniel Hawthorne's son, wrote the books taken from Byrnes' cases. This series of five novels based on Byrnes' files appeared in 1887–1888 and included two novels specifically concerned with the professional underworld: *An American Penman* (1887) and *The Great Bank Robbery* (1887).[14] Hawthorne's series began in the same year that the first Sherlock Holmes story and Fergus Hume's *The Mystery of the Hansom Cab* appeared, and the series was a popular success in America. The skeletal plots are from authentic cases. Hawthorne's major contribution was the creation of plot complications, generally based on romantic love. Julian Hawthorne argued that these nonfiction novels "have the advantage over the conceptions of the imagination, that they are a record of facts, not fancies, and carry the authority and impressiveness of fact."[15]

The series belongs to the older "realistic" tradition of crime literature as well as the newer form of the detective story. The "realistic" crime story reached its greatest popularity in the novels of Charles Dickens and Wilkie Collins, whose books were avidly read in America. These authors shared several concerns and themes with Hawthorne such as the deceptiveness of appearances and the sources of criminal deviance. They also shared the practice of using policemen as sources of material and as important characters.

The judgment of contemporaries on this type of writing was ambiguous. Certainly it is questionable as to whether or not books of this type contributed to the growth of realism as a literary mode in America. Hjalmar Hjorth Boyesen, (a Norwegian immigrant and friend of William Dean Howells) who wrote realistic novels dealing with business morality and corruption, such as *The Mammon of Unrighteousness* (1891), *The Golden Calf* (1892), and *The Social Strugglers* (1893), argued in 1894 that "a realist is a writer who adheres strictly to the logic of reality, as he sees it; who, aiming to portray the manners of his time, deals by preference with the normal rather than the exceptional phases of life, and, to use Henry James's felicitous phrase, arouses not the pleasure of surprise, but that of recognition."[16] Boyesen argued that the public created its authors in its own image and that such novelists as Wilkie Collins and Gaboriau reflected an abnormal pleasure and taste as they ransacked the records of police courts and lunatic asylums for startling incidents. Such fiction is worse than useless as a picture of life, Boyesen argues, and he places the "grewsome [sic] detective stories" of Byrnes and Hawthorne in this class, while at the same time expressing the hope that Hawthorne will soon return to serious literature.[17]

Howe and Hummel, the notorious Bowery lawyers, treated these nonfiction novels at length in their chapter on detectives, contrasting the detective of fiction and his almost "preternatural" powers with the detective of life who depends on his knowledge of the underworld and his personal ties with criminals for success. These lawyers acknowledge the fascination of crime and contend that the romancer magnifies this interest through the use of his imagination.[18] Then, in a curious passage containing a mixture of satire, irony, and nationalistic pride, Howe and Hummel address the collaboration of Byrnes and Hawthorne directly and assert that the most popular American detective stories are a "great advance" on the "effete style" of the French who "simply" compose imaginary narratives of fictitious characters: "To satisfy the exacting palate of our reading people, we require a real flesh-and-blood detective, with a popular name and reputation, to pose as the figurehead, while an ingenious scribbler does the romancing." Howe and Hummel refer ironically to the "realistic" nature of this method and its convincing air of truth. In spite of their obvious disdain, the famous "fixers" for New York's underworld conclude on a note of nationalistic pride, for "as in almost everything else there is a pervading breeziness and expansiveness of horizon about the American product that is totally lacking in the *blasé*, frousy, over-geometrical Gallic detective romance."[19] In spite of the concluding note, Howe and Hummel, with their broad experiences of criminal life, clearly view these stories as romances with little basis in fact.

The Great Bank Robbery is perhaps the best of this series and contains one of the most extended discussions of professional crime found in American fiction before the twentieth century. This examination of professional crime and the professional thief provides much of the novel's interest. The book recounts the robbery of the Manhattan Savings Institution on October 27, 1878, the largest bank burglary of the nineteenth century, which netted almost three million dollars for the burglars. Contemporary reviews of the book were good, although reviewers consigned it to the class of "railway" novels. The reviewers did, however, point out the peculiarly "modern" character of this new mode of detective story. The reviewers also noted the disjunction between the work of the detective and the work of the romancer.[20] While the reviewers saw this disjunction as a flaw, especially in the portrayal of "the woman in the case," these gaps provide some of the best insights into the imaginative response to professional crime in America during this period.

The narrator is a writer whose interest in the case is awakened by a journalist friend. Following an interview, Byrnes gives the narrator permission to relate the story; this book is the result. The style is melodramatic yet also detached. Hawthorne plays heavily on the device of contrast. This contrast marks the world of professional theft as alien to that of respectable society and carries into the romantic interest which develops with the story. Hawthorne opens his story at evening, a transitional period between light and darkness, with a picture of wealthy New

Yorkers going home to dress and have dinner. He follows this image with the sinister one of a different class within the city only now awakening. This class is dedicated to a "secret war against these favorites of fortune . . . a war that had lasted as long as history, and was still in full vigor."[21] This image of the professional criminal as a guerilla warrior engaged in undeclared war runs throughout the book. The image pattern of light and darkness is also a major element in the novel. Hawthorne uses this imagery to emphasize the unnatural quality of professional theft, for he presents the thief's use of darkness as his working element as a perversion of the natural order.

The novel is diffuse, lacking the tautness associated with the modern detective story. The crime does not occur until the sixth chapter, and the inside story of the robbery comes near the end with the confession of one of the burglars and the subsequent arrest of the gang. This, however, is not surprising. Hawthorne was writing for an age used to the leisurely development of a plot. Although Poe, Gaboriau, Collins and Dickens were all well known, the form of the modern detective story with its crime in the first chapter and solution in the last had not yet been established. Wilkie Collins' *The Woman in White* was one of the most popular of these early "detective" stories and contains several parallels with Hawthorne's novel including a concern for the gulf between appearance and reality and a slow unfolding of the plot. Collins uses a multitude of first person narratives to present his complex interweaving of a major plot with several subplots.

Although Hawthorne uses a single narrator to tell his story, his approach is typical of the pre-twentieth century novelist. Subplots, digressions, and tangents that contribute little to the advance of the narrative abound, and while these digressions defuse much of the potential suspense of the novel, they also provide an imaginative context. The outcome of the story was also already known. The novel appeared nine years after a crime which had been a national sensation and whose progress had been avidly followed by newspaper readers; the outcome of the novel was never in doubt. Hawthorne's major interest is in showing how and why the crime occurred, not in posing a mystery to be solved in the last chapter. The novel is essentially an exploration of a hidden area of American society, and its major source of interest is this innovative subject matter. The subplots and digressions serve to heighten interest by providing additional information on the subject of professional crime.

Hawthorne emphasizes the factual nature of the novel. He contends that Byrnes urged him to use as little fancy as possible in the narration and chafes under the constraint of these demands (49–51). He refuses to allow this factual relation complete control, believing that the facts are rigid only externally; once the artist delves below the surface, all facts and characters become plastic and yield to an aesthetic reconstruction. He justifies this imaginative reconception as well as the addition of passages that only occurred in the writer's mind by arguing that "imagination may be as trustworthy as observation, if it be based upon adequate data" (52).

The best examples of Hawthorne's imaginative additions to the incidents of the robbery are in his presentation of Detective Byrnes and in his addition of a romantic angle to the robbing of the bank. The major alteration in his presentation of the detective is the use of Byrnes—according to contemporary newspaper reports the detective in charge of the investigation was actually George Walling.[22] In this novel Byrnes is an individual who on the surface "looked like a prosperous man of business of the higher class" (70). This imagery reveals how much the status of the detective has changed in America since the earlier vision of his occupation as disreputable. He is now ready to take his place among the respectable classes. This businessman exterior conceals a master detective just below the surface. Byrnes makes the transformation as soon as he examines the scene of the crime and continues in this character for the remainder of the novel.

The addition of a woman, Mrs. Nelson, for a romantic love interest is Hawthorne's major imaginative change, however. Quite possibly this was added simply as a sop to female readers in an effort to increase the audience for the novel, but she is an original figure in herself. Hawthorne's use of this woman offended at least one reviewer's sense of propriety; while he agreed that "the idea of an unprincipled woman in the best society driven by maddening pecuniary losses to keep herself in diamonds and laces by hobnobbing secretly with thieves . . . is an ingenious, novel, and not impossible one," Hawthorne carried it too far, especially in the "brutality" of the descriptions of the relations between Mrs. Nelson and her "low accomplice," a diamond dealer and fence named Grady.[23]

Mrs. Nelson opens the novel as a mysterious figure in a brougham. The journalist's vaguely sinister hints about her past excite the narrator's curiosity and cause him to delve for the story behind her, thus resulting in the novel. Mrs. Nelson is one of the earliest examples of the decadent sensibility in American literature. The first detailed descriptions of her by the journalist emphasize that she is world-weary and willing to go to any lengths to feel a new emotion (29). This leads her eventually to a liaison with a diamond dealer from the "night side of life" (39). She forms a "business" partnership with John Grady through which she hopes to recoup her husband's lost fortune. She will furnish opportunities and suggestions for burglaries among the wealthy classes and he will furnish the capital and men. More important than the economic dimension of the relationship, however, is the *frisson* he can provide to her jaded emotions. Through him she will be able to meet "those enemies of the social state, with whom her own calamities had already half allied her in spirit" (39).

The relationship between Grady and Mrs. Nelson is a beauty and the beast love affair. A hideously ugly man, Grady becomes her complete slave, while she thrills at enjoying the wickedest man she can find. Her search for new emotional experiences leads her to rejoice in her degradation as well as in her new double life. According to Hawthorne's account she furnishes plans of the bank to Grady while revelling in her immunity from prosecution, an immunity created by the blinders of the wealthy. She tells Grady, "It would be harder for me to make them [the wealthy] believe me what I am, than for your Jimmy Hope, if he were caught in the vault, putting the securities in his pocket, to make them believe that he was innocent" (122). These self-imposed blinders are a recurrent theme throughout this novel, and the journalist points out the benefits for both sides if a society man were to link himself with professional thieves. The society man, with his access to the most exclusive houses in the city, could scout the premises and inform his fellows of the plan of the house and its routine as well as the location of the valuables without drawing suspicion on himself. This threat of a society "mole" working with burglars is a possibility that the respectable need to guard against. As the journalist points out to Byrnes: "It is at least conceivable—is it not?—that persons of good social position should also be deficient on the moral side— that reputation for virtue should not always involve the possession of it?" (126).

Mrs. Nelson finally plunges into the lowest depths of corruption when she attempts to murder Grady. Following the successful robbery, he begins to bore her with his importunate efforts to force her to desert her true station and become his live-in mistress. She has, however, tired of "common" crime and now plans to use her practised abilities as a lobbyist in Washington.[24] Grady, however, has too strong a hold on her through his knowledge of her dabbling in the underworld, and she tries to poison him. Although the poisoning attempt is unsuccessful, it angers Grady so intensely that he has a fatal heart attack. Again, Hawthorne's attempts at sensation are built on realities, for Grady had indeed died of a heart attack in his "store" not long after the robbery although there was no evidence of a lover's involvement.

The career of a character named Mr. Smith also emphasizes the fascination of the legitimate world with the underworld. This character and the subplot that revolves around him serve as comic relief. A rich young eccentric, Smith was believed to be involved in the bank robbery. Detectives observed him meeting repeatedly with burglars suspected of the robbery as well as with other members of the underworld. Indeed, his indiscriminate mixing with the various criminal classes is a source of confusion for these detectives who know how averse the upper classes of crime are to mingling with such lower classes as river thieves. The mystery is resolved when Smith turns out to be a sort of connoisseur of crime with over thirty scrapbooks devoted to crime in New York City as well as an assortment of criminal relics such as revolvers used in murders, bits of a hangman's rope, and "an anarchist infernal machine (with the explosive extracted)" (158–66). Smith illustrates the general interest of Americans in crime while serving as a warning to the legitimate classes that no matter how strong or innocent this attraction may be, it should be subdued.

The major interest of this novel, however, is in its presentation of the professional thief and the American response to him. Two themes emerge from this depiction: the importance of environment in making a professional criminal and the criminal's absolute freedom. The journalist introduces the professional underworld early in the novel when he remarks that next to journalists, those with the easiest consciences are professional criminals. The narrator expresses shocked outrage at this notion, but the journalist chides him for being superstitious. He argues that simply because the narrator suffers from conscience he should not assume that the professional criminal does. The journalist states that he is not talking about occasional or amateur criminals and then asks the narrator if he has ever seen the Rogues' Gallery.

The Rogues' Gallery becomes fundamental to the exposition of the professional underworld and the novel's central theme of appearance and reality. The journalist asks the narrator to imagine that he has been arrested and is about to join the Rogues' Gallery, "that is, your countenance is to be preserved forever for the contempt, suspicion, and hostility of mankind" (9). When you examine the Rogues' Gallery, however, rather than a series of crestfallen individuals "you will think . . . that you have seldom seen an equal number of intelligent, respectable, self-satisfied persons. Nothing diabolic, nothing brutal, no signs of corroding anxiety or secret agony" (9). The journalist argues that these rascals are able to maintain their innocent expressions simply because "the true burden of sin consists in feeling it to be such" (16). He bases his argument on cultural and moral relativism and after a comparison of America's Puritan settlers with the Sandwich Islanders concludes by arguing that morality is a matter of education and environment: "What to you or me is crime, to the genuine criminal is business, and his mood after committing it is not remorse, but satisfaction" (17). This emphasis on education and environment reveals the response of most Americans to professional crime throughout the nineteenth century. This approach was one based on common sense. It opposed the criminal anthropology becoming increasingly influential in Europe and advanced American academic communities. This emphasis on environment was not something that disappeared in American thought following the emergence of criminal anthropology only to resurface as the progressive response following 1900. It remained throughout the nineteenth century as a vital American response to crime and its origins.

Hawthorne's second major theme in his presentation of the professional criminal, his absolute freedom, helps explain the growing interest in this figure among Americans. Freedom and the nature of freedom has, of course, been one of the major themes in American history. As the nineteenth century drew to a close, the theme took on a growing urgency for Americans as the outlines of corporate capitalism began to emerge and the frontier reportedly disappeared. As America became an urban nation, social freedom seemed more and more of an illusion. The journalist argues that this absolute freedom is the fundamental characteristic of the professional criminal: "His responsibilities begin and end with himself. There's nothing else to hamper him. My dear fellow, just fancy for one moment the state of a man who feels that he owes nothing to society! No fear of social opinion—no obligation—no slavery to it!" (9–10). This absolute freedom not only helps to explain why the professional criminal looks so deceptively innocent but also why he is successful. The journalist argues that the white-collar criminal usually commits his first crime because of social pressures, and that he usually fails because his soul is bound by social obligations. In contrast, the soul of the professional criminal roams free. This, the journalist argues, is the true attraction of a life of professional crime. Men do not become outlaws from greed but from a desire for excitement, variety, and freedom. Unlike the staid businessman, the professional criminal *lives* life to the fullest (13).

The Great Bank Robbery is more than an early example of the detective story. It reveals the form in a state of transition and also provides insight into contemporary perceptions of the professional underworld, a subculture that became of increasing importance to the American novelist.

PROFESSIONAL CRIME AND THE LATE
NINETEENTH CENTURY AMERICAN NOVEL

The presentation of professional crime during the Gilded Age was not confined solely to crime novels and detective stories. This was the era when realism developed as a literary aesthetic. The depiction of crime and corruption was central to the growth of realism in America, especially among those novelists who heeded Zola's call for an experimental novel which would place characters in a situation and then observe their responses. Crimes of various sorts figure prominently in the work of such writers as Rebecca Harding Davis, John William DeForest, Edward Eggleston, Stephen Crane, Frank Norris, Theodore Dreiser, and Mark Twain. Professional crime appeared in the novels of many of these new realists.

Mark Twain put the professional criminal at the center of *Huckleberry Finn* in the character of the frontier confidence man. This roving fraud is a stock figure of much Southwestern humor; he is the familiar swindler who operates on the gullibility of country folk. Twain introduces the King and the Duke as a counterpoint to the sentimentality of the Grangerfords. He thus juxtaposes two strands of popular literature and uses the confidence man to unmask the falsity of the sentimental vision. The King and the Duke depend for a livelihood on confidence games designed to shear hypocrites and fools; among their successes is the camp meeting where the King assumes the identity of a reformed pirate to play on the sentimental notions of his auditors. This assumption of a false role helps define the nature of this character. On the raft the first act of the two confidence men is the creation of a false pedigree. Huck realizes almost at once that they are "just lowdown humbugs and frauds" but, caught in a situation he cannot control, he plays along with them.[25] Twain uses this theme of disguise and deception for comic effect through the Royal Nonesuch episode. The theme underscores the gullibility of an audience loaded with the baggage of sentimental, false ideals. As a counterpoint to the comic quality of these ideals, Twain presents the murder of Boggs by Colonel Sherburn. This episode occurs in the middle of the comic presentation of the King and Duke. Sherburn represents the threatening side of the same deception practiced by the King. He is a man who dons the garb of false ideals such as honor to justify the commission of any act, including murder.

The comic presentation of the Duke and King turns serious after they fleece the audience with the Royal Nonesuch. The Wilks episode presents the underlying threat of the confidence man and his deceptions. The King believes he finally has a chance at a big strike and is determined to win it through whatever means are necessary. He and the Duke drive Jim and Huck into a world of horror built on a sham of respectability. No longer will these frauds be content with petty swindles. These characters have left the fringes of American civilization; they assume the guise of respectability and enter the center of American life as they worm their way into the home and take control of the home's most sacred symbol, the innocent young girl. Twain does not return to a comic portrayal of these figures after their failure at the Wilks' home. Their next act is both petty and destructive. They abuse the frontier virtue of hospitality and destroy the "family" of the raft by turning Jim in for a forty-dollar reward and then disappearing.[26] Twain gave the professional criminal a central place in *Huckleberry Finn*, using him to highlight problems that ran below the surface of the idyllic world on the river.

Unlike Twain, however, most of the realists used this figure and his world as background material. The work of Edgar Fawcett and William Dean Howells exemplifies this fictional use of professional crime and contributes to our understanding of how and why this issue contributed to the development of the aesthetic of realism in America.

Edgar Fawcett's work falls into two categories, romances and realistic novels. Two of his realistic novels are concerned with crime as a fact of American urban life: *The Evil That Men Do* (1889) and *New York* (1898). *The Evil That Men Do*, an early tenement novel, has a grimly deterministic, almost naturalistic tone which centers on Cora Strang's seduction and subsequent decline from working girl to prostitute to death. In this novel professional crime helps establish the tone of certain urban settings. The city itself is a cold, uncaring place dominated by corrupt politicians who have struck a bargain with the criminals of the city for the mutual benefit of both.

In *New York*, Fawcett is centrally concerned with both the professional criminal and his ties to the police. The scope of the novel includes trials, crime, slum life, and political and police corruption. This novel is another study in contrasts and draws much of its framework from the emerging progressive attitude toward crime, reform, and human nature. The central narrative follows the career of George Oliver through three stages. Book One relates his life immediately following his release from prison on a charge of embezzlement. In this first portion, George wants only to negate his old self; he takes the name of Joe Jackson and becomes a handyman in the tenement districts. Unfortunately, his past is inescapable, and a landlord named Lynsko attempts to blackmail him into the crime of arson. George agrees, then informs the authorities and works undercover to bring about Lynsko's arrest. In the climactic scene of Lynsko's capture, George is shot in the chest and almost dies. Book Two moves from the tenement district to the homes of wealthy New Yorkers as George attempts covertly to reintegrate himself into his proper sphere. As the first book detailed crime among the poor, this section focuses on crime among the rich, especially the higher levels of police corruption. It closes with the suicide of Police Captain Cummiskey after his conviction on charges of corruption. The final book presents George's reintegration and marriage after he makes peace with himself and admits his past.

Fawcett thus presents several levels of New York life and crime. The first section is concerned with professional criminals—arsonists—but Fawcett has the same attitude toward criminals in both spheres. No matter what social level the criminal moves in, Fawcett argues that he is essentially a choiceless victim of environment rather than a figure of unlimited freedom. George, for instance, watches the repeated episodes of crime in the slum districts of New York and concludes that in his eyes these criminals are less culpable for their crimes, no matter how heinous, than he is for his own: "The bitter despotisms of birth and environment had allowed them no choice. Their evil had been a necessitous heritage, it would have seemed incredible if they had trodden straight paths when every baleful force of circumstance had dragged them into the zigzags of crooked ones."[27] After Cummiskey's conviction, Fawcett presents the view of both Cummiskey and his family that he is a scapegoat, a sop thrown to a reform government and thus a victim rather than a criminal.

Fawcett agrees: "He was the spawn of an evil code, a political civic grossness, which had nourished him from its poisoned paps and then reared him. . . . His ignorance was the excuse of his vileness; he had been the pupil of blackguardism, not its master" (234). This emphasis on the importance of environment in determining character is a fundamental progressive impulse. Not only does such a view of the criminal as victim of environment bolster the progressive view of human nature as something malleable; it also provides a strong rationale for reform in corrupt government institutions as well as housing conditions.

The underworld also found a place in the novels of William Dean Howells. Both *The Minister's Charge* (1887) and *The World of Chance* (1893) present professional crime as an essential element of urban life in late-nineteenth century America. *The Quality of Mercy* (1892) is a study of the crime of embezzlement and its consequences.

The Minister's Charge is an important novel in the canon of Howells' work, for it marks Howells' transition from the writing of realistic novels of manners such as *The Rise of Silas Lapham* to the writing of "economic" novels and an increasing stress on realism as an aesthetic. In this novel Howells for the first time enunciates the concept of complicity. This idea is crucial to the works usually called his economic novels. For Howells, "complicity" represented his belief that social evil affected all men regardless of their personal involvement.[28] The notion is essentially that all men are *implicated* in social evil, whether the evil be crime or poverty, and that all men share responsibility for the evil.

The Minister's Charge; or, The Apprenticeship of Lemuel Barker is, on one level, a *bildungsroman* which traces the career of Lem Barker, a back-country farm boy, after he comes to Boston with dreams of a literary career. The novel follows both Lemuel and the Reverend David Sewell, a member of the upper middle class who is responsible for Barker's move to Boston since he praised his bad poetry while vacationing in the country. Howells' method of placing the country boy in Sewell's charge proclaims the author's increasingly militant advocacy of literary realism: Howells quickly has a pair of counterfeiters swindle Lem on the common. After this episode Lem roams through Boston's underside where prostitutes proposition him, thieves rob him, and the police jail him on a false charge. Following his trial and discharge, Lem finds refuge in a charity flophouse where Sewell eventually discovers him. One reason for Howells' focus on the "other half" of Boston was apparently a simple desire to shock his readers.[29] He succeeded beyond his hopes, for the novel's presentation of the grim possibilities inherent in the modern city aroused a storm of protest.[30]

Approximately the first third of this novel details Lem's early adventures in Boston. Howells expended much energy to get his sociological details right, visiting both Boston police stations and police courts to observe details of procedure and combing the poorer sections of the city for sociological detail. Howells even draws a portrait of himself as a visitor in the police station at one point in the novel.[31] This first portion of the novel follows Lem after Reverend Sewell's initial rejection. A strong current of satire underlies this section. Howells' satire of the ideals of popular romantic literature is a feature of his work often remarked upon; this kind of writing is a major target for the satire of the last two-thirds of this novel. However, in the first third, Howells satirizes another form of popular contemporary literature and its underlying ideology—the exposé of urban vice.

On a surface level *The Minister's Charge* is the closest Howells comes to the contemporary Alger story. While Howells does present Lem's career according to this pattern, his use of it is fundamentally satiric. The major barb is aimed at the mass of literature designed to expose the vice of the developing urban centers and the threat that these cities pose for American youth. Howells indicates clearly that he is going back to the roots of this false ideal of the virtuous country and vicious city, roots he locates in Thomas Jefferson's virtuous "yeoman farmer." Lem's birth date, for example, is July 4 (48), Jefferson's death date, and the supreme day in the mythology of American republicanism, the day when the myth of the virtuous farmer symbolically became enshrined in the national ideology. Also, Lem's father died in the Civil War (61), a double-edged fact which not only reinforces Lem's republicanism but also points to the death of the "father's" vision of America. This is no longer the Golden Age but the Gilded Age.

Lem's adventures as unprotected innocent in the city are a parody of the threats presented in exposé after exposé of the vice of the metropolis: confidence men, swindlers, prostitutes, vagrants, and thieves lurk behind every park bench. Indeed, after Lem's release from jail, Howells raises one of the central themes of the swindling anatomies as Lem, in his supreme innocence, looks back on the affairs of the preceding day and sees that his troubles were his own fault, for "you might say that if a fellow came along and offered to pay you fifty cents for changing a ten dollar bill, you had a right to take it; but there was a voice in Lemuel's heart which warned him that greed to another's hurt was sin, and that if you took too much for a thing from a necessitous person, you oppressed and robbed him" (66). He thus suffers because of his own greed, that prime necessity for a successful con-game, the desire to obtain something for nothing. Howells is clearly using Lem's thoughts in a satiric manner, for the rhetoric of this passage is laced with biblical rhythms and high-flown phrases strongly inappropriate to the situation.

Howells' satiric purpose becomes clearer as this naive innocent contemplates his changed state. In his rural home in Willoughby Pastures, where he had hardly ever seen a drunken man, "there was no such person as a thief," and the tramps had long since disappeared. "Yet here was he, famed at home for the rectitude of his life and the loftiness of his aims, consorting with drunkards and thieves and tramps, and warned against what he was doing by policemen" (69). This idyllic vision of rural life held a prominent place in the republican ideology of the period as well as the popular literature. Howells later reveals it in its true lights. After Lem has begun to make a place for himself in Boston, he returns to his home in Willoughby Pastures for a brief visit. His optimism about the visit disappears as he understands its true wretchedness. He notices such details as the dirt under the fingernails of his family, and even in his disgust realizes that life had been like that when he was a resident on the farm. Eventually he takes an earlier train back to Boston than he had intended, for "he began to hate this poverty and suffering, to long for escape from it to the life which at that distance seemed so rich and easy and pleasant" (214). Howells thus sets up an imagined pastoralism which he later destroys by forcing the ideal to confront the actual. The "dangers" of the city for the rural innocent lose much of their threatening quality.

Howells expands the target of his satire on American reading materials to include sensational newspapers. These papers were a precursor of the yellow journalism of the nineties, and crime reporting accounted for a large measure of their appeal. Howells presents the Sewells' reaction to the *Sunrise*, a newspaper which they have begun taking as a sort of civic duty to encourage the young publishers. Their response provides insights into the attitudes of the middle class toward crime journalism during this era. Howells himself had begun his career as a newspaper reporter, and this brief presentation by one of the nineteenth century's most acute students of public taste is a noteworthy critique.

The Sewells' response to this paper combines repulsion and pleasure. Reverend Sewell does not care for the paper but his wife will not allow him to cancel the subscription. The paper presents the police reports with a "tone of flippant gayety [sic]" that the minister finds offensive. He also objects to the use of slang in these crime features. Still, the reading of the *Sunrise* becomes a part of their daily routine. Each morning Sewell ritually reads the police report aloud, and he and his wife subject it to a joking criticism until the day when they discover the news of Lem's arrest. No longer are the unfortunate victims of journalistic wit seen as disembodied characters. The world of actuality intrudes upon the Sewells' coziness as the tragedy of the small dramas in the police court comes home to them. Howells' objections to the contemporary journalistic fashion of using the misfortunes of the poor to entertain those more fortunate are evident. This practice not only dehumanizes the object of the reports but also makes a humane attitude toward actual suffering difficult to achieve because the reports turn real problems into aesthetic experiences—no matter how crude.

At the conclusion of this novel Sewell preaches his sermon

on complicity, a sermon which touches a mood of sympathy among the public and brings him fame. The burden of this sermon is simply, "If a community was corrupt, if an age was immoral, it was not because of the vicious, but the virtuous who fancied themselves indifferent spectators" (341). Thus, Howells enunciates his view that all are involved in sin and suffering and all must share responsibility for the criminal.

This theme becomes the central burden of *The Quality of Mercy* as the novel follows the career of John Milton Northwick and the response of the community to his crime. Northwick is not a professional criminal, but he has committed what Howells viewed as the paradigmatic crime of America's commercial civilization—embezzlement. Throughout this novel Howells stresses the complexity of responses to the criminal and his act, yet he argues that the criminal is linked to his culture and that the culture shares his guilt. The true antagonist in this novel is not the criminal but the commercial civilization of America during the Gilded Age.

Howells opens the novel by exposing the hollowness of American culture with a description of Northwick's home, a "wooden palace." This home is a complex symbol of the flimsiness of all wooden structures with the exception of log cabins. The log cabin hearkens back to America's golden age, before the Civil War, an age of individualism, virtue, and the frontier. In contrast to the solid log cabin of the American past, the residence of the Gilded Age is representative of the flimsiness of the apparent wealth Northwick has built through his embezzlements. It thus comes to stand as a symbol of the sham of true wealth, a sham which includes the whole of the commercial civilization of the United States. This civilization may provide "perfect functional comfort," but it offers no comfort of substance.[32] Howells extends this notion to attack the role of appearances in America. Appearance accounts for the commonplace quality of the defalcator in American life. This crime is based on the manipulation of appearances to conceal the emptiness of the true accounts; thus the crime of embezzlement comes to stand for American civilization. Indeed, one may read this novel as an early statement of the development of an ethic of consumerism which was displacing an older ethic of production in America. Howells considered this a central problem of his era as it experienced the rapid erosion of earlier republican ideals of labor and production.

Howells repeatedly drives home the theme of complicity in this novel. Matt, the eccentric son of the president of the mills Northwick has defrauded, says, "Northwick isn't the disease; he's merely the symptom.... It's the whole social body that's sick" (129). The notion of this crime as culturally based is given fullest expression in the report of Northwick's crime by Maxwell, the journalist who wishes to be a playwright. His report argues that Northwick's case is in no way exceptional but should be expected to repeat itself indefinitely: "On one hand you had men educated to business methods which permitted this form of dishonesty and condemned that; their moral fibre was strained if not weakened by the struggle for money going on all around us; on the other hand you had opportunity, the fascination of chance, the uncertainty of punishment." Maxwell continues his report by asserting that the causes would remain the same and so would the effects: "It behooved society to consider how far it was itself responsible" (125—26). Howells thus argues for the theme of complicity and finds the culture as a whole inextricably bound in with the production of crime. Howells does not, however, allow this notion to obscure Northwick's personal guilt. The criminal remains ultimately responsible for his actions. But the major emphasis throughout the novel is on the role society plays in Northwick's crime; the book reveals Howell's increasing awareness of the influence of complex forces in shaping human behavior.

The World of Chance was the last of Howells' economic novels; it shares structural and narrative similarities with *The Minister's Charge*; the two novels frame Howells' work between 1886 and 1893. Both novels tell the story of a young man with literary ambitions and his move from the hinterlands to the city in an attempt to realize those ambitions. Lem comes from rural Massachusetts and with true New England insularity goes to Boston; Percy Bysshe Shelley Ray, on the other hand, comes from the city of Midland and goes to New York, the center of the publishing industry. Both novels are also studies in thwarted ambition, but Lem eventually returns to Willoughby Pastures, while Ray succeeds in conquering the world of literature.

Howells uses professional crime for the same purposes in *The World of Chance* as in *The Minister's Charge*. In both novels crime helps establish the texture of urban life. The major difference is that the earlier novel uses the underworld to satirize the literary theme of the innocent in the sinful city as well as to establish the grimness of the underside of urban life. *The World of Chance* uses crime to set the tone of distrust and economic Darwinism which hangs like a pall over the first half of the novel. When a young mother rewards an old black street musician with a dollar, the overheard remark centers not on her generosity but on the idea that the dollar was probably counterfeit, so the musician lost money.[33] One of Ray's first experiences in the city is forgetting to pay for his supper. When he apologizes, the cashier responds with obvious disbelief since he is "used to such tricks" (18). Immediately thereafter he overhears a conversation about bankruptcy. One of the speakers asserts that the law of supply and demand had "about as much of a law to it as there is to three-card monte" (22). This was, of course, the favorite game of professional swindlers; the implication is that the economic deck is stacked. Ray then sees a scholarly looking man arrested as a thief (34–36), hears about tricks professional thieves use to change their appearance when being photographed for the Rogues' Gallery (38), and learns a valuable lesson from a philosophic stranger: "when we steal, always steal enough" (39). Howells uses the professional underworld and imagery drawn from it once more to establish a tone of distrust. The underworld is representative of the larger system of capitalism. The threat once again is the deceptiveness of appearances, a lesson Lem learned far too late, and one which Ray has trouble mastering.

Professional crime thus emerges as an important element in Howells' economic novels. He uses crime as a method of indicting capitalism which symbolizes the dangers of economic individualism and serves to establish the atmosphere of deceit fundamental to urban life in the new America. Crime also provides one of the bases for Howells' exploration of the larger themes of complicity and appearance versus reality. Howells' exploration and use of professional crime contributed to the developing aesthetic of realism in the American novel. The themes and issues that Howells enunciated would be examined in much greater detail over the next twenty years.

CRIME AND POPULAR FICTION IN THE PROGRESSIVE ERA

Following the turn of the century professional crime moved into the foreground of American fiction. By 1900 the form of the detective story had become established; in September of that year *The Bookman* devoted two articles to examining the formula or conventions of the form[34] as well as the literary figure of the criminal.[35] The second article argued that while the "villain" continued to be important in story papers and cheap novels, "in the future, however, we may look to the novel and the short story for the romance in the life of the 'second-story man,' the 'wire tapper,' the 'welcher,' the 'fence,' and the exponent of the 'gentlemen, find the little joker' game."[36] This is a prophecy that crime will be treated more realistically; it is notable that all of the criminals mentioned are professional criminals. This prophecy was fulfilled. Just as the autobiographies reveal a change in the status of the professional criminal from romantic outsider to victim, the novels of the Progressive Era target the criminal as a symbolic victim produced by American culture.

In the popular fiction of the era two diverse trends emerged in the presentation of theft and professional crime. The first moved toward an increasingly sentimental portrait of the criminal while the second moved toward a more realistic portrayal. O. Henry and Richard Harding Davis provide the best examples of the sentimental mode. Their most famous criminals were, respectively, Jimmy Valentine and Rags Raegen. Both of these characters are burglars, but both are sterling examples of humanity beneath their rough exteriors.

Jimmy Valentine, the hero of "A Retrieved Reformation," was modeled on a safe-cracker named Dick Price whom O. Henry met while in prison.[37] In spite of the hero's actual existence, the outline of the story parallels Davis' "My Disreputable Friend, Mr. Raegen," which appeared in 1891. Both burglars sacrifice themselves for the good of a helpless child in a life-threatening situation and, in both stories, the sacrifice of the burglar leads to his vindication.

This sentimental story pattern had become so firmly established in "household" fiction that O. Henry wrote a pleasant satire of the formula called "Tommy's Burglar." This story pokes fun at the inanities of the form as well as at the gap between this idealized burglar and the real thing. The burglar, soon after entering the targeted home, is approached by the fair-haired, pajama-clad Tommy, an eight-year-old boy. The two discuss the proprieties and editorial demands of the story of a criminal reformed by an encounter with a child which must take place within two thousand words. As the burglar sourly states, "It's the same old story. Your innocence and childish insouciance is going to lead me back into an honest life. Every time I crack a crib where there's a kid around it happens."[38] The play with the conventions continues throughout the story with both Tommy and the burglar bewailing that they get the sorry end of the deal in these stories.

This sentimentalization of the professional thief reinforces the view of the criminal as a victim of his environment. As a victim, the criminal serves as an object of pity and sympathy rather than an object of fear. As he became a staple of women's magazine fiction, the sentimental thief with a heart of gold helped support a concept of human nature based on a belief in the inherent possibilities for virtue within each individual, as well as the hope of reformation for even the most hardened of thieves, a reformation that would come from the stirrings of human sympathy for another human in danger.

In spite of a veneer of fantasy, the detective story took on an added dimension of realism during the Progressive Era. The detective story was becoming established and, as the underlying formula became set, the presentation of surface reality became more fluid. No longer was the master detective pursuing the consummate villain a necessity. Indeed, the detective who solved puzzling cases through logic and observation became ridiculous; O. Henry's Shamrock Jolnes cannot identify a criminal who goes so far as to introduce himself to the sleuth. The new detective, while still a creature of fantasy, often uses realistic techniques and solves realistic crimes.

An example of this new detective is Craig Kennedy, "Scientific Detective," the hero of a series authored by Arthur Reeves. Kennedy is a scientist at Columbia who makes use of the latest advances in forensic science, such as the Unruh test for discovering if a bloodstain is of human origin to solve crimes. The science in these stories is valid, up-to-date, and well presented. The crimes are also intimately connected with the concerns of the Progressive Era and are not always puzzling murders. One of the best stories, for example, concerns a Black Hand kidnapping which Kennedy solves by a crude electronic bugging device. The greatest period of Black Hand extortion plots was in the years between 1900 and 1917, and this terrorist extortion posed a real problem to Italian communities in such cities as Chicago and New York.

The archetypal progressive detective was Average Jones, created by Samuel Hopkins Adams, one of the era's most influential muckrakers. Adams wrote for *McClure's* and also served as its advertising manager. After going to work for *Colliers* in 1904, he produced one of the finest achievements of muckraking journalism in his series of articles on the patent medicine business. This series had direct legislative consequences, for it helped ensure the passage of the Pure Food and Drug Act of 1906.[39] Adams drew heavily on his personal experience for both his novels and the stories about Average Jones, who often seems to serve as a surrogate for Adams. Average Jones is a young man who inherited a fortune from his grandfather on the condition that he live in New York for ten years. The grandfather had been a member of the Tweed Ring, and he imposed this condition in the belief that no man could live in the city for ten years without squandering his life away in dissipation. The money he had stolen from the citizens of New York would thus be returned to them.

In a search for something to keep himself occupied, Jones becomes an "Ad-Visor" dedicated to exposing frauds and swindles in newspaper advertisements. He is, perhaps, the first consumer advocate in American fiction. Among the implicit themes of these stories are the rise of advertising and the growth of the consumption ethic. Central to these stories is the belief that the consumer needs protection in a marketplace dominated by the theory of *caveat emptor*. More specifically, the stories illustrate such themes of Progressivism as a strong dislike for trusts and monopolies, which are presented as corrupt and criminal ("The Red Dot"), medical quackery or, "the cruelest of all forms of swindles" ("The Open Trail"), and corruption in the police and legislatures ("The One Best Bet", "The Million Dollar Dog").

These stories once more raise the question of appearance and the possibilities for deception hidden by appearances. The story "Blue Fires" apparently centers around the operations of a professional hotel thief. The thief later turns out to be a sleep-walker. As the Ad-Visor remarks: "Bacon's principle—an admirable principle in detective work—is that we should learn from things and not from the name of things.... Because the law, which is always rigid and sometimes stupid, says that a man who takes that which does not belong to him is a thief, you've got your mind fixed on the name of 'thief,' and the idea of theft."[40]

The best of the Average Jones stories, "The Man Who Spoke Latin," is built solely on this question of appearance and reality. This story centers around a supposed case of metempsychosis involving an ancient Roman who finds himself reincarnated in the early twentieth century. This Roman turns out to be a genteel but dangerous professional thief who, because of his scholarly training, specializes in rare books and manuscripts; in this case he is on the trail of a rare letter from Bacon concerning this " 'vagabond and humble mummer' " Shakespeare. This priceless letter would end the controversy over the authorship of Shakespeare's plays. Jones, the Ad-Visor, exposes the humbuggery of the deception, although he relies on his knowledge of human nature rather than his knowledge of classical Latin to expose the thief.

By the beginning of the twentieth century, the basic formula of the modern detective story was well established. The detective story was one of the more popular forms of entertainment during the Progressive Era. This kind of story helps open a window onto progressive attitudes toward crime and criminals through the manner in which the authors treated such themes as the detective and the professional thief.

PROFESSIONAL CRIME AND THE PROGRESSIVE NOVEL

With the rise of Progressivism serious fiction also began to examine the professional criminal in more depth and detail. As Arthur Stringer, a writer of mystery novels, noted in 1908, the growth of realism in literature "compelled fiction to include the criminal in its reflection of the actual."[41] Stringer attributes this partially to the development of the "philanthropic and scientific view of criminal life" during the latter part of the nineteenth century and partially to the growing "civilization" of humanity. For these highly civilized readers criminal fiction serves as a cathartic safety valve, a "vicarious rebarbarization," and thus prevents the development of an effeminate approach to life.[42]

While most authors would have denied that their goal was the production of barbarians, the concern of serious writers with criminal life did increase dramatically after the turn of the century. These criminal novels were not designed as mysteries or even primarily as crime stories. The authors were attempting to produce serious realistic studies of the development of criminality, of the importance of environment, and of the nature of deviance as well as to probe the weaknesses and inequities of the American economic and penal systems.[43]

Progressivism drew much of its vitality from a concern with the shaping effects of environment on personality. This concern found an outlet in the serious fictional investigation of deviance. These authors were obsessed with such problems as the nature, source, and motivations of deviance. The application of realism to fictional investigations of criminal life has several implications for early-twentieth-century America. Boyesen insisted that the realist followed "the logic of reality" as he saw it and presented the normal rather than the abnormal aspects of life and society.[44] The use of the contemporary underworld to explore American life after the turn of the century indicates a shift from Howells' realism, with its assumption that the world of the ethical upper middle class was "typical," to a darker, more pessimistic view of American society.

Clearly, something is out of joint in a culture that produces, as a normal by-product, a class who makes an occupation of preying on other members of the culture. The major thrust of almost every realistic crime novel of this period is an examination of the forces within American culture that contribute to this occupational normality whether they be corrupt policemen, materialism, economic inequity, or faulty environment. This parallels and contributes to the emerging view of the criminal as victim—a view which contributed to a sympathetic as well as realistic portrayal of this figure.

Still, the fictional character of the rogue continued to find a place in the progressive novel. In a transformation that reveals a great deal about changing social values, the rogue became the successful capitalist rather than the professional criminal. In this new guise he appears in such anti-business novels as David Graham Phillips' *The Master Rogue*, an ironic fictional memoir of the narrator's rise from clerk to millionaire, and Robert Herrick's *The Memoirs of an American Citizen*.

Just as he was in the foreground in the introduction of professional crime to muckraking, Josiah Flynt was among the first to use professional crime as the basis for serious fiction. In 1900 he and Alfred Hodder (who used the pseudonym Francis Walton) published a collection of short stories titled *The Powers That Prey*. This book served as a fictional complement to the sketches appearing in Flynt's series, *The World of Graft*. As in the journalistic exposé, the purpose of these stories was to uncover the league between police and professional thieves. In this book the authors direct their ire principally at the follies of academic criminologists and criminal anthropology but include novelists and romancers in the attack. Flynt and Hodder argue that both "men of science and romanticists have used the outcast as a point of departure for the aesthetic imagination and have taken it for granted that he is not so interesting as they can fancy him." These writers have pictured the criminal as "a simplified human brute, an epitome of the stigmata of degeneration," and the detective as an abstract figure who sees the world as a "magnified chessboard."[45] Flynt and Hodder then argue that heredity is not the important factor, and that instead of being a variant human species, the professional criminal differs only in circumstance, not psychology, from other people.

The stories themselves present incidents that illustrate the links binding the detective and criminal together. Their contemporary impact may be measured from an ambiguous review by Harry Thurston Peck in the *Bookman*. Peck saw the stories as "informal social studies" and stated that "the reader ... will find his sympathy, as a whole, not on the side of those who represent and at the same time make a travesty of the law, but rather with those ... who have the world abidingly against them." In spite of the sympathy the authors create for these professional thieves, Peck notes that the stories also create a sense of unease in the reader, "an uncomfortable, startled feeling, such as one would have did he know that the apparently empty air around him was filled with strange creatures, unclean and menacing and invisible."[46]

Flynt's most detailed study of the professional underworld was *The Rise of Ruderick Clowd* (1903). This novel uses biography as a structuring device and is a *bildungsroman* about the evolution of a thief. Although contemporary reviewers called it Flynt's most important work,[47] the novel is not well written or structured. The sociology is always too close to the surface and emerges full-blown in an interview with the elderly, retired thief, that ends the book. The novel is, however, a revealing document of the progressive view of the professional thief for Flynt takes his hero from his bastard birth in 1850 through his introduction to crime by stealing food, to picking pockets, to stealing silk, to his eventual emergence as a bank burglar. Professional crime is a business, and Flynt examines both the recruitment process and the training of a thief as Clowd becomes a *wunderkind* of the underworld.

The emphasis throughout the novel is on environment. Clowd's parentage is a symbolic union of the upper and lower classes. His father was a rich young wastrel and his mother a hard-working servant. While Flynt uses this parentage to underscore the hypocrisy of the wealthy, he also uses it to discount the importance of heredity. The novel is structured to point up the determining power of environment. The lengthy prologue establishes the environment into which Clowd will be born and the inevitability of his turn to theft as occupation. After four years of trying to make it legitimately, Clowd chooses to become a thief at the age of eighteen. This is the age when a youth from his ward "had to make up his mind very quickly whether he meant to be a thief or forego his ambitions of wealth."[48] The choice is no choice for these young men from the slums: "The criminal environment was such that the only outlet for their energy was thieving: they became the notorious pickpockets, burglars and cracksmen of their day" (103–4). In another environment these youths might have been great leaders, but since such ambitious young men dreamed of ending their days as well-to-do "businessmen of their class," they were "compelled to take advantages of the opportunities at hand" (103–4). These opportunities were criminal.

Flynt approaches naturalism with his emphasis on the lack of human freedom, but he refuses to take the final step of the naturalist and link environment with heredity. For him background is supreme. This enables Flynt to maintain at least the semblance of optimism as well as the stance of a progressive reformer, for environment may be altered and improved while heredity is inescapable. This stress on environment was one of the keynotes of Progressivism, an influence that found expression in such movements as city planning, settlement houses, and the drive to establish playgrounds for poor urban children.

Alfred Henry Lewis, best remembered today for his Wolfville stories of the old West, was another progressive novelist who wrote about urban crime. His *Confessions of a Detective* was, like Flynt's early work, a bitter examination of the links between criminals, the police, and corrupt politicians. This novelette is another *bildungsroman*, but, instead of detailing the education of a thief, it presents the education in corruption of a once-idealistic policeman. One of the most notable aspect of this novelette is the changing definition of crime that emerges. As the reformers of the first years of the twentieth century examined America, they began to apply a measure based on morality rather than legal codes. This shift is evident in greatly increased attention to such victimless crimes as prostitution as well as such issues as Prohibition. This changing approach also included a much broader sense of crime or graft as anything detrimental to the public. The detective in Lewis' book, for example, says: "Graft? You want me to give you a sort of graft-map, do you? There wouldn't be room on Manhattan Island to draw one." He argues that when a building falls down from rotten mortar or when chimneys send up clouds of soft coal smoke, the crime is no different than theft or assault. He implicates the entire legislative process in corruption, stating: "The very ordinances are passed by the City Council, not to protect the city, but to promote graft. Every one of those ordinances gives some department a fresh grip on the public. The ordinance gets in somebody's way; that somebody has to pay."[49] Although the speaker is a cynical and disillusioned cop, Lewis uses him to condemn the petty venalities of municipal officials. He includes their actions as crimes along with those of the less hypocritical thief.

Lewis' second book on professional crime, *The Apaches of New York* (1912), adds another dimension to the progressive vision of the criminal as victim. Flynt's presentation of the professional criminal as outcast fits this changed image, but Lewis takes it a step further. This collection of short stories deals with the lowest orders of professional crime, the urban gangs. These gangs were shortly to emerge as the dominant force in twentieth-century crime. Lewis claimed that the stories were true and argued that his purpose was "to show how the other half lives in New York."[50]

The stories deal with yeggs, strong-arm artists, stickup men, and prostitutes. They provide a contemporary glimpse of the beginnings of organized crime in this country, and the warfare that raged as the gangs attempted to carve out territories. The Five Points Gang of this era soon produced Al Capone, Lucky Luciano, and other infamous gangsters. This stratum of the underworld, in addition to being more degraded than the higher limits, was much more violent. Indeed, violence was the trademark of these gangs and their life-style. The threat of violent death hangs over these pages, and few of the denizens hesitate at murder. Everything, whether it be love or friendship, is secondary to economic gain. Lewis' primary point in his sketches of the lowest levels of crime is the degradation that results from an inhuman environment. These humans forced to live like beasts in the jungle have responded in the only possible way by becoming beasts.

A Man's World, by Albert Edwards (Arthur Bullard), also appeared in 1912. In some ways this is the most "progressive" of these novels.[51] Presented in the form of an autobiography, the book details the search of Arnold Whitman for the best way to serve the world. Whitman's life follows a path typical of the progressive personality. He is born into a home marked by strict Protestant morality. From here he attends a small denominational college and plans to be a Methodist minister. Like most real life progressives such as Jane Addams, and Samuel Hopkins Adams he becomes dissatisfied with his religion and eventually rejects it outright. He turns to scholarship and believes he is happy in this field but soon experiences the psychosomatic illness that was also common among progressive reformers. In Whitman's case this is blindness, an illness which symbolizes the dead end of isolated scholarship unattached to the nation's social problems. After a short period as a settlement house worker, Whitman finds his true calling in the fields of criminology and penal reform. This choice takes on an almost religious significance for Whitman, and he invests it with the significance that his family environment had placed on the ministry. The narrator's life pattern is typical of the actual pattern of most progressives.[52]

Once again, a central theme of this novel is how to define crime. Where Lewis simply expanded his notion of crime to include anything that was detrimental to society, Bullard presents a pragmatic definition. Like most progressive novelists who dealt with professional crime, Bullard delineates academic criminology as both stupid and vicious.[53] The narrator's view of crime is informed by an awareness of the complexity of the subject and a concept of evolution. He writes a book on theft designed to show the gap between the complexity of crime, whether committed by petty sneak thieves or bank robbers, and "the dead and formal simplicity of our penal code" (237). Later he argues that what is really needed is a new terminology of crime. Just as psychologists have substituted "paranoia" for "devils," criminologists must come up with more than "burglary in the second degree" (243). A vision of the complex evolutionary nature of crime motivates this argument. The problem cannot be expressed in a dead language from a dead time.

The clearest statement of Whitman's evolutionary pragmatism comes when he is defending his theory from an attack by a radical feminist socialist who sees economic maladjustment as the root of all deviance. Whitman argues that "crime consists of acts forbidden by the legislature . . . it is an arbitrary conception, which is always changing" (259). This is legal realism with a vengeance, yet it expresses the dramatic shift that has occurred in the American concept of crime from offenses against a stable, universal order to something evolving while rooted in the realities of present-day culture.

Bullard's novel points to other shifts in American approaches to crime as well as to a new approach to penology. After 1890 medical terminology assumed increasing importance in the American vocabulary of deviance.[54] Whitman shares this medical approach to the treatment of criminals. After working in the Tombs, he attacks the barbaric penal codes of America that emphasize punishment rather than rehabilitation. He argues that as Americans become enlightened "we will learn to protect ourselves from the losses and moral contagions of crime as we do from infectious diseases. Our prisons we will discard for hospitals, our judges will become physicians, our 'screws' we will turn into trained nurses" (142). This medical approach, with its optimistic forecast for the future, was an important element in the attitude of emerging professionals who argued that criminal deviance could be solved if men would simply approach it rationally and scientifically.

BRAND WHITLOCK: THE CENTRAL ROLE OF THE PROFESSIONAL CRIMINAL

The best of the progressive novels dealing with the world of professional crime is *The Turn of the Balance* (1907) by Brand Whitlock. This novel is firmly grounded in Whitlock's extensive personal knowledge of the underworld.[55] Whitlock first became interested in professional crime while working for Governor Altgeld in Illinois. Altgeld urged that justice required an examination of the history, environment, and character of the offender and believed that criminals were unfortunate rather than vicious.[56] Whitlock's interest in crime deepened after he became an attorney and developed an acquaintance with Clarence Darrow, but it reached its greatest flowering in his hometown of

Toledo, where Whitlock served with Golden Rule Jones, the well-known reform mayor. Before Whitlock himself became mayor of Toledo, he served as a police court judge and was known as the "great suspender" for his lenient approach to sentencing criminals.[57]

Whitlock's inside knowledge of the world of professional crime came primarily from his correspondence with prisoners and his personal friendship with a yegg, Curly Williams. Curly helped Whitlock learn the argot of the underworld as well as its code and hierarchy. These experiences contributed to Whitlock's vision of crime and criminality, a vision strongly opposed to the scientific criminologist's views of heredity and moral debasement. Whitlock placed himself on the side of the so-called criminal and found the explanations for crime in environmental determinism and the importance of circumstances, especially economics. He stressed the relativism of right and wrong and, in *The Turn of the Balance*, presented an underworld as moral in its own way as the world of business and politics.

The Turn of the Balance is firmly based in Whitlock's own experience. He hoped the novel would show "the spirit of our whole system of dealing with crime and criminals is fundamentally wrong because it is founded in hatred and fear."[58] When the novel appeared it created a sensation. Reviewers touched by Progressivism such as Harry James Smith generally hailed Whitlock's "burning human sympathy and fine idealism." Smith found the novel worthy of Zola and was impressed with Whitlock's portrayal of the modern city as an organism in which everything was interrelated, as well as with his depiction of "all the steps of the slow, inveterate destruction of character under the 'normal' working of the machinery of society."[59] On the other hand, William Morton Payne spoke for a more traditional group when he awarded Whitlock top rank "in the present competition among our amateur sociologists to produce the most distressful possible" portrait of American society. He called the novel a piece of imitation Zolaism that painted the gloomiest picture of contemporary American life yet produced by using carefully selected "horrible details" and "sensational exaggeration."[60] Both reviewers agreed, however, that the most remarkable element in the novel was Whitlock's portrayal of the language, customs, and world view of the underworld.

Three years later, in a review that reads as an explicit rejection of his earlier statement of "smiling" realism, William Dean Howells gave the book strong praise for its realism, vision, and truth. In the earlier statement on realism, Howells had asserted that Americans would never produce books in the Russian vein of realism because of the enormous differences between Russian and American society. In this tribute to Whitlock, Howells argues that Whitlock's master in his education as a realistic novelist was "the great Russian school which embodies an aesthetic recalling the novelist to the study of man as we all know him in the flesh," and rightly identifies Whitlock's model as Tolstoy rather than Zola.[61] Howells states his changed vision of the nature of American life explicitly in his comparison of Tolstoy's Russia and Whitlock's America. He says that *The Turn of the Balance* is not a polemic but shows areas of life Americans prefer to ignore: "If it tears from our eyes the bandage which we fancied on those of justice and shows her winking at the same crimes against criminals in the American courts and the Russian courts, and in their differing procedure arriving at the same wicked and stupid ends, it is certainly not for us to reject it as impossible." Whitlock's accusations against the American system of criminal justice cannot be dismissed as those of a novelist striving for effects, Howells maintains, for the novel is too firmly rooted in the author's own experience.[62]

This engagement with social reality in an active rather than passive manner is one of the fundamental changes that occurred in the aesthetic of realism following the turn of the century. No longer was the realist content to describe the typical and thus provide the pleasure of recognition. The progressive impulse moved the novelist as well as the muckraker. Unfortunately, these novels often become primarily reformist tracts. *The Turn of the Balance*, however, remains "a work of literary art, simple in style, dramatic in the presentation of life; clear, shapely and rounded to the imperative climax," as well as one of the best statements of the progressive aesthetic.[63]

The subculture of professional crime is central to this novel as it presents the history of two families, the Wards and the Koerners, and the network of interrelations that binds them. The novel is a study in oppositions which presents the fortunes of a wealthy family (the Wards) and a poor family (the Koerners) under the economic system of industrial capitalism. Among the oppositions Whitlock uses these two families to explore are wealth and poverty, justice and injustice, business ethics and criminal ethics, romantic love and prostitution, and freedom and imprisonment.

Although Whitlock originally intended to balance his treatment of the two families,[64] his sympathies for the misfortune-laden Koerners come to the fore and the weight of the book tells their tragic history. This story is one of inevitable decline under the brutal heel of a grinding and unjust society, a decline stemming from the patriarch's loss of a leg in a railroad accident. He sues for damages and wins appeal after appeal until the Supreme Court, sympathetic to the rich, overturns the lower court decisions. During the long course of this lawsuit, the family suffers increasingly from the poverty that follows the accident. The oldest son, Archie, becomes a professional criminal eventually executed for murder; the oldest daughter, Gusta, becomes a prostitute. The Koerner family is destroyed when the patriarch, driven insane by the injustice of the law, slashes the throats of the two youngest children and his wife before committing suicide. The police find him hanging from four nails on the kitchen door in a grotesque parody of the crucifixion, "and from his long yellow face hung the old man's tongue, as if it were his last impotent effort to express his scorn of the law whose emissaries he expected to find him there."[65]

Archie's history dominates the story of the Koerners. The depiction of his life allows Whitlock to give the underworld a central place in this realistic novel. Through this depiction he voices several major themes: the injustice of American society and law, the nature of crime, the stupidity of criminology, and the importance of poverty and environment in shaping a criminal.

Whitlock begins his attack on the law early in the novel with the trial and sentencing of young Harry Graves for a charge of embezzlement. Whitlock quickly scans the other prisoners in the court and attacks the lack of justice for any prisoner so unfortunate as to be represented by a court-appointed lawyer when brought before the "withered and dry" breast of the law. Although Graves' employer dislikes the "necessity" of prosecuting this young man, he feels the law must be carried out. Whitlock balances this later in the novel when the employer's son, Dick Ward, is guilty of the same crime on a much larger scale and the father stops at nothing to "fix" the case successfully.

Soon after this introduction to justice, Whitlock focuses on Archie, who is in jail charged with a misdemeanor. Through Archie, Whitlock relates a detailed account of how a youth may be driven into the profession of crime. Archie had served in the army in the Philippines. This career gave him a taste for adventure and skill with firearms but left him unfit for anything else. At home he begins to hang around saloons since they are the only places available to a youth of his class, offering both warmth and the possibility of social activity. In his wanderings Archie eventually connects with a group of young toughs, the Market Street Gang, and, due to this association, is arrested on suspicion of the theft of a box of dried herring. Although Archie is innocent of this crime, he is sent to the workhouse for thirty days with the rest of the gang.

The "great suspender" uses Archie's imprisonment to begin his indictment of the American penal system, an indictment which continues throughout the novel. He states that the system is one designed to develop "the beast" in men and to fill "them with a kind of moral insanity" (128). Imprisonment marks the turning point in Archie's life, for he will ever after be labeled. Whitlock argues that though the judge believed he had only given Archie a thirty-day sentence, he had actually imprisoned him for life: "He was thereafter to be but an umbra at the feast of life"(129).

After Archie's release, he quickly realizes that the only place he can move without encountering the atmosphere of suspicion is in the underworld. In a passage which echoes the autobiographies of thieves of the Progressive Era, it "dawned on Archie that here was a little quarter of the world where he was wanted . . . where that gap in his life made no difference" (131). Like Wellington Scott, Archie turns to the underworld from loneliness and the need for community.

Imprisonment also serves to introduce Archie to the professional underworld. His cellmate is Joseph Mason, who has spent twenty of his fifty years in prison and who follows the calling of the yegg. Mason's specialty is blowing safes in rural post offices, and he proves a willing teacher, instructing Archie in the status distinctions of the underworld and its skills, "but, above all, he had set Archie the example of a patient man who took things as they came, without question or complaint" (134). After Archie's release he continues to associate with Mason at the saloon of Danny Gibbs. Gibbs is a fence whose saloon serves as a clearinghouse for thieves. Here Archie encounters other yeggs, especially Curly Jackson, who had also been a soldier. As he listens to their tales of a wild and dangerous life, Archie experiences a growing desire to join them. Whitlock presents this simply as part of an educational process Archie has entered through force of circumstance and not as an aberration. Because of his false arrest, these are the only men who accept him as an equal. Their example shapes his personality, his language, and his actions.

Archie's initiation into this world is complete when he and Curly don the guise of tramps, ride the boxcars to a rural village, and blow a post office safe. Archie has now destroyed the psychological barriers that connected him to the rest of society. Following the burglary, he experiences a new sense of self, an inner sense of being a thief. He is now "Dutch"; with the new moniker, for which he feels a childish pride, the transformation is complete. This process closely parallels the deconversion experience described by professional thieves in their memoirs.

Archie's life in the underworld continues to dominate the novel until he is executed for the slaying of a brutally sadistic detective, Kouka, in an act of self-defense. The true reason for the execution is a murder that remains in the background throughout Archie's trial, the vicious killing of two old spinsters. Archie did not commit this crime but is blamed for it simply because he is available, has a record, and is a convenient scapegoat for an outraged citizenry.

Whitlock's presentation of the underworld is one of fascinating detail; the delineation provides perhaps the clearest and most intelligent sketch of the world of professional crime at its penultimate moment of glory. The yegg was the last incarnation of the old style bank burglar who took pride in his skills and profession. A more brutal modern avatar who specialized in hit-and-run daylight assault and used the more primitive tools of terror and violence soon replaced the yegg. The emergence of powerful gangs of organized criminals after World War I altered the entire subculture of professional crime. No longer was crime primarily restricted to the "small businessman" and individual entrepreneur. Following World War I the profession of crime followed the dominant current of American capitalism, and a new structure based on the corporate pattern emerged.

Whitlock uses Archie's trial on the murder charge and his execution to expose the inadequacies of American justice and law. The trial is a travesty with a biased jury and witnesses who perjure themselves at the bidding of the police. Archie's fate is finally decided when the one conscientious member of the jury suffers an attack of physical pain. In order to escape the jury room and obtain treatment, he votes guilty. Thus, Whitlock argues that the American system of justice is fatally flawed by the importance it places on the individual personalities of those who take part in the process.

Whitlock also uses the trial to challenge the notions of criminality held by both the general public and "scientific" criminologists. Most of this is expressed through Archie's lawyer, Gordon Marriott, who serves as Whitlock's mouthpiece throughout the novel. Marriott, for example, discovers that in spite of the newspaper extras which present Archie as a hardened criminal, the most desperate character the police have known in years, the whole affair lacks the element of tragedy he expected. Instead, "it all seemed natural and commonplace enough. Archie was the same boy he had known before. The murder was but an incident in Archie's life, that was all" (393).

After Archie's conviction, Whitlock states that "those persons in the community who called themselves the good were gratified" (515) and further exposes their hypocrisy through Doctor Tyler Tilson, the specialist who examines Archie for the stigmata of degeneracy and finds the "homicidal tendency strongly developed" (515). Marriott, however, refuses to accept "the conclusions of a heartless science that had thumped Archie as if he were but a piece of rock for the geologist's hammer" (516) and fruitlessly appeals the case. This image sums up Whitlock's condemnation of criminology, the legal system, and American penology. They are worse than useless, for they all contribute to the brutalization and dehumanization of fellow humans. Repeatedly Whitlock emphasizes that these things strip away whatever good there is in an individual, leaving him unconnected to the broader stream of humanity.

For Whitlock the professional criminal is the quintessential victim suffering not from degeneracy or heredity, but from a brutal environment, from poverty, and from a vicious system of law and punishment. In this novel no criminal appears as a symbol of absolute freedom. Instead, each is imprisoned in a multitude of ways, both mentally and physically, and is able to escape only through death.

CRIME AND THE AESTHETIC OF THE PROGRESSIVE NOVEL

The novelists who gave professional crime a central place in their works succumbed to the same failings that marked the works of other progressive novelists such as Robert Herrick and David Graham Phillips. These authors all shared the progressive climate of creativity. This climate was one marked by a strong moral fervor; it drew much of its creative impulse from a desire for exposé, and social reform. These progressive novelists wanted above all else to speak to their generation, and mainstream American art at the turn of the century was only beginning to escape from its traditional place within orthodox Protestantism. The English novel still exerted great influence over American fiction, and literary taste in America lagged about a generation behind European taste. Thus, those artists who wished to address their own times were forced to speak through older forms. The result was often a novel that was innovative in content and theme but was dressed in an old style. The most talented writers of the period such as Edith Wharton and Theodore Dreiser gave little evidence that they partook of the dominant progressive climate. Wharton's background was upper-class rather than middle-class, and she lived as an expatriate in France during this period. Dreiser came from the lower classes, and his naturalistic determinism with its stress on biology held little appeal to the genteel progressive with his optimistic view of human nature.[66]

Upton Sinclair's *The Jungle* (1906) is the best-known progressive novel, but this work belongs more closely to muckraking. *The Common Lot* (1904) by Robert Herrick provides, however, a key example of progressive realism in the novel. This book is a study of a socially ambitious architect. After he abandons his ethical standards, one of his buildings collapses. This causes many deaths but leads to the architect's spiritual rebirth. The concentration on an individual and the theme of sin and redemption are typical of the progressive novel, as is Herrick's piling up of huge quantities of circumstantial social detail with the aim of presenting a factual view of "real life."

The novelists who dealt with the professional criminal and his culture shared these concerns and problems. They believed strongly in the unique value of each individual and his potential. Human nature was plastic and determined by environment not heredity. Thus a novel such as *The Rise of Ruderick Clowd* expends enormous energy in detailing the environment that produces a criminal. Another impulse behind these novels was reform. These novelists shared the belief of the muckrakers that if Americans were only aware of the true nature of such things as justice and poverty in America, they would rise in outrage to correct the abuses. Thus Whitlock presents detail after detail in his desire to substantiate his vision as a "factual" portrait of America.

Unlike the modernists who superseded them, progressive novelists sacrificed form to content. Their innovative energies found expression in the description of hitherto undescribed areas of American society. The move of the professional criminal from a minor part to a leading role in American fiction stands as a paradigm for this process. The progressive novelists opened new subjects for literature, but a later generation had to find new modes of expression appropriate for the new century.

Diseased, Defective, or Deprived; The Intellectual Meets the Thief

NEW PROFESSIONALS AND THE PROBLEM OF THE PROFESSIONAL CRIMINAL

The years between the Civil War and World War I witnessed the discovery and apotheosis of the professional criminal. The emergence of a group of criminals who viewed themselves and were also viewed by society as professionals is one variation of a major theme of American civilization during this period. The professionalization of crime was a part of the professionalization of America. Not only did criminals adopt the persona of the professional but the professional criminal became one of the symbolic figures in the development of new academic disciplines as well as the redefinition of older fields. The fight for intellectual control of the professional criminal illustrates the struggle of professional groups as they attempted to create intellectual spheres of influence and service for their disciplines.

The notion of professionalism that emerged in America after the Civil War depended on several elements. In a civilization lacking both a rigid class structure and a hereditary aristocracy, a central problem was the definition of self and the location of that self within society. Professionalism provided an answer to this problem. The individual could define himself as a member of a specific group of like-minded people who depended on a career for a livelihood. This career was conceived in vertical terms with well-marked steps on the journey to success. Self-worth, status, and the social place of the individual came to depend on his standing within the "profession." He would be defined by a group of men qualified to pass judgment on his achievements. This notion of professionalism assumed that the individual would master a body of esoteric knowledge, skills, or techniques. He would then offer his skills to the public as a service for which a grateful public would reward him.[1] Another aspect of the rise of professionalism was increased specialization. As the demands for technical competence and skill increased, the professional became a specialist offering an ever-narrowing range of services. For example, a detective might work primarily on homicide, theft, or vice. A physician might specialize in neurology, pathology, or surgery.

One facet of the rise of professionalism after the Civil War was the emergence of new academic disciplines in American universities such as sociology and experimental psychology, as well as a redefinition of older disciplines such as history and economics. A crucial problem for all these disciplines was the establishment of a professional identity that delineated their intellectual boundaries. A second important drive, especially of members of the younger academic fields, was to prove the potential usefulness of their disciplines to a practical society. These disciplines needed pragmatic problems that took them out of the classroom and into the streets.

Older professions were also redefining themselves and attempting to extend their influence into new areas. Medicine provides a good example. After the Civil War its sphere expanded greatly for several reasons. One was the acceptance of the biological model of the universe put forth in Darwin's *Origin of Species* in 1859. A second was the enormous expansion of experimental science with its practical results—especially in the area of biology and applied medicine. Increasing complexity demanded increased specialization, and physicians capitalized on the dependency this created in their patients. As the physician expanded the traditional boundaries of medicine into new areas, he both created work for himself and strengthened his authority. He also began to assume a role traditionally held by the clergy. He became a spiritual advisor and healer as a complement to his work on physical ills.

Crime became one arena of debate for these professional

groups, and an almost symbiotic relationship developed between the professional criminal and the physicians and sociologists who used him. The criminal felt the influence of this
competition and altered his persona and stance to fit the conceptions these professions fostered. This was especially true of
the criminal's relationship with the sociologist who offered an
explanation of deviance based on environmental determinism,
an explanation which served as a palliative for an uneasy conscience. Criminals rejected the biological model although it too
offered the criminal the ability to deny individual responsibility.
Ease of conscience was not an adequate reward for the assumption of a degenerate and inferior status. These competing schools
profoundly altered American notions of crime. The battle for
control over the criminal culminated in the founding of the
American Institute of Criminal Law and Criminology in June
1909. Although the development of a new profession, that of
criminologist, bore witness to the growing importance of the
specialist in crime, it did little to halt the battle between the
environmentalists and the biologists.

This debate highlights several themes in American civilization
between 1870 and 1917. First it helps to clarify the role of evolutionary thought during the period of its greatest influence.
This is especially true for those analysts who carried a biological
orientation but it also holds for environmentalists. Both groups
debated the theme of social engineering and how best to prepare
for and direct evolution into the future. The debate changed the
language of deviance in America and, by changing the vocabulary, altered the limits of the debate itself. This dialogue also
helped Americans grapple with the new notion of "the dangerous classes." Until the middle of the nineteenth century, no one
had ever asked whether there were people who posed a threat
to everyone because of some fault in the way their minds worked
or some process of physical disease.[2] Under the influence of
Darwin in biology and Marx in economics, this became a central
issue in the study of crime in the late nineteenth and early
twentieth centuries.

Both physicians and academics approached this problem, and
their differing perspectives helped Americans clarify their ideas.
Finally, this confrontation reveals a changing conception of de-

viance as Americans adapted to the changed conditions of their civilization in the early modern era: who posed the greatest threat to society—the thief waging open war on society or the businessman covertly destroying the mutual relationship of trust that glued society together? The figure of the professional criminal became a central symbol in this debate.

ENVIRONMENT OR HEREDITY: THE BEGINNINGS OF THE CRUCIAL ARGUMENT

Two influential works of the 1870s established the limits of the American response to crime and prepared Americans for the debates of the following decades. Charles Loring Brace's *The Dangerous Classes of New York and Twenty Years Work Among Them* (1872) was a book that later became a major prop for those who looked to the environment as the primary cause of crime. Five years later, Robert Dugdale's *The Jukes, A Study in Crime, Pauperism, Disease, and Heredity*, appeared—one of the most important studies of crime produced in the nineteenth century. While Dugdale himself was an environmentalist, his book became a major part of the hereditarian arsenal in both Europe and America. Dugdale's work seemed, at least, to prove that crime was strongly linked to biological heredity rather than environment.

Today Charles Loring Brace is remembered primarily for his work with juveniles; still, his book clearly reveals American attitudes toward professional crime in the years immediately following the Civil War. He is typical of an older American response to crime stretching back to the 1850s. While this approach found a place for "suspect" heredity in the etiology of crime, the major emphasis was on environment. This stress on environment was fundamentally different from the environmentalism that later dominated the Progressive Era and viewed the criminal as a victim of his surroundings. For Brace and others of his generation, the individual retained ultimate responsibility for his actions; heredity or environment might contribute to an individual's fall, but the individual remained a morally responsible agent capable of good or bad action. Never was the criminal a victim of circumstances beyond his control; free will properly exercised would always allow one to triumph over any condition. In Brace's

vision the major reason for the development of a class of professional criminals was a mingling of a faulty social environment
and a weak or improperly developed individual moral sense. If
a potential criminal could be removed from a faulty environment
and placed into one that would strengthen his moral sense, he
would escape the effects of the earlier situation.

Dugdale's beliefs were not markedly different from those of
Brace in actuality. However, it was not Dugdale's actual message
that created his enormous impact on American thinking about
crime. It was, instead, the message that many Americans thought
they found in his book. This perceived message was one that
pointed toward heredity as the major cause of criminality. Dugdale's book seemed to prove that if an individual came from
depraved stock, he would almost surely lead a depraved life.
These two themes—bad environment or bad inheritance—would
mark the limits of discussion about criminality in America during
the years between the Civil War and World War I.

Charles Loring Brace was born in 1826 in Litchfield, Connecticut. He trained for the ministry, but abandoned the church
as a potential career in order to work at the Five Points Mission,
located in New York's most notorious slum. In 1853 he was
appointed chief officer of the newly organized Children's Aid
Society. His book recounts his experiences as a child-saver and
the various practical methods he used in his "scientific" charity.[3]
The professional criminal figures throughout this book as one
of the threats to both society and the unreformed juvenile. He
recurrently stands for the ultimate destination of the wild New
York children who are not trained, disciplined, or sent to the
West. The first four illustrations in Brace's book, for example,
are an updating of Hogarth's *Rake's Progress* designed to show
the stages in the natural career of a street waif: he begins by
living without adult supervision, soon moves into petty theft,
and as he matures, is found gambling in a low saloon. His final
end is the prison.

Brace's view of the professional criminal as the natural result
of the untutored street arab matches the emphasis his title placed
on a "dangerous class." This question was central to the writings
of Brace. He took the concept from the sermons of Theodore
Parker and the writings of the English child-saver Mary Car-

penter.[4] A central experience in Brace's formulation of his notion of the "dangerous classes" was the New York draft riots in the summer of 1863. These riots were a week-long orgy of violence and looting through the streets of Manhattan that left over two thousand dead and millions of dollars worth of property destroyed. Foremost among the leaders of the riots were the criminals of the city. This experience was a catalyst in Brace's thought, and he repeatedly returned to the threat posed by these "creatures who seemed to have crept from their burrows and dens to join in the plunder of the city."[5]

This threat posed by the professional criminal and other members of the dangerous classes contributes to one of the dominant strains of the persona Brace adopts in presenting his work. Frequently he assumes a stance reminiscent of the Hebrew prophets, denouncing his culture and its headlong drive toward oblivion. Repeatedly he sounds the note of warning that unless something is done about the young " 'street-rats,' who gnawed at the foundations of society" (99, 318), they will destroy American civilization. He describes these children by using images of vermin or the life of a savage and warns that in the streets they are rapidly being recruited and educated into crime by the professional thieves they admire (346). Indeed, in his guise as warning prophet, Brace asserts that boys growing up in the slums of New York "become, as by a law of nature," thieves, pickpockets, and burglars (56). A major reason for this is simply the undisciplined life these street children lead. Brace continually describes them in images that emphasize their "wildness," their savage natures. He describes the life of a "young barbarian" in New York as a natural process that begins in the idleness that characterizes the life of an untutored savage in the forest. When the child becomes hungry, he imitates his "savage prototype" and steals. He soon makes the acquaintance of professional thieves and learns better methods of theft until he is confirmed in his career (340). A second and peculiarly American problem Brace identifies is the intensity of the American temperament, a threat in itself: the American criminal will rob a bank when the English thief would be content to pick a pocket (27).

This intense American temperament leads to the second strain in Brace's ambiguous persona: optimistic hope for the future.

Brace adopts a tone that approaches civic boosterism as he describes the possibilities America has for dealing with the dangerous classes and the advantages these give Americans compared to the older civilizations of Europe. He argues that America is blessed by a boundless hope which pervades all levels of social life; the corollary of this hope is the lack of fixed classes in America. Not only does the hope of social and economic betterment set a high moral tone, but it also sets up good examples for the lower classes. Brace even finds hope in the American's incessant desire for change, a quality that commentators from de Tocqueville to Dickens had viewed as destructive. To Brace this "mill of American life, which grinds up so many delicate and fragile things, has its uses, when it is turned on the vicious fragments of the lower strata of society" (47). This continual change, for instance, allows individuals to marry outside their class and thus helps break up criminal inheritance. It also destroys the continuity of bad influences. Because of this America has the opportunity of avoiding the class of hereditary criminals and paupers that plague Europe.

The chief threads throughout Brace's work are the importance of the environment and the role of the family in transmitting social values. These are also essential components of Brace's solution to the problem of the dangerous classes. Brace holds that the dangerous classes are a product of faulty social development rather than individual depravity. The central problem is the urban environment with its overcrowding and temptations to evil. As a solution Brace turns to the agrarian myth. He asserts that "the best of all asylums for the outcast child, is the *farmer's home*" (225). The cultivators of the soil, argues Brace, are the most solid and intelligent class in America and form the foundation of American civilization. This is the premier advantage that America has over Europe: the safety-valve of the West is open to receive the effluvia of the East and regenerate this waste into a useful and wholesome product. The result of Brace's belief in the agrarian mythos was his placing-out system. Through this system he found new homes for thousands of street children on western farms; he maintained a firm belief that the disciplined, wholesome life they led in the West had saved them from careers as professional criminals or paupers.

The publication of *The Jukes* by Robert Dugdale in 1877 heralded the approach of a fundamental shift in the conception of crime by American intellectuals. No thinker of this generation, including Cesare Lombroso, had a greater influence on criminology or the young eugenics movement than Dugdale. His brief book traced the history of a family of paupers, prostitutes, and criminals and provided a focal point for the application of evolutionary thinking to crime. Readers who were eager to apply the theories of biology in new ways found in Dugdale's study a confirmation of the notion that criminals posed a biological threat to the future of the human race. Until World War I, a steady current of books and articles that found a starting point in Dugdale's work appeared to keep these ideas alive in the minds of American thinkers.[6]

Ironically, Dugdale himself was an environmentalist who believed that heredity could always be overcome by proper training. Franklin H. Giddings pointed out in 1910 that Dugdale never considered his work a proof of hereditary criminality, but was "profoundly" convinced that environment could modify and even eradicate tendencies toward vice and crime.[7] Dugdale held that environment and heredity simply marked the limits of any discussion of the causes of crime. His fundamental point was that bad heredity tends to perpetuate bad environment and bad environment tends to perpetuate bad heredity; once the vicious cycle has been established the only hope for escape is to destroy it. A change in environment is the most effective way to accomplish this.

In the intellectual climate of the latter nineteenth century, a climate increasingly dominated by a biological framework, what was important about Dugdale's book was its *perceived* message. This was quickly taken to establish the "fact" that criminals were not simply unfortunate products of bad environment but a degenerate breed, distinct from the rest of humankind. The criminal was something depraved and subhuman, a separate species. Dugdale's work provided a homegrown source of evidence and support for the criminal anthropology fathered by Cesare Lombroso. Although this did not begin to have a powerful influence in American thought until the early 1890s, Dugdale prepared a fertile seedbed for its reception. His work helped establish the biological scheme which competed for preeminence among American thinkers until World War I; he also facilitated the dominance of the physician in the study of the criminal in America.

Dugdale's writing is drenched with imagery drawn from the fields of medicine and disease. He was not a physician himself, but he called his work a "study in the pathology of social disorders."[8] American writers on crime had frequently made references to crime as a disease of society, but Dugdale allowed this field of imagery to dominate his work. This metaphor-source is particularly revealing when applied to professional crime.[9] Dugdale argues that the pauper is "the social equivalent of disease" because pauperism is a form of weakness (32). This is not, however, the case with crime. Crime, especially theft, represents a healthy inheritance rather than a degenerate one. Most of the Jukes, for instance, turned to theft as a way of supplementing an unsteady income. These Jukes preferred theft to the poorhouse for it seemed more independent to steal and take the risks. Dugdale associates this with the American virtue of self-reliance and argues that with proper training it can be turned to the benefit of society. Dugdale describes the criminal in terms that few Americans would fail to value: "The ideal criminal is a courageous man in the prime of life who so skilfully contrives crime on a large scale that he escapes detection and succeeds in making the community believe him to be honest as he is generous" (47). Later he describes the requirements a successful burglar must fulfill as "qualities essential to any successful career" (54) and contends that this is a sign of health and vitality which augurs well for the reformation of these criminals. With proper education, "the log huts and hovels which now form hot-beds where human maggots are spawned, will disappear" (61), and these criminals will cease to live off society. Dugdale views the criminal as a vital force. Throughout this presentation, Dugdale uses the language and dominant value system of American civilization. The criminal does not seem alienated; he is simply a result of economics and environment.

Five years after *The Jukes*, Dugdale published three articles in *The Atlantic Monthly* which focused on property crime and professional theft. The essays attempted to show that the amount of property crime a society experienced was intimately related to the material status of that society, that the traditional punishments were ineffective in reducing crime, and that arbitrary legal punishments needed to be replaced by a rational approach to the problem of theft.[10] The keynote throughout these essays is the primary role of environment as a source of crime, as if Dugdale viewed these articles as a chance to clarify his much-abused position in *The Jukes*. He includes such things as disturbances of the social order, competition, and commercial crises under environmental causes. He discusses heredity only in terms of "national character," where he connects the professional "offender" with the "hereditary offender."

The most striking element in these essays is Dugdale's penetrating discussion of professional theft. He reveals his faith in science as he argues that natural laws regulate crime and provide room for optimism. Civilization is progressing because non-violent professional crime is superseding more violent styles of crime. The crimes that typify American civilization are those based on fraud, dexterity, and training rather than force. Thus, crime is becoming a civilized and industrious pursuit (I, 460–62). Dugdale also makes a further connection between professionalism and crime in discussing the ineffectiveness of imprisonment as a response to professional crime. Imprisonment is simply one of the risks the criminal assumes, and even with this risk crime is a much safer career than such legitimate occupations as mining.

As in all occupations, two things are necessary for a successful career in crime. The individual must have the disposition to accept this profession and must have the aptitude for it or he will fail and turn to other ways of making a living. The prison serves as the graduate school for the profession of crime, for it brings "the true teacher and the true scholar together" (II, 740–43).

Finally, Dugdale argues that the skill of the professional criminal is tied to the civilization in which he moves, arguing that without the implicit cooperation of society he could not make a living. He contends that adequate preventive measures already exist in such things as time locks and electric burglar alarms, arguing that crime is the result of two agents: the criminal who is tempted and the victim who tempts. He uses two of the most sensational crimes of the period as proof of this thesis: the robbery of A. T. Stewart's body from his grave and the burglary of the Manhattan Savings Institution. Neither of these would have occurred if the victims had taken even rudimentary precautions. The prevention of crime through protective technology becomes the key to the eradication of theft. If the criminal is unable to make a living at his chosen occupation, he must become either a pauper or worker. Echoing his earlier assertion in *The Jukes* that criminals shun pauperism, he contends that they will become workers and that their predatory instincts will then atrophy. Thus, education and industrial training will eventually end the profession of crime (III, 243–48).

Brace and Dugdale are pivotal figures in the history of the response to crime by thoughtful Americans. Brace pursued a lengthy career as a practical social worker interested in pragmatic social reform. Dugdale followed a divided life. He was a merchant but followed this career chiefly to finance his interest in social problems. Both men were environmentalists though they were also convinced of the importance of heredity. Brace looks back to an earlier American response in his emphasis on the family as the primary transmitter of social values and morality as well as in his firm belief in the pastoral, agrarian ethos of pre-Civil War America. He also looks forward in his notion of a dangerous class and his concept of scientific charity. In his ideas of scientific charity he tried to incorporate the tenets of Darwin's *Origins*, a work he reread thirteen times.[11] Dugdale produced a small book that had a major influence in several areas of American thought until World War I. Ironically, Brace had stated the thesis that Dugdale expanded and documented. In his account, Brace argued that rural life contributed to inherited crime because of the stable quality of rural life. The flux of urban life prevented the establishment of a class of hereditary criminals. Dugdale's work apparently documented the notion of biological degeneration and helped prepare intellectuals for the ideas of criminal anthropology that soon invaded American shores.

PHYSICIANS AND CRIMINALS: THE MODELS OF HEREDITY AND DISEASE

Throughout the 1880s, the attention of intellectuals who thought about crime increasingly turned toward the notion of "professionalism."[12] In 1886 Yale Professor Simeon E. Baldwin delivered an address on the topic to the American Social Science Association. Baldwin claimed that a class of professional criminals had developed in America who "have a social circle of their own; a pride in their profession; a following of respectful admirers; a Police Gazette literature to proclaim their exploits and perpetuate their kind."[13] He argued that the primary cause of this development was urbanization and the lack of enough honest work in the city: "It is thus that crime becomes a profession; that children are bred to it; that it has its own language,—its own tools" (163). His suggestion for treatment of the problem was the passage of habitual offender acts. These acts would not depend on life-imprisonment, but a sort of life-probation with the professional criminal living under perpetual police supervision (167–71). The American Social Science Association also heard papers on professional crime in 1887 and 1888.[14] Indeed, an 1888 address by William Noyes to this association introduced the ideas of Cesare Lombroso to America.

Heredity had long held a place in the thinking of most Americans about crime. One reason for this was the traditional Christian view that the sins of the fathers are visited upon the children. A second cause, especially potent in the middle decades of the nineteenth century, was phrenology. After 1830, the "science" swept through America. Phrenology began as an experimental science based on the assumption that anatomical and physiological characteristics directly influenced mental behavior. Although heredity was the key to these physical elements, phrenology also gave major roles to environment and education in the belief that these could modify heredity. For the phrenologists crime was a symbol of improper brain organization that could be corrected with proper treatment. Crime became a "moral disease" that could best be treated in a "moral hospital" rather than a prison.[15]

After Darwin's *Origin*, thought about the hereditary nature of crime took on a new urgency in America. These years witnessed the emergence of the physician as the major figure in the treatment of crime.[16] No group found the biological model more convincing; the physician discovered in crime another wedge to widen his role as healer within society. The idea of crime as a disease with physiological roots fit easily into a biological world view and contributed to the growth of a language about deviance built on the vocabulary of disease and pathology.

Oliver Wendell Holmes, Sr. in 1875 made an early argument for heredity and crime, holding that "in most cases crime can be shown to run in the blood," and that we should "substitute a moral hospital for a place of punishment" for the criminals. Holmes wanted to determine the proper response for society to make to criminals. The legal problem of responsibility and the definition of insanity were traditionally a crucial part of this issue. For Holmes this problem was irrelevant, for the criminal "is just as innocently acting out the tendencies he inherits as the rattlesnake." Holmes called this "automatism" and mentioned that he had written his novel, *Elsie Venner*, in 1860 "to illustrate this same innocently criminal automatism with the irresponsibility it implies, by the supposedly mechanical introduction before birth of an ophidian element into the blood of a human being."[17] The proper response for society was to protect itself against these criminals. For Holmes, crime became a disease that society should respond to as it would to any other disease.

Other physicians also grappled with the problem of crime and its cause. E. Vale Blake argued in 1879 that only a small percentage of criminals had strong natural tendencies to crime. He found the cause of most crime in the "great natural law of imitation." In spite of his environmental approach, he used the language of therapeutic treatment as he argued for the "curable" class of criminals and told the social scientist to observe "the analogies of Nature," for "the measures taken to produce excellence in the animal and vegetable kingdoms are equally applicable to human beings." Blake used these analogies to argue for environmental cures similar to removing and quarantining a diseased horse, or moving a failing plant to better soil, but he never broached the idea of an actual physiological treatment for crime.[18] American physicians who were concerned about crime were thus sympathetic to a link between biology and crime; they identified this link by such different names as "moral insanity" or "automatism." This hereditarian stance prepared them for the theories of criminal anthropology.

Criminal anthropology developed as an influential strain in American thought between 1888 and 1891. In 1888 Rev. E. P. Thwing, M.D. carried greetings from the International Congress of Anthropology to the annual Congress of the National Prison Association. He announced to the assembled wardens, chaplains, and physicians that "those of us engaged in the scientific or theoretic side of the study of criminal anthropology join hands with those of you engaged in the practical work as custodians of criminals."[19] The work of explaining the new science to American thinkers was left, however, to physicians—who readily assumed the task. Explanations of criminal anthropology appeared in addresses by William Noyes in 1888 to the American Social Science Association, by Hamilton D. Wey in 1890 to the National Prison Association, and by Robert Fletcher, M.D., in 1891 to the Anthropological Society of Washington.[20] All of these speakers were physicians and all three papers were uncritical presentations of Lombroso's theories.

The fundamental appeal that the work of Lombroso and his European disciples held for these American physicians was the contention that the criminologist should shift his attention from the study of crime to the study of the criminal. The scientist should take over the job botched by jurists. Darwin provided the strongest influence on Lombroso, whose theories centered around the notion of the born criminal.[21] Lombroso believed that most crime was a result of atavism or a reversion to a primitive or subhuman type. The atavism was a biological throwback to an earlier stage of human evolution. A number of physiological features reminiscent of primates such as jug-ears, prognathism, a low and receding forehead, and a weak chin were the marks of atavism. This individual also shared characteristics common to savage races such as tattooing. The moral sensibilities of these individuals were inferior to those of modern humans who represented the highest stage of evolution. These biological throwbacks inevitably acted in opposition to the rules of contemporary society; they were congenital criminals.

A corollary to Lombroso's theory of atavism was the theory of degeneration. The degenerate also moved toward an earlier stage of humanity, but he approached primitive man through a process of devolution instead of skipping over generations. The degenerate came from tainted ancestral stock which had branched away from the highway of progressive evolution and followed its own devious path. The criminal was not simply a variation of humanity; he was a separate species—the criminal type.

Central to Lombroso's theories was the need for a shift of attention from the crime to the criminal. The three American physicians who introduced Lombroso isolated this as the major thrust of criminal anthropology. Hamilton Wey used Lombroso's emphasis on biology to argue for a new view of crime as disease, contending that insanity and alcoholism were now classed among "psychoses" due to "defective organization" and that crime "as a collateral degeneracy should be included in the same category." The latter part of his address is drenched with terms taken from medicine such as "diagnostician," "moral disease," "treatment," and "prognosis."[22]

A central aspect of this new focus on the criminal was that his punishment should be appropriate to the danger he posed to society. The study of the criminal and his potential threat should replace the study of law. Fletcher, for instance, stated that the jurists argued there was no criminal without a crime. The criminal anthropologists contended that this was simply sentimentality: "The criminal is here with the intent to commit crime; if the attempt fail he is as much the assassin or thief as if it had succeeded and must be hanged or secluded accordingly."[23] Wey and Noyes also emphasized this point. Indeed, Wey used it to launch an attack on the "sentimental" notions of moral responsibility and free will which criminal anthropology relegated to the garbage dump of history. The role of the penitentiary would no longer be reform but the simple protection of society from those who threatened it. Wey, again, stated "it is the duty of society to eliminate those who are utterly unadapted to society."[24]

This concentration on the threat that a criminal posed helps explain the central role of the professional criminal in these introductory essays. Noyes stated that he was speaking about "only the professional criminal," (32) and he also held a dominant place in Wey's essay. The professional criminal was the most powerful symbol of the failure of traditional approaches to punishment and reformation.

A prime problem for criminal anthropology was establishing a typology of the criminal. Among Lombroso's American followers, only Fletcher agreed that the born criminal was the source of most crime. The early American followers of Lombroso accepted the classification established by Lombroso's disciple, Enrico Ferri. This typology set up five major groups of criminals: the born criminal, the passionate criminal, the insane criminal, the occasional criminal, and the habitual criminal. American essayists concentrated on the habitual criminal—under the guise of the professional thief. Wey, for instance, argued that the only difference between these two was one of degree. The habitual criminal was inferior to the professional who adopted crime as a business with internal divisions and specialties. This professional criminal was "a student of men and acquainted with the ways of the world, polished in manners, and often aesthetic in tastes" (279). The elevation of the professional criminal also illustrates the American concern for property crime. This was the class responsible for most theft while the other groups accounted for most violent crime. Additionally, this criminal posed a continuing threat because the legal response, imprisonment, usually touched him for only a short time before he was released to continue his depredations.

The themes and issues these early criminal anthropologists raised continued to be of importance during the next fifteen years, a time in which criminal anthropology dominated many Americans' thoughts about crime. The notion of atavism spread throughout American culture and even found a place in imaginative literature. Atavism plays a central role in such major American novels as Frank Norris' *McTeague* and Jack London's *The Call of the Wild* as well as such dramatic works as Eugene O'Neill's *The Emperor Jones* and *The Hairy Ape*.

A central issue for the biological approach became the search for the causes of crime. This was crucial to the physicians attempting to expand their influence in American life. The recent discovery of the germ theory and the spectacular successes it had fostered led to an optimism that seems wildly uncalled for today. Using disease as a model, these physicians held that only after the cause of crime had been established could society react with truly effective remedies of prevention. Then society could attack crime at its source and eventually extirpate it completely. This search for cause would replace the barbaric and absurd legal codes of the jurists who could function only after a crime had been committed and the damage accomplished. The search was conducted and explained in the language of medicine; this language became a central part of the imagination of crime with profound and lasting results. It also gave rise to a new persona, a shared persona, adopted by practically all these writers.

The search for the cause of crime was dominated by the figure of the professional criminal. Although Lombroso's first edition found the cause for practically all crime in the theory of atavism, each later edition of his massive work included a broader range of causes such as degeneracy and the environment. Almost all American criminologists influenced by hereditarian ideas used them cautiously. Increasingly, they argued that unique conditions existed in America that modified the usefulness of the European theories. For these writers the professional criminal often served as a pivotal figure. The problem became whether he was an instinctive, natural criminal or a product of a faulty environment and education. This became a growing problem as the debate increasingly assumed a medical framework; the question eventually became whether the professional criminal was diseased or defective. The most influential physicians concerned with crime had little doubt that the professional criminal posed the greatest threat to society because of his repeated assaults and thus, to prove their own usefulness, the anthropologists had to present a plan designed to minimize and, perhaps, eliminate the threat.

In 1893 Arthur MacDonald published the first book-length presentation of criminal anthropology in America. MacDonald had done graduate work in psychology at Johns Hopkins and spent four years in European universities studying experimental medicine, psychiatry, hypnotism, and crime. Although not a physician he was conversant with the latest ideas and methods of medicine and these strongly marked his work—particularly the experimental method. In 1892 he was appointed as a specialist in education for the "abnormal and weakling classes" to the U. S. Bureau of Education. For the next ten years he occupied a central position in the move to advance the use of criminal anthropology in America and in the drive to establish a national laboratory for the scientific study of the "abnormal classes." MacDonald, however, represents the most conservative side of the American criminal anthropologists. Although his first book, *Criminology*, was dedicated to Lombroso, he did not accept him unreservedly. MacDonald divided the new science of criminology into three branches: general, special, and practical. General criminology presented a synthesis of the field while practical criminology dealt with specific problems of the treatment of criminals. MacDonald's own interest was special criminology which adopted a method of studying a few cases in as much detail as possible. The rationale for this intense study of a single case was "that repetition is the rule in crime."[25] The first half of MacDonald's book consists of a summary of Lombroso's theory and findings, or general criminology; even his examples are drawn from European rather than American sources. The second half contains MacDonald's own researches in special criminology; he presents the results of his detailed study of several cases of "pure murder," "pure theft," and "pure meanness."[26]

MacDonald's academic background included four years of work in theology at Princeton, Andover, Union Theological Seminary, and Harvard. This training strongly asserts itself in the second half of his book. Although he has earlier discussed the physical stigmata in the professional criminal's physiology (41), he rejects Lombroso in his conclusion with the assertion that the criminal by nature is a very small proportion of the criminal class. He argues that the French school of criminal sociology proves that most crime arises from social conditions. This emphasis on the social causes of crime is crucial to an individual who still believes in free will and maintains a faith in the possible "reformation" of criminals. MacDonald also supports his work in education by emphasizing the role of changed environment and better education as a palliative especially useful in combatting "habitual" or professional crime. With education, "all men, no matter how old in crime, can at least be improved and benefitted" (272a-c). This qualified acceptance of heredity retained an important place in MacDonald's thinking. Increasingly, however, he stood in opposition to other, more radical American criminologists, for he laid ever more stress on the power of education as a reformative.[27]

August Drähms, the chaplain of San Quentin Prison, paralleled MacDonald's qualified use of criminal anthropology. His influential book, *The Criminal*, appeared in 1900 with an introduction by Lombroso. Although Lombroso says the book is an excellent presentation of his ideas, Drähms continually undercuts them. He is especially wary of the denial of free will and moral responsibility implicit in Lombroso's work. Drähms did not reject the role of biology in criminality, but he did give a great deal of attention to social and psychological causes. He is primarily important for his reevaluation of the criminal typology into the three areas of the instinctive criminal, the habitual criminal, and the single offender.[28]

Drähms argues that the theory of a criminal type has been pushed to extremes; crime overlaps all classes and conditions of men (37–38). The continual theme of his work is sin as opposed to crime. Drähms was, after all, a clergyman, and his book is firmly based on the ideal of an innate concept of right present in all sane individuals. He contends that crime is "essentially psychical" in cause and that the materialistic determinism of criminal anthropology will never be able to cope with it (21–22). He refuses to separate the influence of heredity and environment, especially for the habitual or professional criminal: "Heredity furnishes the capital; environment handles the stock in trade" (155). The great cause of professional crime remains environmental for Drähms, who finds its major threat in "contagion" (230). Drähms realizes the occupational nature of professional crime, and, although this is not central to his work, he argues that the prison is the "finishing school" for the professional criminal (191) and details the steps in the career of a professional thief as he moves from petty pilfering up the ladder to professionalism (158).

Drähms and MacDonald are typical of the more cautious use of criminal anthropology in America. Both accepted the role of biology in the etiology of crime but rejected the deterministic materialism it calls for. They remained firmly convinced that with the proper methods the criminal could be rehabilitated. As physicians moved to a position of dominance in the response to crime, a more radical voice began to be heard. W. Duncan McKim, an M.D., sounded the early notes of a new extreme hereditarianism in 1900 when his controversial book, *Heredity and Human Progress*, appeared. In this book McKim argued that "heredity is the fundamental cause of human wretchedness."[29] He called for the regulation of marriage and argued that the state should make "Judicious" use of the death penalty to eliminate such hereditary degenerates as idiots, imbeciles, habitual drunkards, and incorrigible criminals. He believed that his plan would eliminate poverty, disease, and crime.

Other physicians followed McKim's lead although few carried their ideas to the extremes he recommended. Typical of the physician's approach to crime are Henry M. Boies, whose *The Science of Penology* appeared in 1901, and G. Frank Lydston, who published *The Diseases of Society* in 1904. Boies and Lydston exemplify an increasing tendency to view crime as a physical disease which would respond to proper treatment once the biological causes had been isolated. Boies, for instance, applies the germ theory to crime and argues that the "science" of penology is "similar to the science of medicine and surgery in that its province is not only to cure specific cases of disease, but also to prevent the genesis, recurrence and spread of disease." He argues that "the disease of criminality" will be controlled "as smallpox, cholera, yellow and typhoid fevers ... have been—by scientific investigation and the discovery and application of appropriate remedies and prophylactics."[30] Boies organizes his work in three major sections: Diagnostics, Therapeutics, and Hygienics. He uses his first chapters to establish a distinction between crime as something legally forbidden and the disease of criminality—a disease that he argues has scientifically been proven to be "curable" (106). Crime itself is simply the "unmistakable symptom and evidence of a disease; dangerous, persistent, contagious, and endemic" (90). Everything else in his work flows from this assumption, including his definition of a new criminal type: the presumptive criminal. This presumptive criminal was a person who had not yet committed a crime. However, the criminologist was safe in presuming that he would commit a crime because of his background. The use of the presumptive criminal is typical of Boies' approach. Throughout his book he presents theorems based on the principle of cause and effect. These theorems are the "natural laws" of the disease of criminality. Never does his faith in science and the scientific method waver. He also believes that a totalitarian approach to crime and the sacrifice of inconsequential "freedoms" is a small price indeed for a world without crime.

For Boies, recidivists, or "the professional class of criminal experts," pose the greatest threat to society, for they are responsible for the greatest depredations. Boies contends that the existence of this class is "an anomaly, an absurdity of national penal legislation" and a "reproach upon social intelligence" (96). He identifies the professional criminal with Lombroso's born criminal as well as the habitual criminal (239), and argues that this group is "the anti-social, anarchistic hostiles of civilization, the survivors or atavistic remnants of savagery" who produce children destined to follow in "the criminal trade" (235). This group, "as prone to do evil as to breathe" (238), should be "exterminated with relentless vigor" (239); they should be forbidden to marry or reproduce and never be given unsupervised liberty. (239–43). If the specialists are given a free reign, argues Boies, they will quickly eliminate this reproach and remove the greatest criminal threat from existence.

Perhaps the broadest and most balanced presentation of crime from the physician's point of view came from G. Frank Lydston who had served as resident surgeon to the Blackwell's Island Penitentiary in New York and, at the time of his major work, *The Diseases of Society*, held a chair in criminal anthropology at the Chicago-Kent College of Law. He was among the earliest Americans to make use of the new theories from Europe, publishing his first essay on heredity and pathology in 1883.[31] In 1891 in collaboration with Eugene S. Talbot he published one of the first studies of criminal skulls from an anthropological viewpoint in America,[32] and in 1896 he published one of the earliest calls for sterilization of the criminal as a remedy for crime.[33]

Lydston stakes out crime as the province of medical science and uses such chapter headings as "Social Pathology" to organize his presentation. Lydston argues for degeneracy as the fundamental cause of practically all crime, although he links this with a concept he calls "psychic atavism."[34] He joins the other physician criminologists in denying the sentimental notions of human equality and free will and calls for the adoption of scientific materialism in dealing with crime. The fundamental principle of scientific criminology is to first make the criminal a healthy individual with a well-developed brain and "rich, clean blood" along with a chance to make an honest living. After this the reformers can preach to him if they like.(20). He also shares the physician's reliance on medical imagery and such cures for crime as "asexualization," marriage restrictions, and physical training (556–79).

Lydston differs from the other physicians in several important respects, however. He points out absurdities in the discipline of criminal anthropology, including the excesses of Lombroso (86), and attacks the quacks who use the new science for self-glorification, arguing that one of the major problems of contemporary medicine is the practitioner's desire for fame and originality. This theme is, of course, a part of the current of professionalization flowing through the field of medicine. These quacks hurt the status of respectable surgeons. Perhaps, Lydston cautions, criminology has blinded itself to the awesome complexity of the problem of crime in its almost complete reliance on biological materialism (26–27).

Lydston argues that crime is the natural tendency of all men; only the restrictions of civilization keep these natural tendencies in check for the majority. This argument is not simply the religious view of human depravity under a new banner of scientific materialism. It points toward the coming importance of Freud in American thought. In support of this view of man's essentially savage nature, Lydston often includes sarcastic descriptions of the crimes of the respectable, ranging from stealing towels in hotels to the economic tyranny of industrialists and financiers. Indeed, he includes a long chapter on anarchy built around the argument that although all crime is anarchic in nature, the most flagrant examples are those rooted in government such as the anarchy of municipal corruption, the anarchy of capital and labor, the anarchy of the legal system, and worst of all, the anarchy of war built around a class of professional murderers who function only so that one government may steal from another.

The social causes of crime are particularly important for the professional criminal. Lydston isolates twenty major causes of crime ranging from "hereditary influences" to "the special factors in America of a rapidly increasing general neuropathy" (91–93). Several environmental and social causes are particularly important to the generation of professional criminals: "vicious example and surrounding"; "criminal suggestion"; "unjust dispensation of law"; "alleged detective science of manhunting; Police persecution of discharged criminals"; and "poverty." He argues that it is hardly surprising to find a constant stream of thieves flowing from the "social cesspools" of the slum. The individual from the slum who turns to crime is not responsible; the villain is the society that allows these sewers to survive and furnish a fertile pool for professional recruitment. The slums are "responsible for the system of apprenticeship in vogue in every large city," which provides the foundation for a "career of trained, expert criminality" (96–98). This is but one example of the tie between society and professional crime.

As a physician attacking the absurdities of the legal profession, Lydston lays particular stress on the role of America's legal system in the production of professionals. He argues that "from top to bottom . . . criminal law is tainted with maladministration and unfairness." As a result individuals "acquire a resentment against society that incites to crime" (107). Especially pernicious is the uneven application of law so that the unprotected thief sees the wealthy miscreant or the criminal with 'pull' released while he receives a harsh sentence: "The convict who is the victim of an unjust discrimination is made so rebellious that reformation is, in his case, an iridescent dream, and revenge becomes his watchword" (115). Of course when the physician takes over, this injustice will cease; the physician will treat each case as a specific disease and apply the remedy that will best promise a speedy cure. Finally, many thieves find it impossible to carry out resolves to reform because of police persecution. Unable to make enough money at an honest calling to satisfy the inordinate demands of the police and thus avoid arrest on "suspicion," the thief is forced back to crime in order to live (114).

Lydston also presents a detailed discussion of the occupation of theft in a chapter detailing the characteristics of the criminal.

This chapter is typical of the use the criminal anthropologists made of the professional thief. Lydston chooses the professional thief as his central figure, for he is the truest criminal (498). The most important characteristic of the true criminal is his moral deformity or retardation—a quality that the professional shares with the instinctive criminal. Lydston attempts to account for this in the professional thief who, he admits, has his own peculiar code of ethics among his class. Lydston uses a biological vision of morality: "His moral centres have either never developed or have ceased to functionate, leaving him in a condition of moral atrophy,—or better, perhaps, moral anesthesia" (498). The professional thief must anesthetize his moral sense; life, to him, is a battle he fights against terrible odds. He lacks even the fear of disgrace that serves as a rudimentary conscience among many men. He is already *déclassé* and cares only about his standing among his own class.

As proof of the professional criminal's moral anesthesia, Lydston uses the photographs of the Rogues' Gallery. These no longer stand for the criminal's absolute freedom as in Hawthorne; they have become symbols of his status as savage. Lydston does present his version of the criminal's code of ethics and caste-concept within the profession. This presentation reinforces his stance as the objective, scientific observer. He simply describes the criminal's code, including practically no analysis of the implications of his observations.

The work of Lydston and Boies is typical of another phenomenon among the physicians who used criminology as a means of expanding their influence. This is the development of a shared persona marked by a confident belief in the experimental method and the eventual extirpation of crime. The great *bete noire* for these physicians was the "sentimentality" exemplified by such conservative thinkers as MacDonald and Drähms. These latter authors vehemently denied that crime was a biologically rooted disease to be treated only with a biological approach. They continued to believe in the criminal's potential for reformation and maintained a strong faith in this power of education and religious training.

Lydston feels nothing but contempt for this notion, arguing that the criminal "is simply excrementitious matter that should not only be eliminated, but placed beyond the possibility of its contaminating the body social" (566). This image of the criminal as excrement is typical of the attitude these physicians shared in their descriptions of him. The essential feature is the vision of crime as a disease infecting the social body. Just as the individual is justified in using any measure to cure himself of a disease such as smallpox, society is justified in adopting any measure to cure itself of crime. These physicians adopted a mask of confident optimism in their writings; even here one finds the progressive concern for social regeneration rather than individual salvation. These authors were not concerned about the individual diseased cells of the social body. Indeed, their prognosis here was gloomy. However, they presented a united front in their argument for the eventual cleansing and cure of the social organism.

Embedded in this approach was a battle against the legal profession for the dominant position in treating crime. These physicians argued that the legal system had failed in its response to crime; jurists were bound to an antiquated system based on superstition and sentimental notions of free will and moral responsibility. Now it was time to let the methods of science, which had been so successful in combatting physical disease, attack the diseases of society. This pose demanded scientific objectivity and ruthlessness. Lydston argues that medical science has enormously enhanced its value to society in recent years through the demonstration of its knowledge of the causes and techniques for prevention of disease. This could also be applied to crime. In Lydston's view, "the moralist and the lawmaker have had their innings and have failed ... and hope for the future would seem to hinge on the dominance of medical science in criminology" (557). Boies goes even further. He presents eighty-three theorems or laws which form the basis of penology and concludes by stating that "criminality is a preventable and curable disease (446). The great search for cause is concluded in his view; all that remains is the treatment and quick elimination of the illness.

ENVIRONMENTALISTS AND SOCIAL CRITICS: THE RESPONSE TO BIOLOGICAL MODEL

In spite of its appeal to physicians and physical anthropologists, most Americans did not find the biological approach to crime congenial. The emphasis it placed on biological determinism and the unchangeable nature of heredity clashed with traditional American beliefs in free will and the potential of each individual to better his lot. Many Americans found the irreversible measures physicians called for in exterminating crime repugnant; these measures seemed an affront to the nation's traditional belief in civil rights and individual liberty. Such measures as sterilization and marriage restriction along with such concepts as the "presumptive criminal" skated dangerously close to the state's intrusion into the most intimate corners of an individual's life. A number of thoughtful Americans realized the great potential for abuse these measures contained.[35]

Even among physicians these ideas by no means represented the only approach to crime. Dr. A. Jacobi, a neurologist, presented a lecture on the criminal brain to the National Prison Association in 1892. Jacobi stressed the axiom that nature allowed great latitude within the boundaries of normality. In spite of the researches of Benedikt and Lombroso, Jacobi argued, no special type of criminal brain existed: "Crime is not an entity, an absolute and well-defined manifestation of the same kind and tendency; it is as manifold as human instincts or tendencies in general."[36] Other thinkers also questioned the usefulness of criminal anthropology. Charles H. Henderson, a professor of sociology at the University of Chicago, denied Lombroso's theory of a criminal type in 1894 in an address to the National Prison Association. He contended that Americans must maintain a belief in the power of the human will to choose between good and evil. The most important sources of crime were such social causes as tenements and the business of loan sharks. Rather than turning to medicine, Henderson argued for free legal service for the poor.[37]

Other Americans confronted the theories of criminal anthropology even more directly. In an influential study of the history of punishment, Frederick C. Wines argued in 1895 that crime was not a disease; in spite of attempts to place criminal anthropology on a firm scientific basis, such concepts as the existence of a criminal type were still unproven. Wines argues that one familiar with thieves can indeed detect them by their appearance, but holds that one can also recognize bankers, clergymen,

or editors. None of these are biological types. The key to Wines'
argument is the concept of professionalism; every avocation demands specific exertions that leave their "impress upon the figure, the attitude, the entire bearing of the man."[38] Wines isolates
two major flaws in criminal anthropology. First, a belief in the
hereditary origin of crime easily distorts an observer's vision,
making it too easy to place a criminal in the incorrigible class.
This tendency is pessimistic in its approach to individual rehabilitation and undercuts the will of the social reformer. In contrast to the criminal anthropologist, the sociologist presents a
hopeful belief in the malleability of character through a change
in surroundings and habits (253–54). A second failing is the
pretension of the new science, which maintains that it can pre-
dict future behavior by simple observation of the individual.
Wines points out that the law does not deal with the criminal
in posse but *in esse* and that criminal impulses which do not end
in specific criminal acts are unimportant either to the law or to
society (262–63).

While the physicians based much of their argument for turning
the treatment of crime over to them on the notion of the professional criminal, environmentalists used the same figure to discredit them. Wines identified the "false" notion of a biological
criminal type as an occupational type. Other writers such as
Samuel G. Smith used photographs of professional criminals to
discredit the theory of a biological type. Smith argued that these
theories had never misled the practical workers in the nation's
prisons but had infected much writing about crime. These theories threatened to destroy the concept of individual responsibility, the foundation of social life. Unless these theories were
discredited, Smith argued, Americans would have sound theories but no world in which to use them; they were harbingers
of a wreck of the social order.[39]

These attacks on criminal anthropology are typical of the
broader social response. Biological theories found expression
primarily among experts rooted in medicine. Another group of
experts was on the ascendant, however, who provided a direct
challenge to the theories of crime as a disease, as atavism, or as
degeneration. One of the most important intellectual developments of the Progressive Era was the establishment and profes-

sionalization of academic disciplines such as sociology and experimental psychology. These social sciences bore the strong impress of the climate of Progressivism, and, in turn, exerted a strong influence over the direction of progressive reform. The social sciences redefined the problem of crime with a new emphasis on the social group and environmental determinism.

The social sciences were much more influential in shaping the response of most Americans to the professional criminal than were the writings of the physician criminologists. The physicians wrote for a highly specialized audience. The social scientists, in contrast, carried their battle for ascendancy into the popular press, writing books designed for a broad general readership; they were also intimately connected with the settlement house movement and muckraking. For all of these groups, an indictment of both environment and a flawed social system was a more persuasive answer to the problem of professional crime than heredity.

Such reporters as Jacob Riis, a forerunner of the muckrakers, helped generate interest in the problems of poverty and crime through their exposés of the misery of American slums. Riis, a Danish immigrant, arrived in New York City in 1870. He became a police reporter in 1877, a job he held for the next twenty-two years. This job brought him into frequent contact with the tenement districts and the misery teeming within them. Although he was not a trained sociologist, Riis helped define the issue of the slum as a major problem of urban life for the generation of progressive reformers. *How the Other Half Lives*, published in 1890, was based on Riis' experiences among the tenements. This exposé was a documentation of the horrors of American slum life graphically illustrated by Riis' photographs. The book also contained a warning of the future consequences of the slums if left to themselves.

Among the many threats Riis found in the slums, none was more dangerous than crime. On the first page of his book, Riis calls the tenements "nurseries of crime"; this imagery of nurture and organic growth continues throughout the book.[40] Riis devotes several pages of his work to "the ripe fruit of tenement-house growth," the gang (164). He sees these gangs as endemic to the texture of urban life in New York, a peculiarly American product that "belt[s] city like a huge chain from the Battery to Harlem" (165). These gangs are composed of "toughs" just beginning a career of crime and they serve as the apprenticeship for future careers as professional thieves (163). Riis argues that the central tenet of faith for both these toughs and professional criminals is that the world owes them a living. Continually Riis presents the career of the criminal in imagery based on organic nurture: "New York's tough represents the essence of reaction against the old and the new oppression, nursed in the rank soil of its slums" (164). Riis is appalled at the youth of some professionals, noting that in 1889 the Society for the Prevention of Cruelty to Children listed "eighteen 'professional cracksmen,' between nine and fifteen years old, who had been caught with burglar's tools" (172). Riis has little hope for these toughs; reformation is impossible since no one will hire them in legitimate occupations. Like the other inhabitants of the slum the tough is condemned by its negative influence to an unsuccessful life, even in the profession of crime where "he never rises above . . . the 'laborer,' the small thief or burglar, or petty crook, who blindly does the work planned for him by others, and runs the biggest risk for the poorest pay" (176). Still, Riis argues, if his crimes make it clear that efforts to ameliorate the professional tough "must begin with the conditions of life against which his very existence is a protest, even the tough has not lived in vain" (176). Riis is typical of the line followed by sociological journalists and the later muckrakers in their influential presentation of the professional thief. He continually underscores his belief that the criminal is made, not born. The criminal is a product of a faulty environment and defective education. To eliminate the professional criminal one must first eliminate the conditions that produce him and his anti-social world view.

Josiah Flynt launched one of the ablest attacks on criminal anthropology while it was at the height of its influence. *Tramping with Tramps* appeared in 1899, one of the earliest examples of participant sociology. Flynt was perhaps better acquainted with the criminal in his "natural habitat" than any other writer of the time. He opens this book with a direct attack on criminal anthropology, "The Criminal in the Open." In this introductory essay, Flynt argues that in spite of Lombroso's detailed typology the only criminal class of importance is the professional.[41] Flynt admits the existence of other criminal classes such as the instinctive and occasional, but holds that these are a small percentage of criminals and relatively unimportant. He then begins a process of simply presenting the findings of academic criminology and refuting them from his own experience. Criminologists say that the criminal is physically weak or diseased. No, says Flynt, the criminal is among the healthiest of all people although in prison he often feigns sickness to escape work. Lombroso believes that most criminals are epileptic. Flynt has never known an epileptic criminal. He continues this refutation by arguing that rather than having a weak will the criminal has one of the strongest wills; he is rarely insane; he is at least as intelligent as other people; and he tends to be socially conservative rather than revolutionary.

Flynt argues that the essential flaw in academic criminology is its focus on the convict. The conclusion of prison doctors who have gathered a mass of information is that the criminal is a degenerate human being. Flynt scoffs at this notion. The first object for a "scientific investigation" of the criminal is to study him in his natural surroundings where he will present himself in his usual state of body and mind instead of in prison where he is a "balked and disappointed man" (2). Rather than examining the criminal's skull, criminology should concentrate on his *milieu*. Flynt does concede that after the age of thirty many criminals acquire a peculiar look. He attributes this to prison life and the prison environment instead of heredity. He also argues that "men who are busied in the detection of crime have more or less similar facial characteristics" and are often mistaken for criminals. Thus, the hereditary stigmata of the anthropologists become attributes of environment and occupation.

Flynt is not an environmental determinist, though. He does assert that most professional criminals are from the slums, but he holds that these criminals are the highest product of this environment, for they refuse to settle for a life on the level of subsistence. They desire luxuries and deliberately take chances to obtain them. Flynt views crime simply as one means of moving up the social ladder.[42] The professional criminals who originate in the slum rise above their environment and make use of gifts "which would enable them to do well in any class" (5). Environment contributes to their turn to crime since "the ladder of respectable business has no foothold in their environment" (5). In spite of the fables told by "city missionaries," these men have never seen anyone climb the ladder to respectability through legitimate enterprise; they have seen and read of those from a poverty-stricken background who have made it through crime. These men realize the punishment that waits for them if caught and are anything but morally retarded, "but it is a choice between the miserable slum, which they hate, and possible wealth, which they covet, and they determine to run the risk" (6). Flynt echoes Dugdale in his view of the professional criminal's potential: "He is physically, mentally, and morally responsible; and ... though unhappy in his birth and environment, the very energy which has enabled him to get away from his poverty is the 'promise and potency' of a better life" (27).

THE PROFESSIONAL CRIMINAL ENTERS THE ACADEMY: THE RISE OF THE SOCIAL SCIENCES

Josiah Flynt's popular sociology reflected the growing importance of the social sciences in American intellectual life at the turn of the century. The pivotal year for the establishment of sociology in American universities was 1893, when Franklin H. Giddings became chairman of a new department of sociology at Columbia and Edward A. Ross began teaching at Stanford. The crucial event, however, took place at the University of Chicago where Albion W. Small created America's first department of sociology. This department became the center of sociology in America.[43]

Although experimental psychology had found a place in the American university in the 1870s when William James started one of the world's first laboratories for this discipline at Harvard, the 1890s were also central to its establishment in the American intellectual community. In 1890 James published *The Principles of Psychology* in two volumes of almost 1,400 pages. This work stands as the first major presentation of experimental psychology in America. In 1892 James succeeded in bringing Hugo Münsterberg from Freiburg, Germany to Harvard. Like William James,

Münsterberg had studied under Wilhelm Wundt, the founder of experimental psychology in Germany; Münsterberg shared his mentor's belief in the importance of the experimental method. Although Münsterberg's academic specialty was motor activity, he became one of the most widely read popular writers about the uses of experimental psychology in daily life and contributed to the spread of its ideas among Americans.[44]

As these disciplines became established, they acquired all the accoutrements of other academic disciplines, including specialization, professional methodologies and theories, and narrowly focused monographs. The practitioners of these disciplines felt a strong need to prove their usefulness to American civilization, a desire that resulted in popularizations of academic theories and techniques aimed at a wide audience. A sense of excitement pervades the early productions of these young disciplines, an excitement combined with a strong dose of combativeness: this emerges from even the most specialized monographs, such as Frances Fenton's 1911 dissertation at the Universtiy of Chicago, *The Influence of Newspaper Presentations Upon the Growth of Crime and Other Anti-Social Activity*. These academics present their methodologies and techniques in loving detail. They are clearly fascinated by the possibilities of a *scientific* approach to society and are confident that they will obtain results that will help combat such social problems as crime. Crime became an especially useful area for the generation of technologies for these disciplines; the scholars are entranced by the possibilities offered by such technological devices as the "kymograph," created to measure a subject's respiration, or the "algometer," designed to register the sensation of pain.[45] Page after page of their writing is filled with descriptions of these technologies and the process of using them to gather data. Indeed, the one area where these social scientists joined forces with the criminal anthropologists to present a united front was in the call for a national laboratory funded by the federal government for the scientific study of criminals. Like such criminal anthropologists as MacDonald, these scholars strongly believed in the efficacy of the experimental method. They also generated new techniques for the study of crime such as the use of questionnaires and statistical analysis.

As these sociologists and psychologists developed new techniques and technologies to complement the experimental side of their work, they also developed new theories. These theories were often attempts to prove the usefulness of the new disciplines to their civilization. One fruitful area for the generation of theory was crime. Crime preoccupied Americans of the progressive generation as they tried to cope with such problems as rapid urbanization, immigration, and an increasingly inhuman economic atmosphere. In this context the settlement house movement proved to be a powerful magnet that drew thoughtful young Americans to the underside of the city. John Dewey, for example, had a long and fruitful association with Hull House.

Other thinkers attacked contemporary problems from a more theoretical stance. Arthur Hall, for instance, addressed the problem of the increase in crime in the late nineteenth century. If society was indeed progressing as such thinkers as Herbert Spencer argued, why did crime seem to continually increase? Hall optimistically argues that this increase is itself a sign of progress. Crime is a social product which increases as civilization progresses: "The persistent enlargement of the field of crime is a necessity for all truly progressive nations" (vi). Hall views the professional criminal as a sign of this progress since his acts are confined to offenses against property instead of person—a sign of heightened civilization. Also, the professional criminal's tendency toward specialization indicates higher progress (324–34).[46]

Other thinkers used the professional criminal as a figure of importance. G. Stanley Hall, one of the most important psychologists of the early twentieth century, argues in his massive work, *Adolescence*, that juvenile crime results from a youth's problems in adjusting to his environment. Although Hall accepts the work of Lombroso and his followers with few reservations, he emphasizes the role of environment in the evolution of the professional criminal. Hall stresses the importance of imitation, habit, and suggestion in the etiology of professional crime. This career criminal is a result of a gradual developmental process rather than heredity; Hall points out that the American professional is often "of fine and even distinguished form, feature, and appearance, whom it is doubtful anyone could distinguish from the honest classes of the business community."[47] Hall also examines the "philosophy of feral mankind" or the world view of the professional criminal. The pervasiveness of the ideas of progressive reformers emerges in Hall's special emphasis on the thief's view of legitimate business as simply another form of graft (I, 340).

One element behind the rise of psychology and sociology was the attempt of academicians to reach a broad audience and to illustrate the practical uses of their disciplines to this audience. Hugo Münsterberg spent much of his intellectual energies in attempts to demonstrate the usefulness of experimental psychology to society. His book *On the Witness Stand* (1908) is a collection of essays that attempts to show the usefulness of experimental psychology in the legal arena. He argues that psychology could be of great usefulness in questioning witnesses and suspected criminals. He also makes a plea for the usefulness of psychology in preventing crime; most men are born alike and most criminals are simply "men with poorly working minds."[48] Psychology can treat these disordered minds as well as prevent their development. The only problem is the professional criminal who has become a specialist. Even here, though, where one finds specimens of minds different from the normal human, the process is a result of training and not an inborn disposition (241–42). The key is to treat the criminal before he develops a dissociated personality that overwhelms the true self. In the professional this dissociation has already occurred; for this reason Münsterberg believes that he is irreclaimable, and society's only response is how to best protect itself against his damage (265).

Sociology was the academic discipline most influenced by the climate of Progressivism and it, in turn, exerted the strongest influence on the progressive movement. A typical example of the popular use of sociology in a progressive approach to crime is Edward A. Ross' book, *Sin and Society*. Ross, a professor of sociology at the University of Wisconsin when he wrote this book, did not use the scientific methodologies of his colleagues in this brief book. It grew from his insights into the nature of American civilization. America's move into a modern world had created the need for a redefinition of ideas about sin and crime. Ross socialized Christian ethics in this book, insisting that sin was no longer the individualistic concept of theology but had become an anonymous, mutual thing.

Ross borrowed the word "criminaloid" from Lombroso to describe the typical criminal of industrial society. For Lombroso the criminaloid was the occasional criminal, hovering on the edge of an as yet unlaunched professional career. For Ross the criminaloid is an individual who prospers by destructive "practices which have not yet come under the effective ban of public opinion."[49] This criminaloid, like Lombroso's occasional criminal, is not anti-social by nature; his crimes are usually committed at long distance instead of at close range. Like Lombroso's criminaloid, Ross' "is really a borderer between the camps of good and evil" (58). Ross, however, is redefining crime; his criminaloid replaces the old style professional criminal as "society's most dangerous foe, more redoubtable by far than the plain criminal, because he sports the livery of virtue and operates on a Titanic scale" (59). The criminaloid is the typical criminal of modern society, and unlike his "low-browed cousins," he occupies "the cabin rather than the steerage of society" (48). The essential feature of the criminaloid is moral insensibility (50), a characteristic attributed over and over again to the professional criminal. Another parallel is that his crimes are usually against property and always directed toward economic gain. Both are essentially forms that prey on society, but modern crime is based on betrayal rather than aggression, and monstrous treacheries exist on all levels of modern life: "adulterators, peculators, boodlers, grafters, violating the trust others have placed in them" (6).

In his definition of modern, mutualized crime Ross draws heavily on imagery associated with professional theft. He is attempting to broaden the definition of crime, to point out that the sins of modern industrialists are more damaging than the older forms of crime on which people continue to waste their energies. The realization of modern sin takes an act of the imagination, Ross says, and he prods his readers through such imagery-laden passages as: "The man who picks pockets with a railway rebate, murders with an adulterant instead of a bludgeon, burglarizes with a 'rake-off' instead of a jimmy, . . . does not feel on his brow the brand of a malefactor" (7). Americans must realize that the new crimes are more destructive than the old, and redirect their energies to respond to the new impersonal sins. Far more dangerous than the honestly professional criminal is the criminal as professional businessman.

WILLIAM HEALY AND THE EMERGENCE OF MODERN CRIMINOLOGY

In June 1909 Northwestern University sponsored a National Conference on Criminal Law and Criminology to celebrate the fiftieth anniversary of its law school. This conference had profound effects on the intellectual response to crime in America. The aim of the conference was to foster a new spirit of cooperation among lawyers and scientists. For approximately twenty years these professions had followed increasingly divergent paths. The legal system and its most visible symbol, the lawyer, had come under increasingly vehement attacks by those approaching the problem of crime from a "scientific" stance such as physicians, sociologists, and psychologists. This conference aimed to rectify the "crying need for co-operative effort among lawyers and scientists."[50] At this conference the American Institute of Criminal Law and Criminology was founded, and the Institute created its *Journal*, an organ in continuous publication to the present. John Henry Wigmore was the architect of this conference and was elected to serve as the first president of the Institute. Wigmore was the author of the ten-volume *Treatise on the Anglo American System of Evidence*, a monumental legal study. He believed in the necessity of cooperation between all branches of knowledge and brought a true spirit of interdisciplinary cooperation to the Institute.[51]

One of the most important events of this conference was the establishment of a committee to translate the most important works of European criminology into English. This resulted in the nine-volume Modern Criminal Science Series. The committee chose an eclectic variety of the most important European theorists, justifying its selection by stating: "As the science has various aspects and emphases—the anthropological, sociological, legal, statistical, pathological—due regard was paid in the selection, to a representation of all these aspects."[52] This conference and the founding of the new Institute signalled the birth of both a new academic discipline and a new profession in Amer-

ica—that of the criminologist. Americans interested in an intellectual approach to crime had finally limned the limits of a new
"science" that would take what was useful from a multitude of
disciplines and attempt to achieve a synthesis that would break
the ground for the young science.

Although the first volumes of the *Journal of the American Institute of Criminal Law and Criminology* (JAICLC) reveal the continuing importance of criminal anthropology in America, the
death of this discipline was approaching. Two men effectively
destroyed the Lombrosian doctrines of a hereditary type and
the biological interpretation of criminality. The first of these was
Charles Goring, who published *The English Convict* in 1913. Goring, a British psychiatrist, used statistical observations of English
prisoners to discredit the Lombrosian doctrines. The work that
ushered in a new era of criminology, however, was produced
by the American psychiatrist and criminologist William Healy,
who published *The Individual Delinquent* in 1915.

Healy was the director of the Psychopathic Institute of the
Chicago Juvenile Court. He obtained this job when Julia Lathrop,
of Hull House, wrote to William James in 1907 with the request
that he recommend someone to direct a psychological study of
juvenile delinquents for the Juvenile Protective League of Chicago.[53] James recommended Healy, one of his former psychology
students at Harvard. Healy was given the job and began work
in the spring of 1909. Healy's background included an M.D.
from Rush Medical College at the University of Chicago in 1900
and post-graduate work in London, Berlin, and Vienna. While
directing the Juvenile Psychopathic Institute, he also served as
Professor of Neurological and Mental Disease at the Chicago
Policlinic. *The Individual Delinquent* presented the findings of five
years of research at the Institute.

Healy's book moved criminology into the modern era; it is to
contemporary criminology what Lombroso's work was to the
first period of the "science." Lombroso's contribution was the
realization that the criminal should be studied by scientific methods; this is why he is regarded as the father of criminology.
Healy's contribution was the scientific study of the criminal
through the methods of psychiatry and psychoanalysis. Although such thinkers as MacDonald had contributed studies of

individual delinquents earlier, Healy established the use of psychology and the case study in criminology. His work made it clear that theorizing about criminals as a unified type or as a collection of classes was useless. The causative factors of crime were simply too complex and interdependent for one to draw generalizations about a specific cause that could be isolated and treated in the fashion of a disease such as diphtheria. He argued that each offender must be examined from an individual viewpoint, and he set this example in his work. He studied each delinquent from a medical, social, and psychological stance in addition to compiling family histories and sketches of environmental forces.

Healy includes a detailed study of professional criminals as "a most important group" that must be distinguished from all other classes of criminals.[54] Healy contends that habitual offenders must be divided into the non-professional and professional classes and defines the professional class by saying that "their criminalism is deliberate, premeditated and repeated, as compared to that type of action which is the result of the impulse of the moment" (316). The note of caution struck here is central to Healy's persona throughout this work. After a short discussion of the relatively small size of the professional class, Healy points out that it is usually only the "stupid ones" who get caught. He argues that the two central questions for a study of the professional criminal are: what are the foundations of his career? and what holds him to this career?

True to his refusal to present an overarching theory, Healy examines several professional careers for their origins. Although he states that here, if anywhere, the student will come across the deliberate choice of crime, he contends that in over one thousand cases, he has found only six that could perhaps be called deliberate. Healy's view throughout is one of an extremely complex determinism. He does isolate several factors which may contribute to a professional career, including craving for adventure, smallness of size, suggestion, habit, special abilities such as motor dexterity, mental imagery, mental conflict, and various environmental defects. Particularly important are mental conflict and habit. Healy is surprised that students of criminal etiology have paid so little attention to this; he believes that it is a "prime consideration," and that everyone who works in criminology should know William James' essay "Habit." In this essay James discusses the thesis that habit is physiologically based and dependent on pathways through the nerve centers: "An acquired habit . . . is nothing but a new pathway of discharge formed in the brain, by which certain incoming currents ever after tend to escape."[55] Healy argues that this is of crucial importance to the study of habitual professional crime (350).

Healy essentially opens a new area for inquiry when he asks what it is that holds a professional criminal to his career. Earlier criminology was so obsessed by its search for cause that it rarely asked such questions. He relies on interviews with established professionals as well as autobiographies of professional criminals and books by policemen to approach this problem. The older conception that professionals naturally belong to this class has been exploded, Healy argues, and he points out that success in the calling is one clear reason for continuing a career of professional crime (319-20). Criminals would not follow crime as a career if it were not profitable. He then uses a case study of an expert safe burglar who belongs to the "aristocracy of criminality" to show how these thieves rely on official corruption to obtain short sentences if apprehended or to buy police protection. Healy concludes that professional crime is perhaps the one field where deterrent penalties might work since these criminals have developed a morality based solely on profit and loss. He hesitates to recommend this because of the "diagnostic" nature of his study (329), but finally argues that it would be useful to have "swifter, surer and longer penalties for this type of crime" (329). Healy also reveals the progressive impulse in his study of professional crime. He argues that the professional follows a life-style based on migration. He echoes the call of such writers as Flynt for the establishment of a central bureau of identification in Washington; this is the only effective way to combat the migratory professional thief.

Healy takes criminology into the arena of modern thought. He refuses to simplify the causes of crime and argues that the world of professional theft is a subculture that must be studied with techniques similar to those used today by cultural anthropologists. His book appeared on the eve of the event that transformed the world of twentieth-century crime—Prohibition. During the era of Prohibition crime itself entered a modern era based on an organization and structure that mirrored the corporate structure that much of progressive reform tried to tame. After this change the old style professional thief became a figure who bore the same relationship to the economics of crime as the corner grocery bore to the economics of corporate capitalism.

Epilogue

The professional thief played an important role in American civilization between the Civil War and World War I. He was the dominant figure in the American imagination of crime during this era. In autobiographical writings the thieves dramatized themselves in roles designed to meet their own perceptions of what the civilization wanted to believe about their profession. During the Gilded Age these thieves presented themselves as master rogues, adept at their trade but holding the same essential value system as most other Americans. In the Progressive Era a new persona emerged which emphasized the status of these thieves as victims of cruel circumstances, alienated from the rest of American society. This new persona fit the progressive vision of criminality. It helped progressive reformers explain how a person could become a professional thief and reinforced their optimistic vision of human nature.

Just as the thieves used American beliefs in their presentation of self, a variety of groups used thieves to satisfy their own goals. For detectives attempting to enhance their own status as professionals, the thief became a worthy opponent, a threat to American life who demanded a response that only specialized crime fighters could provide. These crime fighters were, of course, the detectives. Detectives such as Allan Pinkerton and Thomas Byrnes created a figure of awesome proportions in their writings about professional theft. The professional thief was presented in ways that dramatized his threat to society while also emphasizing his skills and abilities. He thus became a figure that detectives could oppose while still maintaining professional status.

For reformers the thief came to stand for a plethora of evils in American civilization. These evils ranged from the threat posed by urbanization to the dangers of an all-pervasive materialism that threatened to overwhelm traditional American institutions. The professional thief also came to symbolize the links between so-called legitimate politicians and policemen and crime. In this role he seemed to dramatize the pervasive corruption that many reformers found in American civilization. He was, in a sense, the logical end of the drive for wealth that had apparently infected all areas of American life since the end of the Civil War.

In the literary imagination the professional thief contributed to the development of the modern detective story. Popular authors who narrated tales of the conflict between detectives and professional criminals helped solidify the formula of the detective story. Unintentionally, these authors also left a submerged record of American values during this era. In more serious fiction the professional moved from a position as a supporting actor who helped establish the texture of American life to a place at the center of the progressive novel. In this new role he exacted revenge on the detectives and reformers who presented him as a danger to American life and came to stand as a symbol of both economic and legal injustice—the quintessential product of a society in need of spiritual regeneration.

The professional thief was also central to a more overtly intellectual response to crime in America as physicians waged a debate with the young social sciences over the right to "treat" the criminal. These groups were attempting to extend the boundaries of their influence in American life and to consolidate their positions as useful professionals who could serve their society in practical ways. The debate over who could best deal with the problem of crime provides important insights into both professionalization in American life and the American vision of crime and human nature during this period.

In spite of the changed nature of American crime, the professional thief continues to be a important figure in the twentieth-century imagination. The themes raised in the early writings about this figure remain of importance in American civilization.

The professional criminal is still central in crime novels directed toward a general audience. He often serves as a comic figure designed to satirize contemporary notions of professionalism. Donald Westlake's caper novels are a good example of this use of the professional criminal. More important, however, is his continued presence in a long line of serious examinations of crime in American life. These run from Dashiell Hammett and Raymond Chandler to such current authors as Robert Parker. The professional criminal has also held onto a position in more literary fiction such as Ralph Ellison's *Invisible Man* (1952) where the figure of Rinehart, the "hustler," stands for an illusory and deceptive world. The professional criminal is today, as he was one hundred years ago, a useful symbol of the deceptive quality of appearances and the problems of leading a double life.

This figure also remains important to the sociological imagination in America. In 1937 Edwin Sutherland, a sociologist at the University of Chicago, collaborated with Chic Conwell to produce *The Professional Thief*. Sutherland's seminal work encouraged other sociologists and criminologists to use the professional criminal in a variety of ways. These scholars began to use the professional thief to examine such questions as occupational career patterns, the nature of subcultures, and professional vocabularies. A central assumption behind such studies is the belief that crime sheds a strong light on the essential patterns of a culture. The old debate about the causes of crime has also resurfaced in recent years as some criminologists have once more looked to biology as a potential cause and "cure" for crime. The born criminal has returned as the individual with a defective genetic structure. Such surgical techniques as the frontal lobotomy have also been advanced as responses to crime.

The professional criminal has continued his long-standing relationship with detectives and reformers. No figure better illustrates the continuity of this link than Mel Weinberg, the confidence man who served as the "hero" of Abscam. The questions raised over one hundred years ago about the nature of this relationship have not been solved; most Americans continue to feel a touch of squeamishness at the dirty hands of detectives who use criminals to serve supposedly legitimate ends. This same case also points to the use of professional criminals by such "reformers" as critics of the Federal Bureau of Investigation who find in Abscam a vicious assault on the Bill of Rights.

The autobiographies of professional thieves continue to address the central issues of American culture. One of the most important autobiographies of the 1960s, *The Autobiography of Malcolm X*, illustrates the continued usefulness of this form. Other books like *Assault With a Deadly Weapon* (1975) raise many of the same issues that the progressives tried to address. These include environmental determinism and the promise of crime as a way out of the slum. Clearly, many of our concerns remain the same.

Perhaps the central issue for the study of the contemporary professional criminal is the continuity that links him to such forbears as Langdon W. Moore and Jim Caulfield. Professional crime has changed in America. In most cases the individual entrepreneur has been subsumed as a part of the corporate structure of organized crime. Some styles of professional crime, however, continue practically unchanged. These types of crime, such as picking pockets, depend on human skill rather than technology and are essentially static technically. Other types of professional crime have undergone fundamental changes. Perhaps the most important of these changes is the increased role of violence in the profession. The armed robber's move from amateur status to professional status typifies this change. For this criminal, violence is simply functional, another skill to master on the road to success.

One way of learning more about the nature of both professional crime and crime in general is by historical study. Crime, like all other aspects of human behavior, exists in a historical continuum. Although crime is surely not a "problem" that will ever be "solved," we can discover things about this kind of behavior by studying the forms deviance took in the past. We can also learn more about our culture by examining the types of deviant behavior it has experienced. Potentially, one of the most exciting uses of crime in a historical sense is the use of crime as a text—a text that scholars can read and use to discover meaning in our past and, perhaps, our present.

Notes

INTRODUCTION

1. The development of professional crime in nineteenth-century America is examined in both James A. Inciardi, *Careers in Crime* (Chicago: Rand McNally, 1975) and David R. Johnson, *Policing the Urban Underworld: The Impact of Crime on the Development of the American Police, 1800-1887* (Philadelphia: Temple University Press, 1979), esp. pp. 41-67. Other books that examine the history of American crime include Eric H. Monkkonen, *The Dangerous Class: Crime and Poverty in Columbus, Ohio, 1860-1885* (Cambridge, Mass.: Harvard University Press, 1975); Roger Lane, *Violent Death in the City: Suicide, Accident, and Murder in Nineteenth Century Philadelphia* (Cambridge, Mass.: Harvard University Press, 1979); and John C. Schneider, *Detroit and the Problem of Order, 1830-1880. A Geography of Crime, Riot, and Policing* (Lincoln: University of Nebraska Press, 1980). For contemporary discussions of professional crime the seminal work remains Edwin H. Sutherland, *The Professional Thief* (Chicago: University of Chicago Press, 1937). Other books which treat this topic are Ned Polsky, *Hustlers, Beats, and Others* (Chicago: Aldine Publishing Company, 1967); Bill Chambliss, ed., *Box Man: A Professional Thief's Journey* (New York: Harper & Row, 1972); and Peter Letkemann, *Crime as Work* (Englewood Cliffs, N.J.: Prentice-Hall, 1973).

CHAPTER 1

1. For examples of this early gallows literature consult Thomas M. McDade, *The Annals of Murder: A Bibliography of Books and Pamphlets on American Murders from Colonial Times to 1900* (Norman: University of Oklahoma Press, 1961).

2. Some examples of the professional criminal's autobiography in current America are John Allan, *Assault With a Deadly Weapon* (New York: Macmillan Co., 1975): Albie Baker, *Stolen Sweets* (New York: Saturday Review Press/E. P. Dutton & Co., Inc., 1973); and Willie Sutton, *Where the Money Was* (New York: The Viking Press, 1976).

3. James Olney, ed., *Autobiography, Essays Theoretical and Critical* (Princeton: Princeton University Press, 1980), pp. 29-30.

4. *Ibid.*, p. 36.

5. Other examples of this type of criminal autobiography include *Charles Mortimer, Life and Career of the Most Skillful and Noted Criminal of his Day* (Sacramento: n.p., 1873); Silas Doty, *The Life of Sile Doty*, compiled by J. G. W. Colburn (Toledo: Blade Pr. Co., 1880); George Bidwell, *Forging His Chains* (Hartford: S. S. Scranton, 1888); and Dick Lane, *Confessions of a Criminal* (Chicago: Prairie State Pub. Co., 1904).

6. For example, "Wellington Scott" and Jim Caulfield both "retired" in their mid-thirties or at least tried.

7. Other examples are Tom Fogarty (alias), *The Story of Tom Fogarty; the Autobiography of a Criminal*, written down by Thomas Sullivan (Chicago: Cannon, 1900); George C. Contant, *A Pardoned Lifer*, written down by Opie L. Warner (San Bernardino: Index Print, 1909); Thomas L. Maslin, *From Saloon to Prison, From Prison to Pulpit* (Ashland, Pa.: printed by G. Kyler, 1912); William H. Flake, *From Crime to Christ* (Binghampton, N.Y.: Business-Art-Press, 1915); and George Leighton Bartlett, *Through the Mill by "4342"* (St. Paul: McGill-Warner, 1915). This last document is a strange work that was written to defend the Minnesota state prison system against charges of corruption and cruelty. This prisoner expatiates on the gentle qualities of the system. He was of course one of the lucky ones who had a job in the library and was segregated from the more dangerous cases.

8. Langdon W. Moore, *His Own Story of his Eventful Life* (Boston: Langdon W. Moore, 1893), p. 46. Eldridge and Watts referred to Moore's autobiography as the most faithful presentation of criminal life from the inside yet published. Hereafter cited in text as Moore.

9. George Miles White, *From Boniface to Bank Burglar; or, the Price of Persecution* (Bellows Falls, Vt.: Truax Printing Co., 1905), pp. 5, 23, 59. Hereafter cited in text as White.

10. Michael D. Marcaccio, *The Hapgoods: Three Earnest Brothers* (Charlottesville: University Press of Virginia, 1977), pp. 71-72.

11. Josiah Flynt, review of *The Autobiography of a Thief*, by Hutchins Hapgood, *Bookman*, 17 (July 1903), pp. 514-15.

12. Hutchins Hapgood, *A Victorian in the Modern World* (New York: Harcourt Brace and Co., Inc., 1939), p. 173.

13. Hutchins Hapgood, *The Autobiography of a Thief* (New York: Fox, Duffield & Company, 1903), p. 12.

14. Hapgood, *Victorian*, pp. 166-72.

15. Wellington Scott (pseudonym), *Seventeen Years in the Underworld* (New York: Abingdon, 1916), pp. 12-15. Herafter cited in text as Scott.

16. Allan Pinkerton, *Criminal Reminiscences and Detective Sketches* (1878; rpt. Freeport, N.Y.: Books for Libraries Press, 1970), pp. 121, 132.

17. A very brief discussion of the picaresque novel and its vision of crime is found in James Michael Adams, "Picaresque Elements in American Fiction," Diss. University of South Carolina, 1979 (University Microfilm #8002226).

CHAPTER 2

1. Allan Pinkerton, *Criminal Reminiscences and Detective Sketches* (1878; rpt. Freeport, N.Y.: Books for Libraries Press, 1970), pp. 16-51.

2. *Ibid.*, pp. 39-40.

3. David R. Johnson, *Policing the Urban Underworld: The Impact of Crime on the Development of the American Police, 1800-1887* (Philadelphia: Temple University Press, 1979), pp. 41-42, 59-60. Johnson provides an extended discussion of the opposition encountered by both the public and private detectives in this era.

4. See the autobiographies of Langdon W. Moore, George Miles White, and the exposé by Edward Crapsey discussed in Chapter 3.

5. Edward Crapsey, *The Nether Side of New York* (New York: Sheldon & Company, 1872), pp. 53-56.

6. William F. Howe and A. H. Hummel, *In Danger; or Life in New York* (Chicago: J.S. Ogilvie & Co., 1888), pp. 187-202.

7. Morris Friedman, *The Pinkerton Labor Spy* (New York: Wilshire Book Company, 1907), p. 2.

8. Phil. Farley, *Criminals of America; or, Tales of the Lives of Thieves* (New York: Author's Edition, 1876), p. xiii.

9. Thomas Byrnes, *1886: Professional Criminals of America* (1886; rpt. New York: Chelsea House Publishers, 1969), p. v.

10. *New York Times*, 12 March 1876, p. 5, col. 2.

11. George Miles White, *From Boniface to Bank Burglar* (Bellows Falls, Vt.: Truax Printing Co., 1905), p. 286.

12. Austin Bidwell, *From Wall Street to Newgate* (Hartford: Bidwell Publishing Co., 1895), p. 244. Bidwell gives Farley the name Stanley in this autobiography, pp. 28-34.

13. Normand Berlin, *The Base String: The Underworld in Elizabethan Drama* (Rutherford, N.J.: Fairleigh Dickinson University Press, 1968), pp. 212-14, discusses the use of the lower classes for comic effect in the English theater during the Renaissance.

14. Farley, p. 526.

15. James F. Richardson, *The New York Police: Colonial Times to 1901* (New York: Oxford University Press, 1970), pp. 209-13.

16. Lincoln Steffens, *The Autobiography of Lincoln Steffens* (New York: Harcourt, Brace and Company, 1931), p. 201.

17. *Ibid.*, p. 222.

18. Julian Hawthorne, *The Great Bank Robbery* (New York: Cassell & Company, Limited, 1887), p. 74.

19. Arthur Schlesinger, "Introduction" to *1886: Professional Criminals of America*, p. xvi.

20. *New York Daily Tribune*, 30 October 1886, p. 11, cols. 4-5.

21. Hutchins Hapgood, *The Autobiography of a Thief* (New York: Fox, Duffield & Company, 1903), pp. 66, 191.

22. *New York Times*, 1 October 1886, p. 8, col. 1.

23. Byrnes, pp. 1-5. Hereafter cited in text.

24. *New York Times*, 30 October 1887, p. 9, col. 6; *New York Daily Tribune*, 30 October 1887, p. 11, cols. 5-6.

25. Pinkerton, *Criminal Reminiscences*, pp. 88-90.

26. George W. Walling, *Recollections of a New York Chief of Police* (1887; rpt. Montclair, N.J.: Patterson Smith Publishing Corporation, 1972), p. 209.

27. Allan Pinkerton, *Thirty Years a Detective. A Thorough and Comprehensive Exposé of Criminal Practices of All Grades and Classes* (New York: G. W. Carleton & Co., Publishers, 1884), p. 265.

28. *Ibid.*, p. 17.

29. Walling, pp. 321-22.

30. Pinkerton, *Thirty Years a Detective*, pp. 264-65.

31. Benjamin P. Eldridge and William B. Watts, *Our Rival the Rascal* (Boston: Pemberton Publishing Co., 1896), pp. 51-52.

32. *Ibid.*, pp. 341-45.

33. *Ibid.*, pp. 319, 348.

34. *Ibid.*, pp. 348-53.

35. Walling, pp. 332-33.

36. Allan Pinkerton, *Professional Thieves and the Detective* (New York: G. W. Carleton & Co., Publishers, 1880), pp. 68, 14l, 147, 156; also "A Modern Eugene Aram," in *Bank-Robbers and the Detectives* (New York: G. W. Carleton & Co., Publishers, 1882), p. 261; and *Criminal Reminiscences*, pp. 52-53.

37. George S. McWatters, *Knots Untied: or, Ways and By-ways in the Hidden Life of American Detectives* (Hartford: J. B. Burr & Hyde, 1871), p. 194.

38. *Ibid.*, pp. 21-97.

39. *New York Times*, 17 May 1871, p. 2, col. 1.

40. Walling, p. 3.

41. McWatters, Preface, pp. 322-40, 341-48.

42. *Ibid.*, pp. 192-93.

43. Walling, pp. 517-21.

44. Pinkerton, *Criminal Reminiscences*, pp. 297, 282.

45. Eldridge and Watts, p. 338. Hereafter cited in text.

CHAPTER 3

1. Frank Wadleigh Chandler, *The Literature of Roguery* (New York: Houghton, Mifflin, 1907), p. 87.

2. In the *Anatomy of Melancholy* (1621), Robert Burton uses the term in this way: "What it is, with all the kinds, causes, symptoms, prognostickes, and severall cures of it." And Lawrence Babb, *Sanity in Bedlam: A Study of Robert Burton's Anatomy of Melancholy* (East Lansing: Michigan State University Press, 1959), p. 1, points out that the word frequently appears in Renaissance titles. Chandler's definition is extremely broad and includes almost any descriptive or analytical nonfiction dealing with crime and criminals. The term was resurrected by Northrop Frye, *Anatomy of Criticism. Four Essays* (Princeton: Princeton University Press, 1957), pp. 311-12, where he proposes the word be used to replace the term "Menippean satire," a form which he says deals with "intellectual themes and attitudes" and "piles up an enormous mass of erudition" around the themes. Frye essentially, though, keeps Burton's meaning of dissection or analysis for the word though he does emphasize the "intellectualized approach of his form."

3. Thomas W. Knox, *Underground or, Life Below the Surface* (Hartford: J. B. Burr & Co., 1874), pp. 28-34.

4. Judson Achille Grenier, Jr., "The Origins and Nature of Progressive Muckraking," Diss. University of California at Los Angeles, 1965 (University Microfilm #65-13,855), proved helpful in this discussion. This section also draws on Robert M. Crunden, *Ministers of Reform* (New York: Basic Books, 1983). Crunden allowed me to examine the manuscript of this study of Progressivism before publication.

5. This class includes such books as the anonymous *How 'Tis Done* (1890) and such exposés of vice as John P. Quinn, *Fools of Fortune; or, Gambling and Gamblers, Comprehending a History of the Vice in Ancient and Modern Times* (Chicago: The Anti-Gambling Association, 1892).

6. A. J. Greiner, *Swindles & Bunco Games in City & Country* (St. Louis: Sun Publishing Co., 1904), p. 9.

7. Anonymous, *How 'Tis Done: A Thorough Ventilation of the Numerous Schemes Conducted by Wandering Canvassers, Together with the Various Advertising Dodges for the Swindling of the Public* (Syracuse, N.Y.: W. I. Pattison, Publisher, 1890), p. 8.

8. Harry Houdini, *The Right Way to Do Wrong: An Exposé of Successful Criminals* (Boston: Harry Houdini, 1906), p. 58.

9. O. Henry (William Sidney Porter), "Modern Rural Sports," in *The Gentle Grafter* (1904; rpt. Garden City, N.Y.: Doubleday, Page and Company, 1926), pp. 35-36. Hereafter page numbers follow the quotation in the text.

10. *How 'Tis Done*, p. 7.

11. J. B. Costello, ed., *Swindling Exposed from the Diary of William B. Moreau King of Fakirs* (Syracuse, N.Y.: J. B. Costello, 1907), p. 214.

12. H. K. James (James Henry Keate), *The Destruction of Mephisto's Greatest Web or, All Grafts Laid Bare Being a Complete Exposure of all Gambling, Graft, & Confidence Games* (Salt Lake City: The Raleigh Publishing Company, 1914), p. 5.

13. Chandler, pp. 129-31.

14. Mrs. Helen Campbell, Thomas W. Knox, and Thomas Byrnes, *Darkness and Daylight, or Lights and Shadows of New York Life* (1895; rpt. Detroit: Singing Tree Press, 1969), p. ix.

15. *New York Times*, 24 June 1872, p. 2, col. 1.

16. John H. Warren, Jr., *Thirty Years' Battle with Crime, or the Crying Shame of New York, as seen under the Broad Glare of an Old Detective's Lantern* (Poughkeepsie: A. J. White, 1875), p. 31.

17. Edward Crapsey, *The Nether Side of New York* (New York: Sheldon & Company, 1872), p. 9. This is a compilation of articles that originally appeared in *The Galaxy* from 1869 to 1870. Hereafter cited in text.

18. David R. Johnson, *Policing the Urban Underworld* (Philadelphia: Temple University Press, 1979), pp. 2-3, 41.

19. *The Little Brother* antedates Jack London's *The Road* by four years; although London is usually credited with introducing the hobo to American literature, this is a "distinction" that rightfully belongs to Flynt. London capitalized on an audience Flynt created. See for example the introduction by Glen H. Mullin to Jack London, *The Road* (1907; rpt. New York: Greenberg, Publisher, 1926). Mullin claims that though London was not the first American to write about the tramp, he was the first to "lay any claim to literature" (xiv). Richard W. Etulain in *Jack London on the Road: The Tramp Diary and Other Hobo Writings* (Logan, Utah: Utah State University Press, 1979), p. 25, asserts that London was the first important American writer to deal with hoboes. Etulain does not mention Flynt. London himself dedicated *The Road* to "Josiah Flynt, The Real Thing, Blowed in the Glass." *The Road* originally appeared as a series in *Cosmopolitan*.

20. Philip Wiener, *Evolution and the Founders of Pragmatism* (Cambridge: Harvard University Press, 1949), p. 102.

21. Josiah Flynt (Josiah Flint Willard), *Tramping with Tramps* (1899;

rpt. Montclair, N.J.: Patterson Smith Publishing Corporation, 1972), p. ix.

22. Wiener, p. 26.

23. Wiener, "Conclusion."

24. Josiah Flynt, *My Life* (New York: The Outing Publishing Co., 1908), p. 298.

25. Peter A. Lyon, *Success Story: The Life of S. S. McClure* (New York: Charles Scribner's Sons, 1963), p. 179.

26. Louis Filler, *The Muckrakers* (University Park, Pa.: The Pennsylvania State University Press, 1976), p. 77, identifies this book as the first document of muckraking.

27. Josiah Flynt, *The World of Graft* (1901; rpt. College Park, Md.: McGrath Publishing Co., 1969), pp. 1-2. Hereafter cited in text.

CHAPTER 4

1. Ian Watt, *The Rise of the Novel* (Berkeley: University of California Press, 1957), p. 15. Watt points out that Defoe's novel introduced the subordination of plot to the pattern of autobiography.

2. M. E. Grenander, "The Heritage of Cain: Crime in American Fiction," *Annals of the American Academy of Political and Social Science*, 423 (January 1976), p. 48.

3. David Brion Davis, *Homicide in American Fiction, 1798-1860* (Ithaca: Cornell University Press, 1957), p. 119. Although Davis is concerned with murder, he does make passing references to professional crime. He finds that most of these novels dealt with urban crime and appeared in the 1830s and 1840s, a period of accelerating urban growth and disorder. Typical examples of these early novels are Ned Buntline's *The B'hoys of New York* and George Lippard's *The Quaker City*. See also, Thomas M. McDade, "Lurid Literature of the Last Century," *Pennsylvania Magazine of History and Biography*, 80 (October 1956), pp. 452-64.

4. Warwick Wadlington, *The Confidence Game in American Literature* (Princeton: Princeton University Press, 1975) and Susan Kuhlmann, *Knave, Fool and Genius: The Confidence Man as He Appears in Nineteenth-Century American Fiction* (Chapel Hill: University of North Carolina Press, 1973), discuss the uses of this figure in American fiction.

5. H. Bruce Franklin, *The Victim as Criminal and Artist: Literature from the American Prison* (New York: Oxford University Press, 1978), p. 33.

6. Frank Luther Mott, *A History of American Magazines, 1865-1885* (Cambridge: Harvard University Press, 1938), pp. 27-28. See also Mary Noel, *Villains Galore: The Heyday of the Popular Story Weekly* (New York: The Macmillan Company, 1954). Among the magazines Mott and Noel list as capitalizing on the interest are the *National Police Gazette, Frank*

Leslie's Illustrated. Munro's *Fireside Companion*, Beadle & Adams' *Star Journal, Beadle's Weekly* (later *Banner Weekly*), *Day's Doings*, and the *Boston Police News.*

7. Anthony Comstock, *Traps for the Young*, ed. by Robert Bremner (1883; rpt. Cambridge, Mass.: The Belknap Press of Harvard University Press, 1967), p. 21; see also William Graham Sumner, "What our Boys are Reading," *Scribner's Monthly*, 15 (March 1878), pp. 681-85, and Thomas Byrnes, "City Traps for Country Boys," *Youth's Companion*, 65 (November 3, 1892), pp. 582-83.

8. Comstock, *Traps for the Young.* pp. 22-23.

9. Sumner, "What Our Boys are Reading," p. 684.

10. Edmund Pearson, *Dime Novels; or, Following an Old Trail in Popular Literature* (Boston: Little, Brown, & Co., 1929), pp. 138-218. Also, McDade, "Lurid Literature of the Last Century."

11. Back cover of Will Winch, *The Murdered Heiress or Tracing the Crime of the Stage-Coach*, no. 595 in The Old Cap Collier Library (May 4, 1895), published by Munro's Publishing House, New York.

12. This discussion of the detective story's origins draws on the contemporary study by Frank Wadleigh Chandler, *The Literature of Roguery* (New York: Houghton, Mifflin, 1907), pp. 524-27.

13. James D. Horan, *The Pinkertons: The Detective Dynasty that Made History* (New York: Crown Publishers, Inc., 1967), pp. 238-39. Representative titles include *The Expressman and the Detective* and *The Molly Maguires and the Detectives.*

14. Other titles in the series are *Section 558 or, The Fatal Letter; A Tragic Mystery*; and *Another's Crime.*

15. Maurice Bassan, *Hawthorne's Son: The Life and Literary Career of Julian Hawthorne* (Columbus: Ohio State University Press, 1970), pp. 183-84.

16. Hjalmar Hjorth Boyesen, *Literary & Social Silhouettes* (New York: Harper & Brothers, 1894), p. 71.

17. *Ibid.*, pp. 50-51, 67-68.

18. William F. Howe and A. H. Hummel, *In Danger; or Life in New York* (Chicago: J. S. Ogilvie & Co., 1888), p. 187.

19. *Ibid.*, pp. 191-92.

20. Reviews in *The Critic.* 11 (O.S.) (October 8, 1887), pp. 174-75 and in *The Nation*, 45 (November 17, 1887), p. 403.

21. Julian Hawthorne, *The Great Bank Robbery* (New York: Cassell & Company, Limited, 1887), p. 6. Hereafter cited in text.

22. According to both the *New York Times* and the *New York Daily Tribune*, October 29 and 30, 1878, Detective Walling handled this case. Walling later became superintendent of police and wrote the historical anatomy discussed Chapter 2. Byrnes is usually given credit by modern sources and may have actually solved the case.

23. Unsigned review, *The Critic*, 11 (O.S.) (October 8, 1887), p. 174.

24. The character of the corrupt female lobbyist fascinated American writers of this period. She also appears as Laura Hawkins in *The Gilded Age* by Mark Twain and Charles Dudley Warner and as Josie Murray in *Playing the Mischief* by John W. DeForest.

25. Mark Twain, *Adventures of Huckleberry Finn* (New York: W. W. Norton & Company, Inc., 1961), p. 102.

26. William Ernest Lenz III, "Fast Talk and Flush Times: The Rise and Fall of the Confidence Man as a Literary Convention in Nineteenth-Century American Fiction," Diss. University of Virginia, 1980 (University Microfilm #8022672), pp. 270-90 provides a good discussion of the King and Duke.

27. Edgar Fawcett, *New York* (New York: F. Tennyson Neely, 1898), pp. 30-31. Hereafter cited in text.

28. Robert L. Hough, *The Quiet Rebel: William Dean Howells as Social Commentator* (Lincoln: University of Nebraska Press, 1959), p. 33 provides a limited discussion of this concept in Howells' work.

29. Edwin H. Cady, *The Realist at War: The Mature Years, 1885-1920, of William Dean Howells* (Syracuse: Syracuse University Press, 1958), p. 4 discusses the opening of this novel as a part of the battle for realism in America.

30. Kenneth S. Lynn, *William Dean Howells: An American Life* (New York: Harcourt Brace Jovanovich, Inc., 1970), pp. 286-88.

31. William Dean Howells, *The Minister's Charge* (Bloomington: Indiana University Press, 1978), p. 52. Hereafter cited in text.

32. William Dean Howells, *The Quality of Mercy* (Bloomington: Indiana University Press, 1979), pp. 5-6. Hereafter cited in text.

33. William Dean Howells, *The World of Chance* (New York: Harper & Brothers, Publishers, 1893), pp. 15-16. Hereafter cited in text.

34. "The Making of the Detective Story," *The Bookman*, 12 (September 1900), p. 107.

35. "The Criminal as Literary Copy," *The Bookman*, 12 (September 1900), p. 10.

36. *Ibid*.

37. Al. Jennings, *Through the Shadows with O. Henry* (New York: A. L. Bart Company, 1921), p. 135. For the story of Dick Price see pp. 135-58. This tale originally appeared in the April 1903 issue of *Cosmopolitan*.

38. O. Henry, "Tommy's Burglar," in *Whirligigs* (Garden City, N.Y.: Doubleday, Page & Company, 1925), p. 217.

39. From the manuscript of Robert M. Crunden's study of Progressivism, *Ministers of Reform* (New York: Basic Books, 1983).

40. Samuel Hopkins Adams, "Blue Fires" in *Average Jones* (Indianapolis: Bobbs-Merrill, 1911), pp. 179-80.

41. Arthur Stringer (John Arbuthnot), "The Criminal in Fiction," *The New York Times Book Review*, April 11, 1908, p. 209.

42. *Ibid.*

43. Among the novels and collections of short stories that explored the underworld seriously that I do not treat are Nathan Kussy, *The Abyss* (New York: The Macmillan Company, 1916) and John A. Moroso, *The Quarry* (Boston: Little, Brown, and Company, 1913).

44. Boyesen, pp. 71-72.

45. Josiah Flynt and Francis Walton, *The Powers that Prey* (New York: McClure, Phillips & Co., 1900), pp. v-vi.

46. Harry Thurston Peck, review of *The Powers that Prey*, *Bookman*, 12 (January 1901), p. 506.

47. The book was reviewed favorably in both the *Bookman*, 17 (May 1903), pp. 219, 222 and the *Critic*, 43 (October 1903), p. 379.

48. Josiah Flynt, *The Rise of Ruderick Clowd* (New York: Dodd, Mead & company, 1903), p. 101. Hereafter cited in text.

49. Alfred Henry Lewis, *Confessions of a Detective* (New York: A. S. Barnes & Company, 1906), p. 72.

50. Alfred Henry Lewis, *The Apaches of New York* (New York: M. A. Donohue and Company, 1912), p. 5. For a good discussion of Lewis see Abe C. Ravitz, *Alfred Henry Lewis*, Boise State University Western Writers Series, no. 32 (Boise: Boise State University Press, 1978).

51. This novel draws heavily on Bullard's own experience. In addition to fiction Bullard wrote scholarly essays with a strong reform bent. His experience included probation work with the prison association of New York, parole work for the Elmira Reformatory, and investigative work for both the New York State Commission on Immigration and the Russell Sage Foundation. For additional parallels between Bullard's scholarly interests and this novel see A. Bullard, "The Need of a New Criminological Classification," *Journal of the American Institute of Criminal Law and Criminology*, I (1910-1911), 507-10.

52. This analysis of the typical life pattern of the progressive reformer is drawn from Robert M. Crunden, *Ministers of Reform*.

53. Albert Edwards (Arthur Bullard), *A Man's World* (New York: The Macmillan Company, 1912), p. 102. Hereafter cited in text.

54. David Rothman, *Conscience & Convenience: The Asylum and Its Alternatives in Progressive America* (Boston: Little, Brown and Company, 1980), pp. 59-66 and Anthony M. Platt, *The Child Savers: The Invention of Delinquency*, 2nd ed. (Chicago: The University of Chicago Press, 1977), pp. 29-36 discuss the role of medical terminology in the American response to deviance.

55. Robert M. Crunden, *A Hero in Spite of Himself: Brand Whitlock in Art, Politics, & War* (New York: Alfred A. Knopf, 1969), pp. 158-60. All

biographical material on Whitlock is taken from this source and from Brand Whitlock, *Forty Years of It* (Cleveland: The Press of Case Western Reserve University, 1970).

56. Crunden, *A Hero in Spite of Himself*, pp. 52-53.

57. *Ibid.*, p. 97.

58. *Ibid.*, p. 161.

59. Harry James Smith, review of *The Turn of the Balance*, *The Atlantic Monthly*, 100 (July 1907), p. 130.

60. William Morton Payne, review of *The Turn of the Balance*, *The Dial*. 42 (16 May 1907), p. 314.

61. William Dean Howells, "A Political Novelist and More," *North American Review*, 192 (July 1910), p. 100.

62. *Ibid.*

63. *Ibid.*

64. Crunden, *A Hero in Spite of Himself*, pp. 165-66.

65. Brand Whitlock, *The Turn of the Balance* (Indianapolis: The Bobbs-Merrill Company Publishers, 1907), p. 612. Hereafter cited in text.

66. This discussion draws on Crunden's analysis of the progressive novel in *Ministers of Reform*.

CHAPTER 5

1. Burton J. Bledstein, *The Culture of Professionalism* (New York: W. W. Norton & Co., Inc., 1976), pp. 4-5, 86-90 was useful for this discussion of professionalism. Another useful source is *The Organization of Knowledge in Modern America, 1860-1920*, ed. by Alexandra Oleson and John Voss (Baltimore: The Johns Hopkins University Press, 1979). This collection of essays examines the professionalization of scholarship in America. The essay by Dorothy Ross, "The Development of the Social Sciences," pp. 107-38, is particularly relevant to this chapter.

2. Ysabel Rennie, *The Search for Criminal Man: A Conceptual History of the Dangerous Offender* (Lexington, Mass.: D. C. Heath & Co., 1978), p. 55.

3. Joseph M. Hawes, *Children in Urban Society: Juvenile Delinquency in Nineteenth-Century America* (New York: Oxford University Press, 1971), pp. 88-111 and *passim* provides a good account of Brace's work with children as well as an assessment of his overall role as a thinker in the nineteenth century.

4. *Ibid.*, p. 109.

5. Charles Loring Brace, *The Dangerous Classes of New York and Twenty Years Work Among Them* (New York: Wynkoop & Hallenbeck, Publishers, 1872), p. 30. Hereafter cited in text.

6. The works which used Dugdale's book as a starting point include:

Rev. Oscar C. M'Culloch, "The Tribe of Ishmael: A Study in Social Degradation," *Proceedings of the National Conference of Charities and Corrections*, 15 (1888), pp. 154-59 and Frank W. Blackmar, "The Smoky Pilgrims," *American Journal of Sociology*, 2 (January 1897), pp. 485-500. Both M'Culloch and Blackmar were more concerned with the theme of social degradation or degeneration than the theme of crime and its inheritance. M'Culloch, a minister, is notable for his sympathy toward the lower classes and his crusty persona. He makes continual overt parallels to biology and follows William Graham Sumner in arguing that the soft-hearted women who "give to begging children . . . have a vast sin to answer for" since they thus perpetuate pauperism, and that charity inevitably begets a life of vice and crime. Other studies of degenerative families include Henry H. Goddard, *The Kallikak Family— A Study in the Heredity of Feeble-Mindedness* (New York: The Macmillan Co., 1912); Charles B. Davenport and Florence H. Danielson, *The Hill Folk: Report on a Rural Community of Hereditary Defectives* (Cold Spring Harbor, New York: Eugenics Record Office, Memoir No. 1, 1912); Arthur H. Estabrook and Charles B. Davenport, *The Nam Family: A Study in Cacogenics* (Cold Spring Harbor, New York: Eugenics Record Office, Memoir No. 2, 1912); Elizabeth S. Kite, "The Pineys," *Survey*, 31 (October 4, 1913), pp. 7-13; and Arthur H. Estabrook, *The Jukes in 1916* (Washington: Carnegie Institution, 1916).

7. Franklin H. Giddings, "Introduction" to the 4th edition of Robert L. Dugdale, *The Jukes* (New York: G. P. Putnam's Sons, 1910), pp. iii-iv.

8. Robert L. Dugdale, *The Jukes*, 4th ed. (New York: G. P. Putnam's Sons, 1910, orig. pub. in 1877), p. 11. Hereafter cited in text.

9. Dugdale himself generally used the term "habitual" to designate the professional criminal in *The Jukes*. In later writings he began to use the term "professional."

10. Robert L. Dugdale, "Origin of Crime in Society," *The Atlantic Monthly*, 48 (1881), pp. 452-62; 735-46; and 49 (1882), pp. 243-51. Page numbers are hereafter given in the text.

11. Mark H. Haller, *Eugenics: Hereditarian Attitudes in American Thought* (New Bruswick: Rutgers University Press, 1963), p. 33.

12. As other portions of this study make clear, this attention was not confined to intellectuals. The police also made use of the professional criminal during the 1880s, and this was also related to their drive for professional status.

13. Simeon E. Baldwin, "How to Deal with Habitual Criminals," *Journal of Social Science*, 22 (June 1887), p. 162.

14. Francis Wayland, "Incorrigible Criminals," *Journal of Social Science*, 23 (November 1887), pp. 140-44; Francis Wayland, "The Incorrigible,—Who He Is, and What Shall be Done with Him," *Proceedings of*

the Annual Congress of the National Prison Association, 1886, pp. 189-97; William Noyes, "The Criminal Type," *Journal of Social Science*, 24 (April 1888), pp. 31-42.

15. John D. Davies, *Phrenology, Fad & Science* (New Haven: Yale University Press, 1955), pp. 3-5, 90-100.

16. Travis Hirschi and David Rudisill, "The Great American Search: Causes of Crime, 1876-1976," *Annals of the American Academy of Political and Social Science*. 423 (January 1976), p. 15.

17. Oliver Wendell Holmes, "Crime and Automatism," *The Atlantic Monthly*, 35 (April 1875), pp. 466-81.

18. E. Vale Blake, "Spontaneous and Imitative Crime," *Popular Science Monthly*, 15 (September 1879), pp. 656-67. Three years later William A. Hammond, M.D., also addressed the problem of disease and crime using kleptomania and professional theft as his field of inquiry. The article was "A Problem for Sociologists," *The North American Review*, 135 (1882), pp. 422-32.

19. *Proceedings of the National Prison Association*, 1888, pp. 140-41.

20. William Noyes, "The Criminal Type," *op. cit.*; Hamilton D. Wey, "Criminal Anthropology," *Proceedings of the National Prison Association*, 1890, pp. 274-91; and Robert Fletcher, "The New School of Criminal Anthropology," *The American Anthropologist*, 4 (July 1891), pp. 201-36. Noyes was assistant physician at Bloomingdale Asylum and Wey served as the physician to the New York State Reformatory at Elmira. Other reports on criminal anthropology of this time include a lengthy presentation by Thomas Wilson, "Criminal Anthropology," *Annual Report of the Board of Regents of the Smithsonian Institution* (1890), pp. 617-86; and Eugene M. Aaron, "Recent Researches in Criminology," *Scientific American Supplement*, 33 (June 18, 1892), 13727-28.

21. The term itself comes from Lombroso's disciple and son-in-law, Enrico Ferri. Other ways of referring to this concept were the congenital criminal or the criminal by instinct.

22. Wey, pp. 285-86.

23. Fletcher, p. 210.

24. Wey, p. 287.

25. Arthur MacDonald, *Criminology* (New York: Funk & Wagnalls Company, 1893), p. 169. Hereafter cited in text.

26. Nothing better illustrates the criminal anthropologists' emphasis on the potential threat of the individual criminal instead of his actual crime than MacDonald's chapter on "pure murder." He spends thirty pages examining a youth who did not kill anyone as a typical case of the murderer. The youth had been guilty only of an assault on an old woman who had told him to stop throwing snowballs at her.

27. Other major publications of MacDonald include *Abnormal Man*

(Washington, D.C.: Government Printing Office, 1893) and *Hearing on the Bill (H.A. 14798) to Establish a Laboratory for the Study of the Criminal, Pauper, and Defective Classes* (Washington, D.C.: Government Printing Office, 1902). MacDonald is also important for the extensive bibliographies he included in each of his books. These included both European and American writings of all kinds that even touched on crime. From his position in Washington, he exerted a steadying influence on the more radical offshoots of criminal anthropology in the U.S. and their proposed legislative remedies.

28. Stanley Grupp, "Introduction" to August Drähms, *The Criminal: His Personnel and Environment* (1900; rpt. Montclair, N.J.: Patterson Smith, 1971), p. xvii. Drähms is hereafter cited in the text.

29. W. Duncan McKim, *Heredity and Human Progress* (New York: G. P. Putnam's Sons, 1900), p. 120.

30. Henry M. Boies, *The Science of Penology. The Defence [sic] of Society Against Crime* (New York: G. P. Putnam's Sons, 1901), p. 14.

31. G. Frank Lydston, "A Contribution to the Hereditary and Pathological Aspect of Vice," *Chicago Medical Journal and Examiner*, 46 (February 1883), pp. 131-48.

32. G. Frank Lydston and Eugene S. Talbot, "Studies of Criminals. Degeneracy of Cranial and Maxillary Development in the Criminal Class, with a Series of Criminal Skulls and Histories Typical of the Physical Degeneracy of the Criminal," *Alienist and Neurologist*, 12 (October 1891), pp. 556-612.

33. G. Frank Lydston, "Asexualization in the Prevention of Crime," *Medical News*, 68 (May 23, 1896), pp. 573-78.

34. G. Frank Lydston, *The Diseases of Society. The Vice and Crime Problem* (Philadelphia: J. B. Lippincott Company, 1904), p. 86. Hereafter cited in text.

35. In the *Hearing on the Bill . . .* MacDonald asserted strongly in 1903 that crime was not a disease; those who argued that it was were simply speculating and confused about the nature of crime by the problem of incorrigibility and crime, i.e., professional crime; p. 13.

36. Dr. A. Jacobi, "Brain, Crime and Capital Punishment," *Proceedings of the National Prison Association*, 1892, p. 179.

37. Professor C. H. Henderson, "Practical Issue of Studies of the Criminal," *Proceedings of the National Prison Association*, 1894, pp. 119-34. In 1899 Henderson served as president of the National Conference of Charities and Correction where he delivered an address titled "Relation of Philanthropy to Social Order and Progress," *Proceedings National Conference of Charities and Correction* 1899, pp. 1-15. He admits that there are social causes but now contends that the sources of "defect . . . are largely biological, deep in our relations to nature." He has also been

infected by the threat most criminal anthropologists saw in the "dangerous classes" as he argues that pauperism, insanity, and crime are about to overwhelm American civilization: "We wish the parasitic strain, the neuropathic taint, the compulsive tendency, the foul disease, to die out."

38. Frederick Howard Wines, *Punishment and Reformation: A Study of the Penitentiary System*, 2nd ed. (orig. pub. 1895; New York: Thomas Y. Crowell Company, Publishers, 1910), p. 231. Hereafter cited in text.

39. Samuel G. Smith, "Typical Criminals," *Popular Science Monthly.* 56 (March 1900), pp. 539-45.

40. Jacob A. Riis, *How the Other Half Lives: Studies Among the Tenements of New York* (1890; rpt. New York: Hill and Wang, 1957), p. 1. Hereafter cited in text.

41. Josiah Flynt, *Tramping with Tramps* (1899; rpt. Montclair, N.J.: Patterson Smith, 1972), p. 3. Hereafter cited in text.

42. Daniel Bell's famous essay on crime as a social ladder in *The End of Ideology* (Glencoe, Ill.: Free Press, 1960) is a modern statement of the same theory.

43. Albion W. Small, "Fifty Years of Sociology in the United States," *American Journal of Sociology*, 21 (May 1916), 769-70, Harry Elmer Barnes, *The History and Prospect of the Social Sciences* (New York: Alfred A. Knopf, 1925), pp. 763, 820. Hawes, *Children in Urban Society*, provides a good discussion of the rise of academic sociology and psychology, pp. 198-212. I have also benefitted from Robert M. Crunden, *Ministers of Reform* (New York: Basic Books, 1983).

44. Bruce Kuklick, *The Rise of American Philosophy* (New Haven: Yale University Press, 1977), pp. 180-95.

45. The "kymograph" and the "algometer" are two of the machines used by Frances A. Kellor in *Experimental Sociology* (New York: The Macmillan Company, 1901), pp. 51-78. Kellor was a graduate student in sociology at the University of Chicago. Although her book did not treat professional criminals, it was one of the most important early works in American criminology. She was strongly influenced by the French school of criminology. Her book is a continual sniper's attack on criminal anthropology. She studied female delinquents imprisoned in both the North and the South as well as college women for a control group. She was the first to use experimental techniques on a large group of black criminals and to compare the findings with those for whites. A central theme of her book is the need for a scientific laboratory to study the individual criminal.

46. Arthur Cleveland Hall, *Crime in Its Relations to Social Progress* (New York: The Columbia University Press, 1902).

47. G. Stanley Hall, *Adolescence: Its Psychology and its Relations to Phys-*

iology, Anthropology, Sociology, Sex, Crime, Religion, and Education, 2 volumes (New York: D. Appleton and Company, 1922), I, p. 366. For a biography of Hall see Dorothy Ross, *G. Stanley Hall: The Psychologist as Prophet* (Chicago: The University of Chicago Press, 1972).

48. Hugo Münsterberg, *On the Witness Stand: Essays on Psychology and Crime* (New York: Doubleday, Page and Co., 1908), p. 48. Hereafter cited in text. A recent intellectual biography is Matthew Hale, Jr., *Human Science and Social Order: Hugo Münsterberg and the Origins of Applied Psychology* (Philadelphia: Temple University Press, 1980); pp. 111-21 deal specifically with *On the Witness Stand*.

49. Edward Alsworth Ross, *Sin and Society: An Analysis of Latter-Day Iniquity* (New York: Houghton Mifflin Company, 1907), p. 48. Hereafter cited in text.

50. James W. Garner, Introductory Editorial, *Journal of the American Institute of Criminal Law and Criminology*, I (May 1910), p. 2.

51. Wigmore also published an annotated guide to novels that dealt with the law, "A List of Legal Novels," *Illinois Law Review*, 2 (April 1908), pp. 574-93.

52. Report of the Committee on Translations, Bulletin no. 3 of the Institute, April 1910, *JAICLC*, I (September 1910), p. 452. The works chosen for translation were: Hans Gross, *Criminal Psychology*; Bernaldo de Quiros, *Modern Theories of Criminology*; Enrico Ferri, *Criminal Sociology*; Raymond Saleilles, *The Individualization of Punishment*; Cesare Lombroso, *Crime, Its Causes and Remedies*; Gabriel Tarde, *Penal Philosophy*; W. A. Bonger, *Criminality and Economic Conditions*; Raffaelle Garofalo, *Criminology*; and Gustav Aschaffenburg, *Crime and its Repression*.

53. Hawes, pp. 249-51.

54. William Healy, *The Individual Delinquent: A Text-Book of Diagnosis and Prognosis for All Concerned in Understanding Offenders* (Boston: Little, Brown, and Company, 1915), p. 316. Hereafter cited in text.

55. William James, "Habit," in John J. McDermott, ed., *The Writings of William James: A Comprehensive Edition* (New York: Random House, Modern Library, 1968), p. 9.

Bibliographical Essay

An interdisciplinary study of this nature presents many topics that can only be treated briefly. One of the purposes of this essay is, therefore, to point to sources useful in following up points raised here. A second purpose is to indicate sources that I found particularly useful. A study of this sort, which attempts to examine the "public" response of Americans to the concept of professional crime, depends on a wide variety of published sources. Many of these books are, by their nature, works addressed to a specific moment; since they deal with the underside of American life, a large number of them have been "lost" to the student of American civilization. One of the difficulties this work presented was the task of assembling a body of sources to examine. Several works proved useful in this endeavor. Arthur MacDonald conceived his task in the 1890s as introducing Americans to the emerging notions of the infant discipline of criminology. As part of this task his three major works, *Criminology* (New York: Funk and Wagnalls Company, 1893); *Abnormal Man* (Washington, D.C.: Government Printing Office, 1893); and *Hearing on the Bill (H.A. 14798) to Establish a Laboratory for the Study of the Criminal, Pauper, and Defective Classes* (Washington, D.C.: Government Printing Office, 1902), included extensive bibliographies of writing devoted to crime and criminology. The bibliographies in the latter titles are especially interesting for their annotations which provide valuable insights into contemporary judgments of the literature. A recent book that proved useful in locating sources is Bruce Davis, comp., *Criminological Bibliographies: Uniform Citations to Bibliographies, Indexes, and Review Articles of the Literature of Crime Study in the United States* (Westport, Conn.: Greenwood Press, 1978). Louis Kaplan, comp., *A Bibliography of American Autobiographies* (Madison: The University of Wisconsin Press, 1961), was invaluable in locating autobiographies of both professional criminals and detectives. This bibliography is annotated, although the annotations are often so brief as to be almost useless. Arthur E. Fink, *Causes of Crime: Biological Theories in the United States, 1800-1915* (Philadelphia: University of Pennsylvania Press, 1938) is a good review of the literature of biological thinking about crime. Fink recounts these writings in some detail but includes practically no analysis or interpretation. His bibliography is extensive and useful for anyone interested in medical or biological theories of crime causation. Two books were useful as bibliographic sources concerned specifically with professional crime: Edwin Sutherland, *The Professional Thief* (Chicago: The University of Chicago Press, 1937) and James A. Inciardi, *Careers in Crime* (Chicago: Rand McNally, 1975).

Sociologists have produced practically all of the writing about professional crime in America. In addition to Sutherland and Inciardi, several works contributed to my ideas and are useful for students interested in pursuing other aspects of this topic. The most helpful of these are Ned Polsky, *Hustlers, Beats, and Others* (Chicago: Aldine Publishing Company, 1967); Bill Chambliss, ed., *Box Man: A Professional Thief's Journey* (New York: Harper and Row, 1972); and Peter Letkemann, *Crime as Work* (Englewood Cliffs, N.J.: Prentice-Hall, 1973). For the general concept of professionalism, the work I found most useful was Burton J. Bledstein, *The Culture of Professionalism* (New York: W. W. Norton and Co., Inc., 1976).

Little scholarly work has been done on the history of American crime and practically nothing of scholarly value has been written about professional crime as a historical phenomenon. Most historians who have written about crime use as a thesis the principle that deviance is shaped by the specific conditions of a civilization. The historical works on American crime include Raphael Semmes, *Crime and Punishment in Early Maryland* (1938; rpt. Montclair, N.J.: Patterson Smith Publishing Corporation, 1970); Douglas Greenberg, *Crime and Law Enforcement in the Colony of New York, 1691-1776* (Ithaca: Cornell University Press, 1974); Roger Lane, "Crime and Criminal Statistics in Nineteenth Century Massachusetts," *Journal of Social History*, 2 (Dec. 1968), pp. 157-63, and *Violent Death in the City: Suicide, Accident, and Murder in Nineteenth Century Philadelphia* (Cambridge, Mass.: Harvard University Press, 1979); and Eric H. Monkkonen, *The Dangerous Class: Crime and Poverty in Columbus Ohio, 1860-1885* (Cambridge, Mass.: Harvard University Press, 1975). These studies address the effect of large social forces on crime but provide little treatment of the professional underworld. A book that does briefly address professional crime is Frank Browning and John Gerassi, *The American Way of Crime* (New York: G. P. Putnam's Sons, 1980). This work is, however, sketchy and generally undeveloped.

Autobiographical writings are a source that both cultural historians and literary critics are finding of increasing importance. Most studies of autobiography concentrate on major figures in intellectual, political, and literary history. Little work has been done on criminal autobiographies as a literary genre except for Frank Wadleigh Chandler's *The Literature of Roguery*, 2 volumes (New York: Houghton Mifflin, 1907). Chandler is more concerned with biography than autobiography and concentrates on British observers rather than American. Two works were useful in the general formulation of my ideas on autobiography: James Olney, ed., *Autobiography: Essays Theoretical and Critical* (Princeton: Princeton University Press, 1980) included a translation of Georges Gusdorf, "Conditions et limites de l'autobiographie," which originally appeared in *Formen der Selbstdarstellung* ed. by G. Reichenkron and E. Haase (Berlin: Duncker and Humboldt, 1956), pp. 105-23; and Robert F. Sayre, "The Proper Study—Autobiographies in American Studies," *American Quarterly*, 29 (1977), pp. 241-62. Sayre includes a good bibliography of writings about autobiography. Fredric V. Bogel, "Crisis and Character in Autobiography: The Later Eighteenth Century," *Studies in English Literature, 1500-1900*, 21 (1981), pp. 499-512 was also helpful for my theories about the form of autobiography.

The role of the police and the history of police in America is a topic of growing interest to American historians. This work often deals with the administrative history of police departments. The best of these books are Roger Lane, *Policing the City: Boston, 1822-1885* (Cambridge, Mass.: Harvard University Press, 1967) and James F. Richardson, *The New York Police: Colonial Times to 1901* (New York: Oxford University Press, 1970). Several studies have attempted to examine police history by using a theme such as professionalization or reform to organize their approach. These include Wilbur R. Miller, Jr., *Cops and Bobbies: Police Authority in New York and London, 1830-1870* (Chicago: The University of Chicago Press, 1977); Jerald E. Levine, "Police, Parties, and Polity: The Bureaucratization, Unionization, and Professionalization of the New York City Police, 1870-1917," Diss. University of Wisconsin, 1971; and Joseph G. Woods, "The Progressive and the Police: Urban Reform and the Professionalization of the Los Angeles Police," Diss. University of California, Los Angeles, 1973. John C. Schneider, *Detroit and the Problem of Order, 1830-1880, A Geography of Crime, Riot, and Policing* (Lincoln: University of Nebraska Press, 1980) examines the development of the police in response to urban geography. Most useful for this study was David R. Johnson, *Policing the Urban Underworld: The Impact of Crime on the Development of the American Police, 1800-1887* (Philadelphia: Temple University Press, 1979). Johnson includes a detailed examination of professional crime and its impact on the development of the American police as well as treating more casual street crime and vice.

The "pre-muckraking" exposé poses a peculiar problem for the student of American culture. Practically no scholarly work exists which examines the "mysteries and miseries" literature written by the journalists who explored America's emerging urban centers after the Civil War. Two works that proved to be of some use in tracing these writings were Frank Luther Mott, *A History of American Magazines, 1865-1885* (Cambridge, Mass.: Harvard University Press, 1938) and Mary Noel, *Villains Galore: The Heyday of the Popular Story Weekly* (New York: The Macmillan Company, 1954). The nonfiction exposé of the professional criminal and his methods has received no treatment as either a literary form or as a cultural document.

On the other hand, muckraking is a topic that has evoked a large response from both historians and literary scholars. Often these works are primarily surveys of the era's writing such as C. C. Regier, *The Era of the Muckrakers* (Chapel Hill: University of North Carolina Press, 1932) and Louis Filler, *The Muckrakers* (University Park, Pa.: The Pennsylvania State University Press, 1976). Louis Filler, *Progressivism and Muckraking* (New York: R. R. Bowker, Co., 1976) provided a helpful bibliographic guide to the writings of this era. The works I found most useful were Robert H. Bremner, *From the Depths: The Discovery of Poverty in the United States* (New York: New York University Press, 1956); Judson Achille Grenier, Jr., "The Origins and Nature of Progressive Muckraking," Diss. University of California, Los Angeles, 1965; and Robert M. Crunden, *Ministers of Reform* (New York: Basic Books, 1983). Crunden examines muckraking as one aspect of the progressive climate of creativity and discusses what it shared with such other forms as the progressive novel and painting.

An enormous body of scholarship is devoted to the years between the Civil War and World War I in American literary history. The most useful work dealing with crime is still Frank Wadleigh Chandler, *The Literature of Roguery*, 2 volumes (New York: Houghton Mifflin, 1907). Though dated, Chandler's work is filled with useful information and insights. Jay Martin, *Harvests of Change: American Literature, 1865-1914* (Englewood Cliffs, N.J.: Prentice-Hall, Inc., 1967) is the standard survey of the literature of this era. Unfortunately, no adequate study of the "Progressive" novel has been written, nor is there a guide to the fiction produced by progressive writers. These writings have been almost completely neglected by literary scholars and critics. The best discussion of this form of fiction is in Robert M. Crunden's book, *Ministers of Reform*.

As students of literature have become more interested in the genres of popular fiction, the body of commentary on detective fiction has grown rapidly. Rarely, however, have literary scholars attempted to relate this category of writing or the use of crime by novelists to the traditional canon of American literature. A notable exception to this is David Brion Davis, *Homicide in American Fiction, 1798-1860: A Study in Social Values* (Ithaca: Cornell University Press, 1957). Although Davis treats an earlier period and is concerned with murder rather than professional crime, his book provided helpful background and insights for my study. M. E. Grenander, "The Heritage of Cain: Crime in American Fiction," *Annals of the American Academy of Political and Social Science*, 423 (January 1976), pp. 47-66, is a sketchy but useful guide to crime in major American fiction. While literary scholars have not dealt with the figure of the professional criminal in imaginative writing, other themes related to crime have been scrutinized. H. Bruce Franklin, *The Victim as Criminal and Artist: Literature from the American Prison* (New York: Oxford University Press, 1978) examines writing produced by Americans guilty of violating the law and finds this theme important to such major writers as Herman Melville. The criminal figure who has most engaged the mind of the literary critic is the confidence man. The best of the works to examine this figure in American fiction are Susan Kuhlmann, *Knave, Fool, and Genius: The Confidence Man as He Appears in Nineteenth-Century American Fiction* (Chapel Hill: University of North Carolina Press, 1973); Warwick Wadlington, *The Confidence Game in American Literature* (Princeton: Princeton University Press, 1975); and William Ernest Lenz III, "Fast Talk and Flush Times: The Rise and Fall of the Confidence Man as a Literary Convention in Nineteenth-Century American Fiction," Diss. University of Virginia, 1980.

A large body of writing treats the specific category of detective fiction. H. Douglas Thomson, *Masters of Mystery: A Study of the Detective Story* (1931; rpt. New York: Dover Publications, Inc., 1978) is one of the earliest of these and is typical of most of the studies which followed it. Usually, these works are mainly concerned with the evolution of the form and its conventions, giving at best a passing nod to the cultural context enveloping the genre. Although Thomson does treat nineteenth-century detective fiction, he is again typical of most of these works in his concentration on writing after World War I. Some recent studies have, however, attempted a more complex approach to the form which illustrates an awareness of the effect of larger cultural concerns on the genre. These include John Cawelti, *Adventure, Mystery, and Romance: Formula Stories as Art and Popular Culture* (Chicago: The University of Chicago Press, 1976) and William Ruehlmann, *Saint with a Gun—The Unlawful American Private Eye* (New York: New York University Press, 1974). These books deal mostly with contemporary literature, and in Ruehlmann the polemical approach occasionally overwhelms the substance of his argument. More closely related to my study are Ian Ousby, *Bloodhounds of Heaven: The Detective in English Fiction from Godwin to Doyle*

(Cambridge, Mass.: Harvard University Press, 1976) and Stephen Knight, *Form and Ideology in Crime Fiction* (Bloomington: Indiana University Press, 1980). Neither of these excellent works treats the professional criminal, but both examine the interrelationships between cultural and social institutions and fiction and how developments in the host society shaped the concerns of imaginative writers.

Three contemporary sources were invaluable to the examination of the American intellectual response to professional crime. *The Proceedings of the Annual Congress of the National Prison Association* provide a detailed account of the way Americans who dealt with the professional criminal on a daily basis viewed this figure. These *Proceedings* include speeches by prison wardens, chaplains, and physicians. Of special use in gaining insights into the way thoughtful Americans in general saw this figure was the *Proceedings of the National Conference of Charities and Correction* which often addressed the issue of crime. For the years between 1910 and 1917, the *Journal of the American Institute of Criminal Law and Criminology* provides an excellent sample of the beliefs of the emerging professional criminologists about crime.

A number of later studies have examined the various responses of American intellectuals to crime. These books were generally tangential to my study, for they rarely discuss the professional criminal, but they were invaluable in providing information on the larger issues of criminal deviance in America. Three books were especially useful for academic criminology: Arthur E. Fink, *Causes of Crime: Biological Theories in the United States, 1800-1915* (Philadelphia: University of Pennsylvania Press, 1938); Hermann Mannheim, ed., *Pioneers in Criminology*, 2nd ed. (Montclair, N.J.: Patterson Smith Publishing Corporation, 1972); and Ysabel Rennie, *The Search for Criminal Man: A Conceptual History of the Dangerous Offender* (Lexington, Mass.: D. C. Heath and Co., 1978). An outstanding survey of the eugenics movement in America with lengthy passages on the attempts to use this as a way of treating crime is Mark H. Haller, *Eugenics: Hereditarian Attitudes in American Thought* (New Brunswick, N.J.: Rutgers University Press, 1963). Several other books were useful in providing background on the American response to crime in the nineteenth and early twentieth centuries. David J. Rothman has treated the institutional response to deviance in two books: *The Discovery of the Asylum: Social Order and Disorder in the New Republic* (Boston: Little, Brown and Company, 1971) and *Conscience and Convenience: The Asylum and its Alternatives in Progressive America* (Boston: Little, Brown and Company, 1980). A fascinating examination of the relationship between psychiatry and crime in the nineteenth century is Charles Rosenberg, *The Trial of the Assassin Guiteau: Psychiatry and the Law in the Gilded Age* (Chicago: University of Chicago Press, 1968). Two works on the response to juvenile delinquency before World War I also proved useful to the study of the intellectual response of Americans to crime. Anthony M. Platt, *The Child Savers: The Invention of Delinquency*, 2nd ed. (Chicago: The University of Chicago Press, 1977) treats juvenile delinquency between 1870 and 1900 by focusing on the development of the juvenile court. A broader work is Joseph M. Hawes, *Children in Urban Society: Juvenile Delinquency in Nineteenth-Century America*, the Urban Life in America Series (New York: Oxford University Press, 1971). Hawes uses an interdisciplinary approach to examine the notion of juvenile delinquency; his study, like Platt's, culminates with the establishment of the juvenile court as a deeply entrenched social institution.

Newspapers and periodicals played an important role in determining the responses of Americans to the works I have examined as well as providing accounts of some of the more infamous crimes of the era. I relied most heavily on the *New York Times*, the *New York Daily Tribune*, the *Nation*, the *Critic*, and the *Bookman*. My debts to these sources are acknowledged in the notes.

Index

About the Author
LARRY K. HARTSFIELD is an Assistant Professor of English and Communications at Fort Lewis College in Durango, Colorado. He is the co-author of the *American Studies Association Annotated Historical Bibliography* and author of articles in *Proceedings* and *The Handbook of Texas*.